Book Anatomy

A VOLUME IN THE SERIES

Studies in Print Culture and the History of the Book

EDITED BY

Greg Barnhisel, Joan Shelley Rubin, and Michael Winship

Book Anatomy

BODY POLITICS
AND THE
MATERIALITY OF
INDIGENOUS
BOOK HISTORY

Amy Gore

University of Massachusetts Press
Amherst and Boston

This book will be made open access within three years of publication thanks to
Path to Open, a program developed in partnership between JSTOR, the American
Council of Learned Societies (ACLS), University of Michigan Press, and
The University of North Carolina Press to bring about equitable access and impact
for the entire scholarly community, including authors, researchers, libraries,
and university presses around the world.
Learn more at https://about.jstor.org/path-to-open/.

ISBN 978-1-62534-749-7 (paper); 750-3 (hardcover)

Designed by Sally Nichols
Set in Adobe Garamond by Westchester Publishing Services
Printed and bound by Books International, Inc.
Cover design by adam b. bohannon
Cover art by Nicholas Galanin, *Everything We've Ever Been, Everything We Are Right Now
– Untitled (Black Figure)*, 2019. Monotype on paper, 30×22 inches (76.2×55.9 cm).
Courtesy the artist and Peter Blum Gallery, New York.

Library of Congress Cataloging-in-Publication Data
A catalog record for this book is available from the Library of Congress.

British Library Cataloguing-in-Publication Data
A catalog record for this book is available from the British Library.

Any views, findings, conclusions, or recommendations expressed in this book do not
necessarily reflect those of the National Endowment for the Humanities.
An earlier version of chapter 3 appeared as "Pretty Shield's Thumbprint: Body Politics in
Paratextual Territory," *Western American Literature* 55, no. 2 (Summer 2020): 167–92.
Used by permission of the University of Nebraska Press.

FOR MY MANY TEACHERS
AND AMONG THEM, FOR JESSE ALEMÁN,
WHO GUIDED THIS BOOK TO
HIGHER GROUND

CONTENTS

ILLUSTRATIONS

ACKNOWLEDGMENTS

In my doctoral program, I grew fascinated by academic acknowledgments. Not many in my family had gone to college, and those who had earned their degrees later in their lives through correspondence or a senior citizen program at the local community college, so reading acknowledgments became a way for me to peer behind the veil of academic life. As it turns out, what academics wrote in their acknowledgments didn't always match public appearances or common perceptions. Their thanks expressed joy in their work instead of the complaint, drudgery, or frustrations I had commonly heard about the profession in public forums and academic guidebooks. They spoke of the financial, emotional, and intellectual help they had received, rather than what they had not. They spoke of their families as integral support, not obstacles, to their professional lives. And while those working in academia undeniably face serious obstacles and inequities, these academic acknowledgments, along with friendly individuals and organizations who supported me along the way, helped me see more of the human in the humanities—the warm intellectual conversations that generate inspiration, the supportive writing groups, the patient librarians and editors, the pets and babysitters and shared meals and hospitality that all conspire in the academic's quest to write a book. I came to see writing a book, and likewise, receiving a terminal degree, conducting research, and landing a job, as a community effort.

As such, I welcome the opportunity to thank the many communities that made my academic life, and the book it produced, possible. As a scholar of the paratext, I also welcome the opportunity to utilize the acknowledgments genre in the way in which I learned to read it, as a means of accessibility and transparency to academic processes upon which I self-consciously reflect here. I hope that my transparency, my educational journey, and my book's journey might serve others in the way that the acknowledgments of others served me.

Especially because my book centers embodiment, I begin with my positionality: I am a phenotypically white, cis-gendered, able-bodied, heterosexual female with Italian American heritage who grew up lower-middle class in Connecticut. I earned high grades, but I did not attend excellent or even adequate schools for the majority of my education. Due to the absence of close relatives in my life who could share with me their traditional college experience, I consider myself to be a first-generation college student who, after a rough start, learned how to navigate a college degree and then later three graduate degrees and a tenure-track job. My family, deeply committed to local history and community, passed on their passions on to me, but from my childhood I knew that, despite the colonial-house plaque up the road that read "Established in 1740," there remained a much earlier and continuing Native history of the land on which I lived that had been missing in my education. An undergraduate class on "The Heritage of Native North Americans" by Dr. Chris Hummer started me on a journey that continues to draw me deeper into the ethics of place and the response-ability, to use Toni Morrison's phrase, of community.

Since I have now spent almost every year of my life in school, I have a host of academic communities to thank. At the beginning of my life, my primary and secondary classmates initiated me into academic competition and pushed me to achieve. When I entered higher education, my instructors and classmates inspired my intellectual awakening and introduced me to concepts that continue to shape my worldview, especially my formative experience at The Oregon Extension. The Bread Loaf School of English, based out of Middlebury College, gave me access to professors at the top of their respective fields and gave me a first glimpse of the highest academic excellence and prestige. During my time as an adjunct instructor at Montana State University, Emily Edwards and Ryan Storment showed me how to be an outstanding educator, and their model of how to teach teachers and how to engage students shaped my career trajectory. And after over a decade of university teaching, I thank my students, who remain one of my favorite aspects of my job—their dedication and joy for learning makes me look forward to the start of each new semester, and it is for them that I push myself to be a better scholar, researcher, and teacher.

I have a number of tireless librarians to thank. Despite a library fire and a worldwide pandemic, Roger Adams at Kansas State University's

Morse Department of Special Collections never gave up trying to connect me with one of only two known surviving reprints of S. Alice Callahan's *Wynema* during the final revisions of my manuscript. Jolie Braun of Ohio State University also connected me to *Wynema* when I could not travel, immediately answering my email, personally calling the books from off-site storage, and kindly sending me digital images of the only known extant copy of the first edition of *Wynema*, as well as the only other extant copy of the reprint. At North Dakota State University (NDSU), Beth Twomey, John Hallberg, Susanne Caro, Maddison Melquist, and the many librarians behind the scenes of interlibrary loan made sure I had access to the research materials I needed and helped me feel welcome at my new job. In the NDSU Germans from Russia Heritage Collection, Michael Miller and Jeremy Kopp went out of their way to be welcoming and even brought in kuchen during a class visit to the archives so that my students and I could try it for the first time. At the University of New Mexico (UNM), librarians Glenn Koelling, Sarah Kostelecky, Paulita Aguilar, and Kevin Brown continually inspired me with what the archives held and how it could empower. I also thank the librarians at the New York Public Library, Newberry Library, University of Virginia, Connecticut Historical Society, Montana State University, Pennsylvania State University, Beinecke, and Harvard for granting me access to the materials I needed to examine for this book.

The community in Native American Studies and the American Indian Center (AIC) at Montana State University meant the world to me. I had the privilege of being taught by Native instructors and classmates, listening to Native languages being spoken in person, and learning about Native history and stories from the community members themselves. Thank you to my many teachers there, both inside and outside of the classroom, especially Matthew Herman and Linda Karell, who guided by example my earliest endeavors as a non-Native scholar of Native literature. The Indian Pueblo Cultural Center (IPCC) in Albuquerque gifted me with invitations to visit Pueblo lands, to listen and learn from Native peoples, and to hear Native languages. The IPCC sets an extraordinary example of sovereign intertribal collaboration on a number of fronts—land recovery, education, entrepreneurship, food sovereignty, community outreach, and so much more. My memories of connecting tourists to Pueblo stories as a docent (including trying to give a museum tour during a power outage blackout!), two magical Annual Galas that sparked my passion for Native haute couture, and an incredible day with friends at the Taos Pueblo Feast Day will remain some of my most cherished memories from my time in New Mexico. Many thanks to Bianca Mitchell, Jonathan Cabada, Leo Vicenti, George Arthur, Monique Fragua, and Jon Ghahate for their warm welcomes and guidance into a deeper knowledge of Pueblo cultures. All of these Native communities have trusted me with their stories and to share their stories with other peoples, a response-ability that I have dedicated my life to honoring. While I hope that this book reflects the knowledge that they entrusted to me, any mistakes or misrepresentations I make in this book will show how much I still have to learn.

In my doctoral program, Jesse Alemán guided me through my dissertation and professionalization. Over the course of six years, his voice became the voice in my head, pushing me to greater achievements and holding me to a high standard. He became my model of professionalism, demonstrating how to never once phone it in or rest on one's laurels but considering each opportunity as worthy of one's best efforts. As anyone who knows him can attest, his research, conference presentations and lectures, and lifetime of academic achievements demonstrate the success he models by example. His support, along with that of my dissertation committee members Beth Piatote, Phillip Round, and Aeron Haynie, enabled my achievements. In addition to my committee members, my appreciation goes out to Kathleen Washburn and Joe Kraus, who also wrote letters of recommendation on my behalf. Outside of the English department, the UNM Women's Resource Center became a haven in the storm and a beacon of free chocolate, beverages, and printing, not to mention a community of extraordinary holistic support and women's empowerment. I also appreciate the support I received from the UNM Graduate Resource Center, which gave me access to a bevy of academic resources, including a women's-only job seekers workshop that drew together a number of female graduate students across campus. I thank those women, even though we met each other only briefly, and my friends and peers in the English Department graduate program who shared their support with me during our difficult journeys.

While reflecting on my dissertation, my advisor quipped that I wrote it not chapter by chapter, but conference paper by conference paper. Thank you to the funding sources, which I will mention by name in the next paragraphs, that allowed me to attend between two and four conferences a year as a graduate student. A number of welcoming conference environments I joined also made this book possible, most notably the Native American Literature Symposium, the Society for the Study of the Multi-Ethnic Literature of the United States (MELUS), the Western Literature Association (WLA), the Society for the Study of American Women Writers (SSAWW), and yes, even the Modern Language Association (MLA). My immense gratitude goes to the hosts, organizers, staff, faculty, panel chairs, and participants whose service work continues to make academic conferences a vital component of our careers. The MLA, SSAWW, and MELUS all provided professional development workshops over the years that shaped my success; thank you to all the panelists who volunteered their time and who continue to do so for the future of the profession.

This book would not have been possible without a great deal of money. My parents, due to their Christian beliefs, invested a great deal of their thinly spread income to send me to a K–12 church school, which did not provide me with a strong education but did provide me with the academic skills of self-discipline, self-directed study, and perfectionism that allowed me to succeed in college and beyond. I received a combination of merit scholarships and student loans, some taken on or cosigned by my parents, that allowed me to attend college and then graduate school. In my doctoral program at UNM, my professionalization found support from English Department funds and often from the American Literary Studies Arm's funds. I also actively sought and received funding from UNM's Office of Graduate Studies, the Center for Regional Studies, the Office of Teaching and Learning, Career Services, Graduate and Professional Student Development, and the Feminist Research Institute. Outside of the university, I received funding from the Association for the Study of American Indian Literatures, the Rare Book School, the MLA, MELUS, WLA, and the Newberry Library Consortium in American Indian Studies. While struggling to live at poverty level on my student loans, continually write grant applications, and excel in my schoolwork, I both taught at the college level and worked in the service industry.

For the time and financial resources to complete a crucial round of revisions on my book project, I thank NDSU for their generous pre-tenure sabbatical and the National Endowment of the Humanities (NEH) who awarded me a Summer Stipend. I am grateful to Damian Fleming; the North Dakota State University College of Arts, Humanities and Social Sciences NEH review committee members; and Jesse Alemán and Beth Piatote for supporting my NEH application. I also received research funding in the final stages from my department and NDSU's Research and Creative Activity office, including a book subvention. Without these many financial contributions, I flatly would not have succeeded in my education or my research. Even so, my federal student loans for four degrees total nearly $200,000, and I will rely on my continued status as a state employee and on the unassured Public Service Loan Forgiveness federal program in order to financially survive my education. I hope that sharing my financial information will continue to bring attention to the student debt crisis that our country faces.

I have several people and organizations to thank for helping me to land a tenure-track job which afforded me the personal and financial stability that enabled this book. First, Jonathan Davis-Secord worked tirelessly to provide professional development preparation to UNM graduate students. I benefited enormously from the workshops on job materials and the variety of job market experiences shared in his classes, especially the individual experiences shared by Beth Davila, Jesse Constantino, Tiffany Bourelle, Cristyn Elder, and Sarah Townsend. Thank you to everyone who critiqued my job materials and made them stronger. From the start, Aeron Haynie became a respected mentor and friend who believed in me no matter what the job market looked like. Julie Newmark also became a cherished friend and a continuing member of my support system. Derrick Spires not only volunteered his time during a SSAWW conference to give me a mock job interview, but also took the time to follow up with additional feedback. He also encouraged me to consider more carefully the language of "firsts." During the job interview process, Bruce Maylath, Alison Graham-Bertolini, Adam Goldwyn, Kelvin Monroe, and Amanda Watts modeled an organized, professional, and transparent search. My additional thanks to Kelvin, who encouraged me to consider the role of temporality in my project.

In the last stages of my book revisions, I am deeply grateful to Brian Halley, the executive editor at the University of Massachusetts. He welcomed my project into the Studies in Print Culture and the History of the Book series, and he shepherded this first-time author into publication with a warm blend of friendliness and professionalism. My heartfelt thanks to Cari Carpenter and my second anonymous reviewer who gave of their time generously and provided supportive and valuable comments that aimed to strengthen my work. Cristina Stanciu kindly pulled me aside during the 2022 MELUS conference to offer her mentorship to me, despite a hoarse throat, on the publication and manuscript peer-review process, and my NDSU colleague Don Johnson demystified the end stages of book publication with a classy camaraderie.

As a first-generation college student, my family may not have always understood what I was doing, but they cheered and supported me at every step. My dad David encouraged my curiosity about the world and taught me to learn by observation, in effect teaching me agency in my own education. My mom Cori placed herself in the thick of things with me every day, supported me unconditionally, and recognized patterns of my academic life, mental health, and stress long before I did. My great-uncle Dom Bosco taught me by example how to love community and how to care for the land. He shares with me my love for history, old books, classic Hollywood film, place-based community, and the land, and he has been one of the few intrepid souls in my family to ask me what my book is about, listen carefully when I told him, and ask follow-up questions. My sister Mindy, my grandmothers Lucy and Ann, my grandparents Jay and Janet, my aunt Luann, and my in-laws Guy, Ruth, Wendy, and Mark all encouraged my education, even when it relocated me and later my husband far away from them. My husband Tony patiently carried moving boxes full of heavy books across the country multiple times without complaint, and he understood when my work kept me indoors more than we both would have liked. He gifted me with both companionship and independence while writing this book, and he supported me when neither of us knew what a life driven by a woman's career would look like or where it would take us. All my love and thanks to him and my extended family.

I also wish to extend my thanks beyond the human world. Minute by minute, hour by hour, day after long isolated day of working from home, especially during the pandemic, my dogs Molly Brown and Forest gave their love and companionship and kept me sane. When Molly Brown died, Reuben came along and brought springtime to our lives again. They all shared their space and their mom with friend Millie and, at various times, our foster dogs Buxton, Shay, Gary, Bobby, Parker, Alex, Longmire, Archie, Moose, Donatella, Giada, Giovanna, Michelob, Diesel, Cascade, July, Delta Dawn, Trixie, Ariat, Duval, Stetson, Tony Lama, Punky Brewster, Yahztee, Lotte, Axton, Bexley, Elsie, Vivian, and Evelyn, all of whom brought an extra portion of love and joy into our household. Whenever I hit a writing block, the strong New Mexico sun lent me the strength to push through. The vistas of Cedar Crest lifted my spirits and patiently readjusted the strained nearsightedness of graduate school, both physiological and psychological. And everywhere I relocated, the trees offered their stability when so much felt precarious.

All royalties from this book will be donated to the Indian Land Tenure Foundation.

Book Anatomy

INTRODUCTION

Material Matters

M ORE THAN ANY other object, the book takes up the language of the body as well as the mind: as teachers we refer to the "body" paragraph; as critics we acknowledge a shifting literary canon or "corpus"; and as readers we recognize a book's "face," hold its "spine," and pour over its pages populated with typed "characters" made by "typefaces." It can be no coincidence that the physical features of the book correspond to the physical features of the body; in fact, bibliography commonly labels its descriptions as "book anatomy." Recalling Foucault's concept of bodily self-discipline in modernity, reading and writing also teach the body to engage with the printed word in specific disciplinary ways, involving hands, eyes, and body posture. The book, in other words, embodies discipline, power, agency, and control in both physical and imaginary worlds, and it materially carries our humanity, as well as our human stories—from the stains and marginalia of its readers to the socially, culturally, institutionally embedded means of its production.

Book Anatomy theorizes the material connection between books and bodies to argue that the reprints, editions, and paratextual elements of Indigenous books matter: they embody a frontline of colonization in which Indigenous authors battle the public perception and reception of Indigenous books and negotiate the representations of Indigenous bodies.[1] While Daniel Heath Justice offers in *Why Indigenous Literatures Matter* (2018) that Indigenous writings matter for the ways in which they teach readers about past, current, and future relationships, I add that the *materiality* of Indigenous literatures also matters, not only in the transmission of the stories they contain but also as a documentation for the material conditions of Indigenous relationships, corporeal existence, and structures of power. Renée Bergland's *The National Uncanny* (2000) and Joshua David Bellin's *The Demon of the Continent* (2001), for example, foreground the power relations at stake in the presence, or liminal presence, of Indigenous bodies as national-ist textual representations in early American books. Representations of bodies also figure prominently in Indigenous writing, as Native authors struggled to be perceived within American society as living, modern, and embodied intellectuals while using their writing to speak out against injustice. Yet while numerous scholars find the ideas expressed in books to be a source of Indigenous power, I claim books themselves as a source of *embodied* power. Books contain more than corporeal representations and symbolism; whether fiction or nonfiction, books facilitate bodily encounters. Their words invoke bodies as actors of agency and as the inevitable outcome of ideas—words *create* imaginary bodies, and words imaginatively act *upon* bodies of the past, present, and future. As Michelle Coupal, Aubrey Jean Hanson, Sarah Henzi, and many Native literary scholars continue to attest, "stories are inseparable from the sovereignties, bodies, and traditional territories from which they arise," and as such books act in relationship with, and bear witness to, the material worlds in which they circulate.[2] Accordingly, my project looks to the book itself and its paratextual elements—its graphic design, illustrations, typefaces, pref-aces, appendices, copyright, frontispieces, and so forth—as an embodied expression of print culture power relations.

Paratexts rise as the neglected spaces of Indigenous literature. As medi-ators of their texts, paratexts speak to the complex nature of the literary marketplace for Indigenous books and attest to what I contend must be the political nature of bibliography, despite, and because of, its historical neglect in the study of marginalized literatures. A book's textual content might undergo revisions, but paratexts often undergo the most drastic changes over time and between editions, revealing what the Multigraph Collective describes as the "layered sites that bear the traces of ongo-ing change and of the various interactions they have experienced and enabled—like humans, perhaps."[3] The paratext documents, for example, whether or not an Indigenous writer retained legal copyright, as I dis-cuss in my first chapter with Cherokee author John Rollin Ridge's *The Life and Adventures of Joaquin Murieta* (1854). An introduction or pref-ace speaks to a text's reception among readers and the dynamics of the literary marketplace, and changing cover images can reveal the ongoing tensions in marketing Indigenous literary products and representations of Native peoples, as the texts discussed here demonstrate. Rather than mere wrapping, paratexts not only frame the text but signify its meaning.

My research advances book history and bibliography by joining other scholars in revising the field's relationship to multi-ethnic and Indigenous literary studies, what Beth McCoy describes as "forging a crucial coalition between bibliographic scholars and those studying the intersections of race, power, and culture." Bibliography took a cultural turn in the late twentieth century with the aid of D. F. McKenzie's *Bibliography and the Sociology of Texts* (1985): originally given as a series of lectures, McKenzie urged book history scholars to "consider anew what bibliography is and how it relates to other disciplines," a consideration that more thoroughly places texts within their cultural, social, and historical contexts. McKenzie reflected upon the paradigm shift that had occurred during his time from the practice of bibliography as a book science concerned with "signs" to the concern of "meaning" in a practice of bibliography as necessarily informed by historical context. Later research such as Round's *Removable Type* (2010) answers McKenzie's call to demonstrate the productive application of book history to Indigenous studies, and scholars such as Marcy J. Dinius, Brigitte Fielder and Jonathan Senchyne, Jacqueline Goldsby, Leon Jackson, Kinohi Nishikawa, Dan Radus, and Caroline Wigginton continue to transform the study of books in relation to its negotiations of race and power, inspiring my own scholarship here.[4] Yet much work remains in fully realizing the relationship between the paratext, book production, and Indigenous authors. My research takes up the interdisciplinary work of conjoining the paratext and body studies with Indigenous literary studies to make the case that Indigenous books themselves embody the marks, traces, and scars of coloniality and survival within Indigenous literary history.

As an example, the surrounding paratextual elements that accompany the published text of *Pretty-shield: Medicine Woman of the Crows* (1932) wage war over representations of Pretty Shield's body: while the book's illustrations depict Indigenous women's bodies in primitivist black-and-white drawings, one of the opening paratextual pages of the book stresses Pretty Shield's agency over her own body with an inked impression of her thumb and the assertive caption, "I told Sign-talker the things that are in this book, and have signed the paper with my thumb"[5] (Figure 1). Pretty Shield's thumbprint marks the text that follows as her own, imprinting her body on the very pages of what could have been an ethnographic exploitation under other circumstances. Pretty Shield draws from her body's experience not only as a means of sharing her life story, but also as a source of authority, and she inserts an impression of her body as a paratextual element in order to proclaim her authority over the written word.

While the paratext is intended to be the "non-story" of the book, a means to highlight the narrative, it nevertheless tells a story of its own

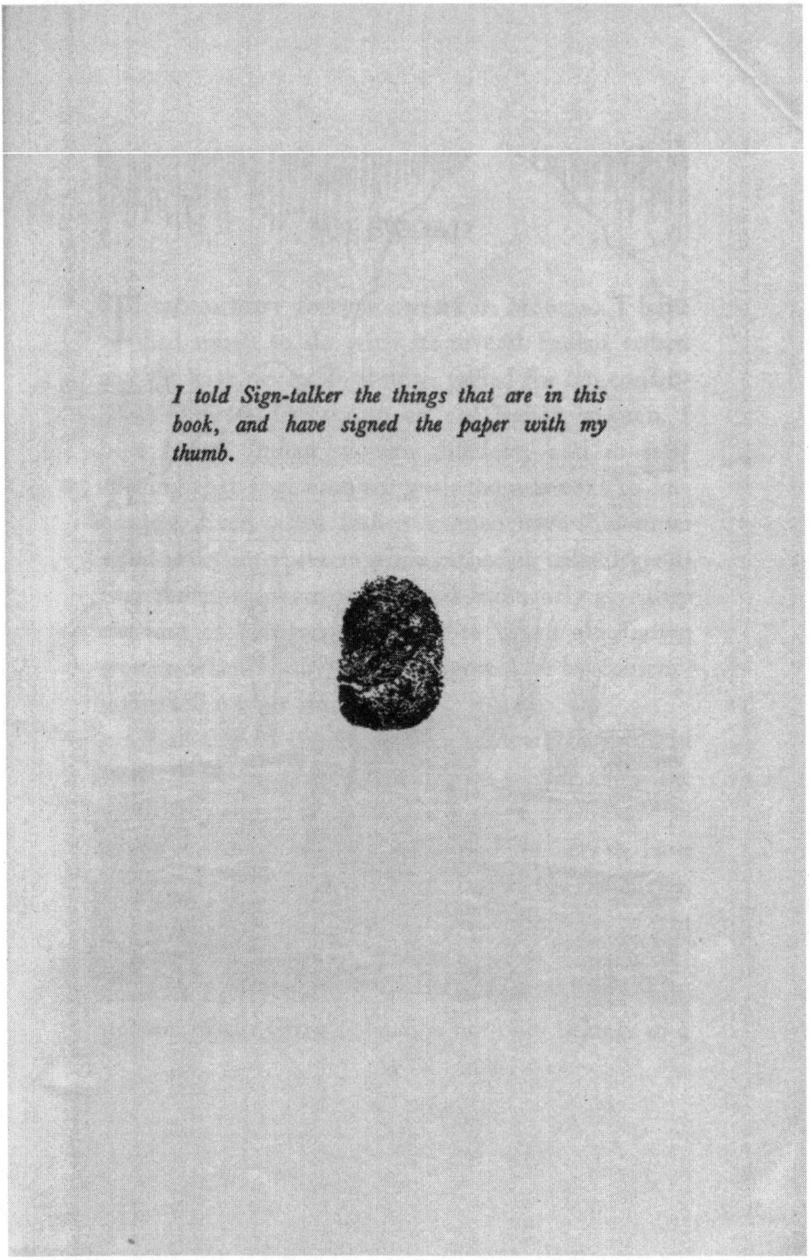

I told Sign-talker the things that are in this book, and have signed the paper with my thumb.

FIGURE 1. Pretty Shield's thumbprint from the 1972 facsimile edition. Author's collection.

that must be present for the narrative to exist. The paratext often remains outside the purview of literary criticism; however, my research joins a growing number of scholars who consider the paratext to hold essential meaning for the interpretation of literature and its historical context, especially in regard to race and gender. John Matthews provides a helpful explanation of the paratext's undervalued function as he writes, "[The frame] is at once outside the reader's field of concentration and the determinant of that field, beneath one's notice yet the foundation of it. By indicating all that is not-the-story, the frame's marginality becomes indispensable to providing the ground which defines the figure of the narrative." Rather than tangential or supplementary elements in relation to the text proper, the paratext provides a critical framing meant to instruct the reader's reception of the text. Elements such as the acknowledgments, foreword, preface, and introduction set the tone of the text and the authority of the author(s). Any of these elements may also imply the text's genre (fiction, nonfiction, scholarly, popular) and, most significantly to my project, the paratext may also signify the author's race or gender. Whatever the combination, paratextual elements initially invite the reader and provide the book's opening overture, functioning as "always that which is first to be passed through or beyond." The paratext thus becomes the reader's first encounter with a text and the reader's first engagement of their imagination, influencing their perception and reception of the narrative. In short, to borrow a term from Butler, the paratext provides "normative constraints" on the text, subtly telling the reader how to interpret and receive it.[6]

In looking to the paratext I examine the mutual negotiations, transactions, and perceptions that took place not only in the moment of print but also in a book's continuing reverberations across time. I do not attempt here a comprehensive study of Indigenous book history during the eighteenth, nineteenth, and early twentieth centuries: many Indigenous books by authors such as Samson Occom, William Apess, George Copway, Black Hawk, Joseph Nicolar, Gertrude Bonnin, Luther Standing Bear, Mourning Dove, Ella Deloria, Charles Eastman, and John Joseph Matthews, to name a few, do not appear in the following pages. Instead, *Book Anatomy* concentrates on five books published during an era of Native literary history, the late nineteenth to the early twentieth century, that has arguably received relatively less attention in Native literary scholarship than other eras. Each book marks a significant milestone— John Rollin Ridge's *The Life and Adventures of Joaquin Murieta* (1854), Sarah Winnemucca Hopkins's *Life among the Piutes* (1883), and S. Alice

Callahan's *Wynema* (1891) are the first and only books published by their authors, and they each represent some of the first known entries in Indigenous book history, including the first novel (*Murieta*) and the first autobiography and novel published by Native women. The collaboration of Frank Linderman and Pretty Shield, titled *Red Mother* (1932) and later renamed *Pretty-shield*, represents one of the earliest as-told-to narratives of a Native woman that highlights her own words, using quotes in a dialogue format, and it is one of only two books in Native history to include an inked thumbprint. Like Pretty Shield, D'Arcy McNickle's *The Surrounded* (1936) was the first book he ever produced, and while he would go on to publish a young adult novel and several works of nonfiction in his lifetime, his debut novel and its experiments with modernism made a lasting impression on Indigenous book history.[7]

For each book, *Book Anatomy* focuses thematically by chapter on one paratextual element, highlighting one's particular significance in relation to the book's embodiment over time—copyright with Ridge's *Murieta*, blank space with the first entries of Winnemucca and Callahan, Pretty Shield's thumbprint, and footnotes and citations with McNickle's *The Surrounded*. Crucially, each book I examine here also received at least one reprint or second edition, allowing me to examine the paratextual negotiations present not only within one edition but in multiple editions over time. Reprints reveal interlocutions of power and ongoing relationships, and as such the temporal nature of Indigenous reprints invites an accounting. For better or for worse, the paratextual elements of Indigenous books mediate between author and publisher, reader and writer, past and present, and as such they matter, in the sense of both cultural meaning and materiality, as the largely overlooked frameworks of Indigenous literary history.

Although paratexts may be mediated spaces, they also become spaces of readerly interaction that teach us about a text's social and historical relationships. For Indigenous writers, the paratext often presents their bodies for public viewing in association with their status as authors, exemplifying Michael Warner's claim for publication as "a political condition of utterance." Because publication is political, Warner continues, "No one had a relation to linguistic technologies—speaking, reading, writing, and printing—unmediated by such forms of domination as race, gender, and status." As a result, the paratexts studied in *Book Anatomy* often highlight the author's race and historically tie the narratives with ethnography rather than literary art or talent, as I discuss in Chapter Five

with McNickle's *The Surrounded*. For example, the paratexts of Indigenous literary history have often utilized stereotypical images such as a
tomahawk or feathers in the book's graphic design, and many included
"authenticating" introductions or prefaces from white associates.[8] Yet
other paratextual elements may simultaneously emphasize an Indigenous author's intellectual networks, rhetorical skill, multilingualism,
advanced education, and literary talent. Later editions of their works may
also display changing social attitudes towards Indigenous writers and
document these historic contexts and transformations. Through the
paratext, then, readers of Indigenous literature encounter the contested
space of the corporeal book.

In the following pages I combine bibliographical analysis with the
cultural training and critical analysis of Indigenous literary studies to
uphold the value of Indigenous book history as an act of witnessing.
Book Anatomy stands against what Drew Lopenzina describes as the historic *unwitnessing* of Indigenous literary contributions: their dismissal or
disregard, their marginalization, and the concomitant "rhetorically erasing
[of] the inconvenient truth of the persistence of Native peoples and their
cultures."[9] *Book Anatomy* also works against the historically ubiquitous
Indigenous "deficiency" model, which gives the impression that Native
peoples did not produce storied objects, only produced oral literature,
or did not write very many books, and probably not in English, until
around the 1970s. My book seeks to correct some of that misinforma-
tion by tracing the history of Indigenous books well before the mislead-
ingly named Native American Literary Renaissance. Bringing Indigenous
book history more firmly into conversations with mainstream narratives
about the history of the book, I join the work of previous and ongoing
scholarship to counter the "illegibility" of Indigenous achievements in
regard to the printed word.

Although the critical witnessing of Indigenous literatures and print
culture remains the overall project of Indigenous literary studies, such
scholarship faces a new challenge with the advent of twenty-first-century
digitization. In the early stages of digitization, many primary records reproduced in electronic form, oftentimes imperfectly, were subsequently
deaccessioned by institutions as no longer needed. Printed newspapers,
academic journals, and duplicate copies and reprints of books continue
to be discarded or undervalued when a single copy or even a sole digital
reproduction exists, resulting in a massive reversal in cultural preservation. While institutions must grapple with the persistent and increasing
strains of space and funding, books written by Black, Indigenous, and

people of color remain especially at risk: although some of these and other print culture items currently appreciate at a high market value for collectors, the legacy of canonization and the manifestation of white supremacy in library collections already leave behind vastly inequitable material representations.[10] Single copies, first editions, or a digitized edition instead stand in as representational, obscuring the richness and complexities of Indigenous book history as its books reiterate through time and place.

Such practices prompted the MLA to produce a statement in 1995 on the "Significance of Primary Records," entreating librarians and scholars of the humanities to consider the value of primary documents as irreplaceable and the reproductions as supplementary to archival research and as an incomplete "substitute for the actual physical objects in which those earlier texts were *embodied* at particular times in the past." Their statement holds even more significance for the emergent field of Indigenous book history, as Miriam Fuchs attests: despite the initial ease of digitization, she cites the potential danger to Indigenous book history when researchers come to rely on digitization without examining the original documents. In the case of Queen Lili'uokalani's *Hawaii's Story by Hawaii's Queen* (1898), which Fuchs describes as Lili'uokalani's final attempt to intervene in the political process of the United States that forced the abdication of her throne and the overthrow of Hawaiian sovereignty, Fuchs began to examine reproductions of the diary and began to be convinced by the argument of Lorrin A. Thurston, who discredited Lili'uokalani's authorship. She reflects, "To my regret, the typed copies seemed at first to confirm Thurston's charge" and only after deciding to examine the highly restricted original volumes of Lili'uokalani's diaries did she discover that the odd inconsistencies of the entries were due to corrupted reproductions, not Lili'uokalani's hand.[11] Fuchs's warning reminds scholars of the potential threats, as well as the potential benefits, to Indigenous book history and the political assertions of Indigenous authors from the digitization of Indigenous primary documents, and she implicitly challenges scholars to review the value of print in the midst of digitization. My work answers her call to demonstrate the value of physical copies and reprints to Indigenous literary history and, more broadly, the value of print documents in a digital age.

As the chapters that follow demonstrate, Indigenous literary history remains intertwined within a broader context of American literary production, especially in light of its similar concerns and connections regarding books and bodies. The authors examined here—John Rollin Ridge, Sarah

Winnemucca, S. Alice Callahan, Pretty Shield, and D'Arcy McNickle— did not seek such a separation between literary productions; in fact, they actively sought inclusion into mainstream literary history and readerships in order to join the conversations happening over Indigenous bodies, lands, sovereignty, and human rights. Thus, although the myriad connections between books and bodies begin to make their association look natural and ingrained, the political stakes of their association grow immense. In fact, the "naturalness" of the connection should trigger a critical awareness—as the human body, and specifically the Indigenous body, becomes embedded in the bibliographical object, it reckons with the exploitation of the human subject as an object.

My project rejects the connections between books and bodies as an intellectual exercise divorced from social and political realities. Instead, the trope demands a historical grounding in the nineteenth-century developments of race, challenges readers to probe the boundaries between subject and object, and bridges nineteenth-century with twenty-first-century concerns over changing conceptions of the body as well as the changing technologies and receptions of print. Ultimately, books and bodies provide insight into historical, social, and political movements that impact Indigenous literature and lives. Therefore, through a cultural, historical, and bibliographical examination of Indigenous texts from the mid-nineteenth century to the early twentieth century, I demonstrate that the composition of the book testifies to the physical and social violence inflicted upon Indigenous bodies and, in many cases, also creates the space for Indigenous assertions of their bodily sovereignty and bodily experiences under colonization.

Marginalized Bodies and Mediums of Power

Nineteenth-century Indigenous writers did not stand apart from the power of the printed word; rather, they harnessed the skills of reading and writing to produce books that attempted to counter adverse representations and to promote Indigenous communities and advocacy, all the while negotiating the difficult and often prejudicial publishing world. William Apess's autobiography, for instance, continually expresses an alienation of self from body under colonization, and his book testifies to the way in which the construction of "empire was a significantly corporeal process."[12] As Apess's body and psyche bore the scars of his brutal beating by his grandmother, his poverty, the racial prejudice of his religion, and his indoctrinated childhood fear of Indians, the editions of his books bear the marks of the colonial encounter of Indigenous stories in the mainstream marketplace: for example, his first edition vehemently accuses the Methodist Episcopal Church of refusing his ordination due to racial prejudice, while his second edition edits out his accusations as "parts which some persons deemed objectionable."[13] As Barry O'Connell documents, the differences between Apess's editions bring to the fore tensions of power and voice in American society and letters, and his social scars and their healing transfer to the page as they become embodied within the material manifestation of his life story.[14] As such, *Book Anatomy* advances beyond Indigenous representations in texts to stress the work of empire as a corporeal process: while colonialization most evidently and immediately attempted to control bodies through the violence of war, enslavement, genocide, gender roles and binaries, and assimilation, it also attempted to control bodily sovereignty through the cultural work of the embodied book.

The book—more generally, reading and writing—was conceived as a medium of power for those with socially designated bodies. Colonization inflicted oppression upon certain types of bodies, and its agents enlisted paper as the means to do so—empirical proclamations of "discovery," treaties, laws and legal documents, slave advertisements, wanted notices, and the popular press. As Sandra Gustafson summarizes, European intellectuals created a hierarchical distinction between written and oral literacy, and they enforced their distinction to justify the oppression and persecution of colonized subjects. "Producing Western literacy as a technology of power," she writes, "many European colonialists perceived the lack of alphabetic writing as a fundamental cultural inadequacy that justified the enslavement of Africans and the domination of Native American peoples." While enslaved African Americans were legally prevented from reading and writing, and by extension, owning books, they were concomitantly prevented from legally owning bodies, having a right to their own or those of their family. In contrast, from first contact Indigenous peoples were not only encouraged, but forced, to learn to read and write in English as a means of assimilating and thus "disappearing" the bodies of those who had sovereign rights to the land. As one example, after the Pequot War of 1636–37 in which American settler colonials burned alive, slaughtered, and beheaded a staggering number of Pequot men, women, and children, the 1638 Treaty of Hartford attempted to use the colonial power of paper to destroy the existence of the Pequot Nation by forbidding any official recognition of their continued existence and the use of their name on any documents. Many remaining Pequot survivors were sold into slavery within settler colonial families, and any Pequot runaways who were caught were branded on the shoulder to safeguard against further runaway attempts.[15] The colonial encounter traumatized bodies, set them at war with one another, and indelibly scarred them, all while using paper as an attempted means to destroy tribal sovereignty and Indigenous personhood.

While the power of the popular press may seem to pale in comparison to the impact legal documents may have upon the body, the ubiquitous popular press crafted the imagination, sentiment, and political movements of nineteenth-century American society, which in turn directed the treatment of bodies. In this light, the power of books in general, including captivity narratives, historical romances, sentimental novels, and dime novels, cannot be underestimated. For example, Francis Meynell's book *Typography* (1923) begins with an introduction titled, "'With Twenty-Five Soldiers of Lead I Have Conquered the World,'" a quote that he claims is French in origin and refers to movable type. His title speaks to the power of the printed word in the implementation of colonization, a claim that Febvre and Martin repeat in their foundational contribution to the field of book history as they assert that their primary aim is "to prove that the printed book was one of the most effective means of mastery over the whole world." These provocative statements position the book not only as a method of colonization, but simultaneously as a material manifestation of Indigenous resistance against systemic oppression. Indigenous authors are well aware of the connection between books and colonization: as Vine Deloria famously stated, "when they arrived they had only the Book and we had the land; now we have the book and they have the land."[16] Not only, then, does the materiality of books connect to physical bodies, but books also contain an immense political influence upon the treatment of bodies and the extended physical world.

When Native peoples utilized print materials in their anticolonial struggle, they did so by, to use Warner's phrase, "implicitly locating power on different grounds." This did not necessarily entail an abandonment or assimilation of Native traditions, but a bold engagement in a battle that was not created on their terms. Put another way, when Indigenous authors published, they neither replaced nor undermined Indigenous oral literature and other Indigenous literary aesthetics; rather, they added another venue, one that was neither more nor less authentic, to the already prolific options for Indigenous communication. Yet the printed word simultaneously promotes and erases expressions of power, a process Indigenous writers grappled with as they published into mainstream American literary production, a realm designated as white. In *The Letters of the Republic* (1990), Warner describes the establishment of printing in America as a process that incorporated readers into a system of ownership over book property that intended conceptually to block or limit literary access for nonwhite citizens, especially enslaved Black (who, designated as property, could not own property themselves) and Native peoples (who, designated as participants in oral cultures, could not have a "literary" tradition).[17] Books became key players in the process of the "racialization of print," which Joseph Rezek describes as "the centuries-long, non-inevitable procedure through which printed objects became powerfully associated with white supremacy and ideologies of racial hierarchy." The ability of white writers to produce literature acted as a characteristic of white identity that inducted individuals into higher education, defined them as civilized Christians, and became their ticket into white power and the concerns of a white community.[18] Race often dictated who could access the privilege of writing, whose writing became published, how the publication became marketed and to whom, whose writing became canonized, and who could read it. In short, as Warner puts it, "to do reading was a way of being white" and of establishing white supremacy in what Lauren Berlant identifies as the "anatomy of national fantasy."[19] By publishing, Native authors gained access to power but also contended with the book's embedded associations of whiteness.

While bodies and literary publishing became embedded within white supremacy, I follow the lead of other scholars in referring to the operation of whiteness at the level of power. As John Young explains in *Black Writers, White Publishers: Marketplace Politics in Twentieth-Century African American Literature* (2006), scholars should proceed cautiously with generalizations about marginalized authors in the white-dominated American literary marketplace, for to paint a picture of "oppressive white editors and publishers and ultimately powerless black authors would be both simplistic and inaccurate." Publishing a book is not a "black and white" undertaking—rather, to use Michaël Roy's description, publication is a "product of 'gray' interactions that took place outside the pages of the printed book and that, for that reason, are hard to reconstruct."[20] Similarly, I maintain that we should not understand Indigenous authors as powerless in the production of their books or their editors as singularly oppressive. Rather, my project seeks to parse through the complex relationships revealed through the paratextual pages of Indigenous book history, relationships that do not offer up simplistic understandings of resistance and oppression but instead reveal nuanced interactions of strategy, collaboration, and negotiation.

The racialization of print in the American literary marketplace reflects only one facet of white supremacy. As the operation of racism at work in society, the intensity to mark bodies of difference exposes an underlying anxiety of whiteness and the push to establish white, especially male, bodies as "normal," the unmarked standard explicitly established through anatomical charts and textbooks and implicitly established through the discourse and the act of marking others. In other words, as Jennifer Putzi asserts, "the white male attempts to escape or conceal his own marked body by marking another, by *making an other* out of a noncitizen, a nonperson." To mark bodies of difference, either on the physical body with letters or symbols or through the printed word, perpetrates an act of objectification. Rendering someone or something as an object politically promotes its loss of agency and sentience. In other words, objectifying forms of life limits their qualitative value and makes them disposable. Yet ironically, whiteness also acts as a means of objectification in spite of its attendant white privilege, for, as Cheryl Harris argues, the American legal system "converted an aspect of identity into an external object of property, moving whiteness from privileged identity to a vested interest."[21] Therefore, whiteness as a property to be possessed objectifies one's body, as well as the bodies of others, and adds another layer of complexity to the tension between humans and objects.

The slippage between physical subject and material object comes in part from uncertain categorization of the human body itself. Are we our bodies, the most intimate and tangible evidence of our being? Or do we transcend our bodies, relegating the body as an important but mere container for our personhood? Ultimately, is the body itself a subject or an object, and what might be the political implications of our answer? These questions hold foundational implications on all levels of our existence—political, spiritual, material, ontological—and have often been used as a means to create hierarchies, to deem some human and animal bodies as expendable, and to disenfranchise. Elizabeth Grosz's *Volatile Bodies* (1994) summarizes the difficulty of the body's categorization between subject and object as she writes:

> The body is a most peculiar "thing," for it is never quite reducible to being merely a thing; nor does it ever quite manage to rise above the status of

thing. Thus it is both a thing and a nonthing, an object, but an object which somehow contains or coexists with an interiority, an object able to take itself and others as subjects, a unique kind of object not reducible to other objects. . . . If bodies are objects or thing, they are like no others, for they are the centers of perspective, insight, reflection, desire, and agency.

Her insights of the body as both a thing and a nonthing applies to the special status of the book, the uniquely endowed object invested with our cultural records. Yet the problematic implications of the book and the body's special status come to light through the course of human history and the ways in which society deploys these special entities in relationships to each other. As Jean Bethke Elshtain and J. Timothy Cloyd point out, "We are never *not* our bodies. But we neither own our bodies nor are they simply our own. From birth, indeed well before birth, our bodies are entangled with those of other bodies that, for better or for worse, help to make our body-self what it is, what it becomes, what it may remain."[22] As the entity through which one constructs a personhood or an individuality, bodies embed us in society, and in turn, society constructs the body in relationship to itself and to other bodies.

As increasingly racialized subjects, nineteenth-century Indigenous and other marginalized peoples experienced an acute awareness of their bodies as "the epicenter of political conflict."[23] Print culture portrayed Indigenous peoples in hyper-corporeal ways—their physical strength and resilience, their sexuality, their "savagery" apart from the body-disciplining ways of European societies, and the "exotic" manifestations of culture on their bodies (piercings, tattoos, head and hair shapings, etc.). Perhaps the most famous example of an exoticized Indigenous body occurs within Melville's *Moby-Dick*, as the enigmatic Queequeg displays Polynesian tattoos all over his body, tattoos that Birgit Brander Rasmussen points out as illegible to Ishmael but literate to Queequeg himself.[24] Drew Lopenzina also cites the trauma that alphabetic literacy inflicted upon Native bodies during the practice of branding enslaved Native peoples. He writes,

But the Natives of New Spain were indoctrinated into alphabetic literacy by having it burned into their very flesh, an inscription of their condition of servitude that could not be erased, even as ownership changed hands and new inscriptions were added on top of the old making a palimpsest of Native flesh. The European letter manifested itself as trauma. The marks of alphabetic literacy, seared on the skin, must have appeared as a sign of contagion, a virulent reinscribing of identity transcendent of the mere scars on the surface.[25]

Yet for Indigenous peoples, and for many marginalized groups, the act of authorship became one way in which to assert their humanity and self-advocacy in a society that attempted to categorize their bodies as inferior or subordinate, as nonhuman or subhuman, as savage, or as "three-fifths" of a human being. Flying in the face of these racisms, books evinced logic, reason, artful rhetorical articulation, the full range of human emotions, and the author's authority over their own narratives. In other words, the act of writing oneself into subjectivity in many cases comes ironically through the object of the book and other forms of the printed word.

The language of "book anatomy" reflects a long cultural investment in the link between books and bodies. The bibliographical terms of spine, appendix, header, and footnote permeate the book with human endowments, but they also reflect the significant social and material reality of books as made out of the bodies of plants, animals, and sometimes even other humans, as Sarah Key's *Animal Skins and the Reading Self* (2017), Joshua Calhoun's *The Nature of the Page* (2020), and Megan Rosenbloom's *Dark Archives: A Librarian's Investigation into the Science and History of Books Bound in Human Skin* (2020) provocatively evaluate.[26] Many have considered the book to extend the life of the human body beyond the grave, and we may even expect books to do what bodies cannot: "transcend the invisible forces of time and distance and death."[27] Simultaneously, what Andrew Piper identifies as the "tremendous cultural investment in the corporeal identity of the book" falls back on the faulty ability to "read" the human body, which often rested on false assumptions of race and ability."[28] Taken together, the paratextual examination of Indigenous books across editions remains long overdue for its potential to speak to the multifaceted relationships embodied within Indigenous book history. My project contributes to the scholarly knowledge of Indigenous literary production during the long nineteenth century, speaks to contemporary debates over the value of print, connects Indigenous literary production to colonization's persecution of bodies, and sets the stage for the later outpouring of Indigenous literature in the late twentieth and twenty-first centuries.

The Paratextual Condition of Indigenous Book History

Book Anatomy concentrates on Indigenous prose narratives written in English and published as books between 1854 and 1936, a timeframe that spans nearly one hundred years of changing attitudes toward Indigenous bodies during the simultaneous epoch of print culture. The nineteenth century witnessed some of the earliest Indigenous writers in English, and it includes some of the most intense years of Indigenous history under colonization—bedrock decisions of federal Indian law and policy, removal, boarding schools, reorganization, chronic war, and by acreage the greatest land loss. As such, I emphasize early Indigenous authors as founders, not forerunners, of Indigenous written literature. In addition, the long nineteenth century fixated on the body as a site of difference, experimentation, and proof of an innate hierarchy, to which "scientific" movements such as phrenology attest. In the midst of widespread and diverse debates on the body, American society enlisted print culture as a key means of corporeal persecution. In particular, Indigenous women bore the brunt of hyper-corporeality: for example, in the midst of Sarah Winnemucca Hopkins's literary and political circuit in Washington, D.C., that hoped to influence the U.S. legislative session in favor of Native rights, two regional newspapers attacked her physical appearance by describing her as stunted in stature with unwashed hair, mud-encrusted feet, and "scales of greasy dirt" on her face from which they pretended to calculate her age.[29] Thus not only does the era represent a crucial time frame for Indigenous literary production and book history, it also contains vital context for the way Indigenous books battle both political and corporeal representations.

By focusing exclusively on the book, I acknowledge that I focus on Indigenous authors who had privileged access to certain forms of social, cultural, and/or financial power that enabled the longer form rather than those who published in the often more immediately accessible newspapers, magazines, and other mediums of print culture. Early Indigenous writers engaged much more frequently in newspaper and magazine print culture than book publication, in addition to the numerous types of communication media across Indian country. I also position my project in a different direction than other Indigenous literary scholarship of the long nineteenth century that have brokered new perspectives on the relationships created by print culture and other media, such as Lisa Brooks's *The Common Pot* (2008) and *Our Beloved Kin* (2019), Matt Cohen's *The Networked Wilderness* (2009), Jean O'Brien's *Firsting and Lasting* (2010), Drew Lopenzina's *Red Ink* (2012), Cari Carpenter and Carolyn Sorisio's *The Newspaper Warrior* (2015), and Jacqueline Emery's *Recovering Native American Writings in the Boarding School Press* (2017). This cluster of recent scholarship paves the way in reconsidering early settler colonial and Indigenous exchanges through the printed word, for as Cohen suggests, "If Natives and English were both oral and inscribing peoples, then they constituted each others' audiences in ways scholars have only begun to consider." My project supplements these scholarly movements in finding print culture broadly as an important yet still underdeveloped locus through which to decipher the impact of the printed word on Indigenous lives. Newspapers, too, are meant to interact with the body and represent a crucial medium of Indigenous literary history, one that scholars such as Robert Dale Parker, Carpenter, Sorisio, and many others labor to reveal. Nor do I wish to imply that Indigenous books "spontaneously enter[ed] into print" as isolated events, as Carpenter and Sorisio rightly critique.[30] Rather, books speak in relation to each other as well as many other forms of Native communication. Moving, within, behind, and in front of nineteenth-century Indigenous books were broader Indigenous print cultures and storied media that Indigenous studies scholars continue to put forward in ways that reinvigorate, reexamine, and remap the field.

However, the relative infrequency of early Indigenous books should lend greater weight to those that do appear, as they represent milestones in Indigenous literature. The racial, cultural, and literary breakthrough publications accomplished by these Indigenous authors deserve special recognition, especially as many perceive there to be a dearth of Native literature before 1970.[31] Yet I address Indigenous literary firsts with several factors under advisement: the archival turn of the last several decades in Indigenous literary studies led to the recovery of many of these texts, which cautions us to the ever-changing nature of any literary canon. The field of Indigenous literary studies continues to see tremendous growth in the recovery of all manner and material of Indigenous literature, and I anticipate that what the field now identifies as a "first" may very well change in the coming years.[32] However, the limitations of the field's current knowledge do not diminish the importance of the texts I examine, whether or not they had precedents. I welcome the coming scholarship that may upend any of the current milestones of the known book history, and I see such future recoveries as strengthening and complementing my current endeavors.

My research remains indebted to two foundational works of scholarship: Round's *Removable Type: Histories of the Book in Indian Country, 1663–1880* (2010) and McCoy's "Race and the (Para)Textual Condition" (2006). Round's work surveys the development and importance of Indigenous books and print culture, tracing the power relations enabled through Indigenous deployments of the written word. *Book Anatomy* parallels Round's book in its focus on Indigenous-authored writings during a similar timespan, but my research focuses on the book specifically rather than print culture broadly. My work also inserts the body as a crucial component in the discussion of Indigenous book history and offers one of the first examinations of paratextual elements as a means of understanding Indigenous book production, marketing, and reception. McCoy's article draws upon Gérard Genette's *Paratexts: Thresholds of Interpretation* (1987, English translation 1997) in which he invents the term and exhaustively lists its elements, yet McCoy departs from Genette's evaluation of the paratext as ancillary, a "spatial servant" to the text itself, to argue that "its marginal spaces and places have functioned centrally as a zone transacting ever-changing modes of white domination and of resistance to that domination." Furthermore, she claims, "the American spatial imaginary, after all, still understands white domination almost solely as a series of public, bodily, and, indeed, *textualized* confrontations between white and black. Yet careful attention to texts by and about African Americans challenges this understanding and reveals the hidden, indirect, and *paratextualized* forces impelling and complicating those confrontations."[33] While McCoy focuses exclusively on African American cultural production, I position my scholarship in relation to Indigenous book history and its cultural negotiations over the embodied book.

Chapter by chapter, my project begins with John Rollin Ridge's *The Life and Adventures of Joaquin Murieta* (1854), a book that opens the door to ongoing issues of the printed word, disembodiment, and dispossession within a crucial turning point in nineteenth-century American history. Ridge's novel, which holds the distinction of being the first known novel to be published by a Native man, records a riveting publication history of plagiarism, copyright, and property rights for both Ridge as a Native author and for Indigenous nations during an era of removal and dispossession. Despite Ridge's protests in his author's preface of a later edition, his literary property became appropriated with impunity for over one hundred years after his original publication, at the same time that the property rights of land and labor for the Cherokee Nation, for Mexican Americans, and for California tribal nations also experienced illegal seizure. The multiple editions and plagiarisms of *Murieta* contain paratextual elements that work to alienate or dispossess the author from his novel, and they speak to the difficulties the author of the first known Native American novel encountered when joining the literary marketplace.

My second chapter looks at the political use of blank space in book production, taking up the first two books authored by Indigenous women writers, Sarah Winnemucca Hopkins's autobiography *Life among the Piutes* (1883) and S. Alice Callahan's novel *Wynema: A Child of the Forest* (1891). I begin with the significance of blank space in Indigenous history, often used on colonial maps as an erasure of Native bodies and nations, and then look specifically at the way Indigenous female authors work from within the double-bind of race and gender to repurpose blank space not as erasure but as an invitation to their readers for reflection and alliance. Indigenous women writers faced even greater obstacles on the path to book publication, as evinced by their late entry in the mainstream literary marketplace. Appearing over one hundred years after the first book and over fifty years after the first autobiography published by Indigenous men, Winnemucca's autobiography chronicles not only her activism during the U.S.–Paiute conflict, but also her negotiations to publish within the American literary marketplace. As the first novel published by a Native woman, Callahan's *Wynema* follows soon after to engage with the sentimental genre and record the horrors of genocide. The book history of Indigenous women writers reflects their struggles, under patriarchy and white supremacy, to enter into and control the dominant discourses representing their bodies, and I argue that the authors utilize the blank spaces of their books to work toward a spatial justice in reclaiming lands and bodies.

The subject of my third chapter, *Pretty-shield: Medicine Woman of the Crows* (1932), features a thumbprint in its opening pages that Pretty Shield uses to assert both the veracity of the text and her agency over her body in telling her "woman's story." The marketing, reprinting, reception, and royalties of her narrative may have escaped Pretty Shield's control, but her paratextual thumbprint claims ownership over the text that follows in order to remind readers of her agency. Through the contemporary critical reframing of Native autobiographies, I seek to advance the current autobiographical criticism by conceiving of the paratextual elements in Pretty Shield's life narrative as contested and negotiated bibliographical territory. As such, I offer a theoretical framework that connects spatial theories of the American West to the materiality of the book and argue that the paratextual elements of *Pretty-shield* shine new light on debates over the text's production when examined as a bibliographical territory in which bodies collaborate, battle for agency, and forge new relationships.

Lastly, D'Arcy McNickle's *The Surrounded* (1936) challenges the white gaze through its covers, footnotes, epigraph, and other paratextual elements. Aligning the reader's perspective with a white ethnographic and tourist gaze, McNickle's novel challenges the visual and literary consumption of Native bodies and cultures perpetuated by the twentieth-century tourism of the American Southwest and the rise of primitive modernism. McNickle sought trade presses for his books and published in other national literary venues, urging his mainstream audience of non-Native readers to revise their stereotypes of Indians and reminding them that their perceptions of Native peoples come almost exclusively from Euroamerican rather than Native perspectives. Reinforced by paratextual elements that situate the novel uneasily within ethnographic literature and revise ethnography's citational relations, the narrative of *The Surrounded* redirects the white ethnographic gaze by exposing its failures of vision.

My conclusion extends my analysis into the advent of digitization and its implications for nineteenth-century Indigenous book history scholarship. The process of digitization continues to jeopardize the print record when it is viewed as a replacement for, not a supplement to, the printed word. As a result, the cultural legacy of Indigenous books, not to mention Indigenous print culture broadly and the print culture of other disenfranchised communities, becomes exponentially precarious due to their already underrepresented preservation. Moreover, digitization often neglects to process and make accessible more than one copy or even edition, which then hinders or prevents the comparison of paratextual elements and the work of Indigenous book history itself. I caution against the continuation of these practices, cite ongoing concerns of accessibility and preservation within digitization, and advocate for the future of Indigenous book history.

CHAPTER ONE

Dispossessed

Editorial Dismemberments, Copyright, and Property Rights in John Rollin Ridge's *Murieta*

> [T]he colonizing presence sought to induce a historical amnesia on the colonized by mutilating the memory of the colonized; and where that failed, it dismembered it, and then tried to re-member it to the colonizer's memory. . . .
>
> —Ngũgĩ wa Thiong'o, *Re-membering Africa*

IN THE 2018 edition of Ridge's *The Life and Adventures of Joaquín Murieta* (1854), the publisher includes a lengthy statement in support of copyright. Penguin Books, the paratext announces, supports copyright because it "fuels creativity, encourages diverse voices, promotes free speech, and creates a vibrant culture." Furthermore, it thanks readers for their compliance in copyright law and for doing their part to support writers and the dissemination of books to every reader. The statement's democratic aims for the social good, however, become grimly ironic in regard to the text at hand and its long history of plagiarism. Swept up in the rising popularity of the Murrieta legend that his novel helped establish, Ridge's copyrighted text became alienated and dispossessed from its author: first, his authorized editions contain paratextual elements that work to estrange the author from his novel and speak to the difficulties the author of the first known Native American novel encountered when joining the literary marketplace.[1] Meanwhile, five years after Ridge's initial publication, a salacious crime magazine titled the *California Police Gazette* plagiarized Ridge's text twice by reprinting it in serial form and later in book form in clear violation of copyright. Despite

Ridge's public outrage, his literary property became appropriated with impunity and continued to be reprinted without his byline for over one hundred years after his original publication, at the same time that the land-based properties of the Cherokee Nation, Mexican Americans, and California tribal nations also experienced unjust seizure.[2]

Unauthorized reprints were common during the nineteenth century. In the absence of an international copyright law, world literature and especially British literature could be reprinted in the American literary marketplace without needing to share profits with the author or original publisher, making already commercially successful books, rather than untried American manuscripts, the more profitable choice for publication. As a result, unauthorized reprints and uncopyrighted periodicals dominated the American literary marketplace, leading Meredith McGill to describe the era from 1834 to 1853 as the "culture of reprinting."[3] By the time Ridge copyrighted *Murieta* in 1854, however, the culture of reprinting had shifted. Due to structural changes in the book trades that began in the early 1850s and the increasing commercial viability of American literature, signaled most definitively by Harriet Beecher Stowe's runaway bestseller *Uncle Tom's Cabin* (1852), the culture of reprinting changed as literary property became increasingly legislated.

Yet in the case of Ridge's *Murieta*, a number of conditions make the unauthorized reproductions of his book "plagiarisms" rather than reprints or piracies. *Murieta* was not a commercially successful British book, which had often been the prime target for an unauthorized reprint. Instead, it had been published in the United States and had a U.S. copyright, which did have a protection under domestic law that earlier Native authors, such as Paul Cuffee, William Apess, George Copway, and David Cusick, had pursued. Unlike a piracy, the *Gazette* does not reproduce Ridge's text exactly, although it follows the original plot closely with some additional scenes and details. It does, however, obviously paraphrase Ridge's words and ideas, so much so as to suggest that the writer may have been looking directly at a copy of Ridge's first edition while plagiarizing, as I will demonstrate later in this chapter. These changes, therefore, characterize the *Gazette*'s theft of the novel as a plagiarism rather than an unauthorized reprint or piracy.[4] Moreover, one might additionally label the *Gazette* plagiarisms and many of the republications of Ridge's *Murieta* throughout the twentieth century as ongoing "appropriations," according to Susan Scafidi's definition, since many of them benefit financially by drawing directly from Ridge's stolen plot and characterizations without acknowledging his text as the source.[5]

Plagiarism becomes an economic theft as well as an intellectual one, a point that should not be lost for the first known Native novel as the process of colonization and white supremacy economically impoverished Indigenous nations on multiple fronts. The dispossession Ridge experienced from his novel, therefore, did not reflect the common practices of the literary marketplace but instead more closely mimicked a broader seizure of property, labor, and intellectual and creative output long experienced by Native peoples.

Much of *Murieta* scholarship focuses on the numerous dismemberments in the content and context of the novel, arguing that the decapitation of Murrieta works to animate a number of social issues. Jesse Alemán, for instance, reads the novel as a demonstration of "what happens to the individual and collective racial body politic when they appeal to American ideology for social equality. They end up dispossessed, dismembered, and eventually decapitated." Alemán, John Carlos Rowe, and Mark Rifkin all consider the novel as an "allegory of U.S. expansionism" as the U.S.–Mexican war not only dismembered the Mexican nation, but also exposed the inherent dismemberments present in American democracy and society for marginalized peoples. Erica Stevens traces the theme of dismemberment in another direction through Three-Fingered Jack's hand, which she reattaches to the Caribbean legends of another Three-Fingered Jack: Jack Manson of Jamaica, who also inspired a number of copycat texts. Her essay aims to "study when and how bodies and literary traditions become misshaped, disfigured, or even severed" from their cultural histories. Shelley Streeby and Robert McKee Irwin more broadly argue against the regional and national dismemberment of Ridge's *Murieta* from its larger trans-American context, calling out analyses that elide "a larger, violently divided inter-American field" of literary criticism.[6]

While these scholars trace the appearance of physical, symbolic, and colonial dismemberments in the novel's literary context, I argue that another vein of *Murieta* dismemberments remains at large. Although critics may consider piracy and plagiarism as types of dismemberment, they largely have not considered the omission or replacement of paratextual elements between editions as a series of editorial dismemberments. Yet such paratextual changes often radically repackage a text. They offer new, additional parts that refigure, and sometimes disfigure, the bibliographic body. They may silently remove cover images, an aesthetic design, or illustrations that could otherwise reveal a certain historical moment to critics and readers. They may also obscure the text's history of reception and perception by replacing such items as the introduction, which contributes vital information to the history of the book. These editorial decisions present critical concerns to Indigenous authors and their book history, for as Richard Watts points out, "the paratext often functions as a marker of colonial ownership." He explains, "In the preface of a colonial administrator, the dedication by an author to a colonial governor, and the reduction of indigenous culture to a visual cliché in the book cover's illustration, the authority over the text and the cultures it represents passes from its expected possessor, the author, to the predominant voice in the paratext, that of the colonizer."[7] Such paratextual markers tell a story of colonialism and resistance in the American literary marketplace, a story too easily missed without a critical and editorial attention to a book's paratextual history. Spanning Ridge's authorized editions along with the plagiarisms of his text, the book history of *Murieta* documents the violation of copyright and other paratextual changes across editions as a series of bibliographical dismemberments that estrange the novel from its author and parallel the ongoing fight over the property rights and dispossession of racialized subjects.

Authorship and Ownership: The Nineteenth-Century Editions of Ridge's *Murieta*

In August 1853, a poster appeared in Stockton, California, to advertise the town's newest local entertainment: for one day only, as the poster announces, one can be gruesomely titillated by the dismembered body parts of two infamous California bandits. Joaquín Murrieta's head and Three-Fingered Jack's hand, preserved in large jars, had not been easily obtained and pointed to the continuing violence within the newly formed state of California. In previous years, following the Treaty of Guadalupe Hidalgo, newspapers began to announce the continual raids and murders committed against local citizenry and blamed a man named Joaquín as the ringleader. Yet the newspapers could not agree—at times Joaquín had as many as five different last names, perhaps representing five different men, and he seemed able to commit crimes simultaneously in widely spread geographical locations. The crimes for which Murrieta was accused became so troublesome that on May 11, 1853, the California legislature authorized Captain Harry Love and his group of rangers to capture the elusive Murrieta. After two months of searching, Love and his men triumphantly brought a dismembered head and hand that they claimed belonged to the one and only Joaquín Murrieta and his lieutenant, Three-Fingered Jack, to the governor in exchange for a substantial monetary reward. The controversially identified body parts then made their way around the state in an attempt to convince California citizens of the reestablishment of law and order.

Cherokee writer and expatriate John Rollin Ridge came to California in the heyday of the Joaquín legend. On the run from a murder he allegedly committed in Kansas and fearing retribution, Ridge followed the streams of migrants heading to the farmlands and gold mining camps of the coastal state.[8] There he attempted to make a living with his pen, publishing poems and articles in local periodicals while picking up work as a newspaper editor. As a man with literary ambitions, Ridge soon turned to the novel and decided to capitalize on the romanticized exploits of Joaquín that had been circulating in regional newspapers.[9] The result, a ninety-page sensational novel that anticipates later dime novels, claims to recount with historical accuracy the events of Murrieta's life, from his push into a life of crime to his beheading. Although Ridge's *The Life and Adventures of Joaquin Murieta, the Celebrated California Bandit* (1854) sold well enough to warrant additional reprintings, the book itself and its author would eventually lose the limelight to the international popularity Ridge's creative writing generated for Murrieta, whose legend became reworked and retold into plays, films, dime novels, mysteries and romances, an epic poem, children's books, a Soviet rock opera, and the inspiration for both Batman and Zorro.[10]

Ridge's *The Life and Adventures of Joaquin Murieta* inserts readers into the intense violence of mid-nineteenth-century California. As the novel opens, the narrative paints a sympathetic portrayal of Murrieta, who enthusiastically crosses the border from his boyhood home in Sonora at the conclusion of the U.S.–Mexico war in hopes of becoming an American citizen. He immediately encounters racial prejudice, however, and after a series of brutalities in which Americans rape his mistress, lynch his half-brother, run him off his farm, and whip him, Murrieta turns against his "generous and noble nature" and into a life of crime. Because of the similar injustices experienced by other Mexicans in California, a number of men begin to join Murrieta's band and initiate what in effect becomes an organized crime unit with the sadistic Three-Fingered Jack as Murrieta's right-hand man. The bulk of the novel then relays their daring adventures and close encounters with vigilante law as they exact revenge on the America that denied their equality. The novel ends with Murrieta and Jack's dismemberment at the hands of Captain Love and translates the tragedy of Murrieta's life into a moral lesson: "there is nothing so dangerous in its consequences as *injustice to individuals*—whether it arise from prejudice of color or from any other source; that a wrong done to one man, is a wrong to society and to the world."[11] *Murieta* leaves the reader entertained by the bandit's daring exploits, but it rewraps the gratuitous sensationalism in the sober message of tragic injustice.

Three known nineteenth-century printings of Ridge's novel with his byline exist: a first edition, published by W.B. Cooke in 1854, and a posthumous edition published by Frederick MacCrellish in 1871 (reprinted in 1874) which advertises a narrative "revised and enlarged" by the author before his death.[12] Very few copies of the 1854 edition survived, and they did not reappear in bibliographic history until the 1930s, allowing early twentieth-century scholars to question Ridge's protestations of the novel's plagiarism or to dismiss such claims as unimportant.[13] Even after published scholarship on the 1854 edition appeared, scholars continue to debate Ridge's role in the creation of the Murrieta legend, dismembering text from author by focusing on the folk figure's transcendence over one original source or genre. Streeby, for example, argues for Murrieta's preexistence in newspaper accounts and its continuance in a variety of popular cultural productions, in summary considering "traditional notions of individual authorship" in regard to the Murrieta legend to be "untenable." Her argument counters Joseph Henry Jackson's assertion that Ridge "actually created both the man, Murrieta, and the Murrieta legend" and the attributions of other scholars who acknowledge Ridge's book as the first text to combine circulating oral stories and disparate newspaper accounts into a single extended narrative that provided a baseline for the vast majority of subsequent retellings.[14] While Streeby correctly asserts Murrieta's cultural existence before and beyond Ridge's novel, his legal copyright supports his claim of individual authorship over his text. In other words, Ridge did not claim rights over the exclusive invention of the Murrieta folk figure, but he did claim copyright over his literary product. Consequently, Ridge's accusations of plagiarism must be considered important, tenable, and worthy of examination in the scope of Indigenous book history.

Before *Murieta*'s first plagiarism, the paratextual elements of Ridge's bylined editions reveal preliminary dismemberments of Ridge from his copyright, the full profits of his literary product, and his prominence in Indigenous literary history. In the 1854 edition, for example, the author's byline points to the racism embedded within copyright law. The cover page lists the author as "Yellow Bird," which is the English translation of Ridge's Cherokee name, Cheesquatalawny. The copyright, however, does not give legal authority to the Cherokee name but to Ridge's Euroamerican name, bracketed in fine print at the bottom of the title page: "Entered according to Act of Congress, in the year 1854, by Charles Lindley and John R. Bridge [*sic*] in the Clerk's Office of the District Court of the United States, for the Northern District of California." Although Ridge published under both names in his lifetime, the copyright law favors his Euroamerican name as eligible for property rights rather than his Cherokee name. The bibliographical exchange of the names also implies a play toward the marketability of a Native author's byline, at the same time that the authority, expected financial gain, and credit go first to Lindley and then only secondly to the misspelled name of "John R. Bridge."

Several critics have pointed out the oddity of a shared copyright, though none have discovered why Lindley, a white lawyer from Connecticut and Ridge's supervisor at the Yuba County office, might both receive credit and potential profits from Ridge's literary labor.[15] James Varley speculates that Lindley may have been advocating for Ridge by helping to finance the project and negotiate the publishing contract, but if that were the case, Lindley's labor appears to be more on his own behalf since his name appears first on the copyright. Additionally, there is no known evidence of Lindley's assistance in the project and no subsequent claims of authorship or copyright by Lindley have ever been found.[16] Another possibility for the shared copyright, I offer, might be as additional insurance for Ridge against the precarity of Native citizenship in the United States, as American copyright law only protected its citizens. Yet in any case, the oddly shared copyright serves as an example of the ways in which American law, including copyright law, is never neutral. Ian Hany López puts it simply: "law constructs race at every level," which extends to the influence of race in shaping and molding copyright law. The law works to maintain colonial appropriation and wealth acquisition in favor of white supremacy, and it accords rights to "those who had the capacity to exercise them, a capacity denoted by racial identity."[17]

As racialized nonwhite subjects, Ridge, the Cherokee Nation, and the California tribal nations had little rights to property or to human rights, for that matter, within the U.S. judicial system, and Ridge had personal as well as tribal experiences in the machinations of dispossession. Due to increasing pressure from the U.S. government and the state of Georgia to vacate the thriving plantations of the Cherokee Nation, Ridge's father, grandfather, and others of the Ridge faction signed the Treaty of New Echota in 1835, which agreed to the removal of the Cherokee people to designated lands west of the Mississippi and initiated what was to become the genocidal Trail of Tears. As the Cherokee Nation had made it illegal and punishable by death for any citizen to sign away any more of the nation's land, upon signing the treaty Ridge's father reputedly remarked, "I have signed my death warrant." Ridge's family history with the Treaty of New Echota gave him direct experience with the power of paper to sever a nation. The federal and state pressure to remove purposefully intended to fracture, alienate, and ultimately dispossess the Cherokee Nation and its citizens from their land and their human rights, and the New Echota treaty conspired in that goal. Several members of Ridge's family were indeed assassinated for their role in the treaty, including his father, who was beaten and stabbed to death in front of young Ridge and his mother. Indeed, one possibility for the book's name change between the byline and the copyright may be Ridge's personal struggle with his estrangement from the Cherokee Nation, from which he continued to be alienated for the remainder of his life, as well as his struggles as an Indigenous person to grapple with the assimilation policies he experienced during his lifetime. As James Parins puts it, Ridge's personal life remained "full of contradictions. He was proud of his Cherokee heritage, yet he also espoused the Euro-American doctrine of progress, with all its racial baggage."[18]

After his father's assassination, Ridge and the surviving members of his family fled to Arkansas, where Ridge studied law for a brief time before giving it up to become a writer, perhaps in frustration over the incessant miscarriages of legal justice he had endured in his life. Such injustices only continued when he witnessed the layers of theft and dispossession in California, starting first with the dispossession of California tribal nations and then of Mexican Americans in the aftermath of the Treaty of Guadalupe Hidalgo, during which the newly formed state government "quickly moved to legislate white supremacy by imposing racially targeted laws." The new American laws disenfranchised voters, restricted gold mining to "legal" citizens, prohibited people of color from testifying in court, charged Native peoples with "vagrancy" and subjected them to forced labor, and unofficially sanctioned lynchings and mob violence. For example, the 1850 Foreign Miners' Tax took aim primarily at Mexican miners and levied against them a hefty tax that effectively banned them from mining and its economic opportunities. In 1851, the California Land Act required every land claim in the state to be reviewed and approved in court, a process which resulted in an average of seventeen years of costly litigation for Mexican American landowners. As a result, most Californios lost their wealth to the exorbitant fees of white attorneys and to the squatters who eventually took possession of their lands. Although the Foreign Miners' Tax was repealed and then reinstated with a less oppressive tax, Timothy Powell describe the changes in the law as a means of extracting cheap labor from Mexican Americans and then Chinese immigrants rather than a corrective to a discriminatory law. Meanwhile, the state of California explicitly condoned the genocide of Indigenous California Nations by creating a state-wide bounty for the scalps of Native men, women, and children while white nativists targeted them for rape, lynching, the destruction of their villages by fire, and rifle target practice. Even if a California law did serve to protect Native peoples, the state government, courts, and citizens "ignored it whenever it collided with their own interests," as Sabine Meyer reports grimly.[19] Yet as Damon Akins and William Bauer, Jr. eloquently detail in *We Are the Land: A History of Native California*, Indigenous peoples in California (and across the world) fought and continue to fight for their property rights and human rights in the face of horrific dispossession and violence.

Ridge's alienated copyright parallels the alienated property rights of the Cherokee Nation and many other tribal nations under American colonization and its judicial system. Multiple scholars cite that the "model for copyright is real property," and as Cheryl Harris argues in her foundational essay on whiteness as property, "Possession—the act necessary to lay the basis for rights in property—was defined to include only the cultural practices of whites." Such legal systems of racialized discrimination and oppression extended not only to racially contingent forms of property and property rights but also to copyright in the white-dominated literary marketplace. Authorship signified ownership within the increasingly legislated American literary marketplace of the nineteenth century, and copyright effectively functioned as a "white man's right," promoted within the structures of whiteness as a type of property, a means of claiming rights, and a mark of citizenship. Recognizing it as such, colonized, enslaved, and marginalized citizens pursued authorship and ownership as a key opportunity for enfranchisement, for, in Isabel Hofmeyr's words, "one route into being a rights-bearing subject was to become a book-bearing one." Race-based property rights remain part of what makes Ridge's novel so perpetually compelling, as it unsettles racist U.S. law and imperial policies through what Jason

Berger describes as the novel's violent assertion of "what the law and imperial polices intentionally foreclose: a Mexican/Mexican American seizing and reappropriating capital."[20] In this context, then, the foul play toward Ridge's copyright stands as especially egregious: for Ridge to write and attempt to publish a book under his own copyright made a provocative statement, in the midst of the overwhelming dispossession of his era, that threatened a disruption (however small) in the continued disenfranchisement of Native peoples as citizens, subjects, and fully realized human beings. In response, the machinations of the publishing industry effectively sidestepped Ridge's individual property rights by misspelling his name on the copyright page, sharing his copyright with a presumably white lawyer, and negating his rights to the written story so that other white, and then later nonwhite, individuals could profit off of his written version.

Ridge first claims to have had his book's profits stolen from him by his publishers in a disgruntled letter sent to his cousin, Stand Watie. In his letter, he laments the severing of his labor and profits from his book's first edition after the suspicious dissolution of his book's publishing company, profits which would have been considerable if his allegation of 7,000 copies sold was not exaggerated.[21] Jackson later casts doubt on Ridge's claim to the bankruptcy of his book's publisher, W.B. Cooke, by saying in his 1955 introduction to *Murieta* that no record of his bankruptcy has yet been recovered. Documents from advertisements and the San Francisco business directory during this time strongly indicate, however, that Ridge's publisher dissolved their business (and their financial obligations) sometime within the year 1853, only to have both partners take up separate print shop businesses down the street from their original shop in the following years.[22] Such dishonest business practices were common in the unstable publishing market of San Francisco in the 1850s, and this could easily be the duplicitous scheme that Ridge refers to in his letter when he tells his cousin of being cheated out of his novel's profits.

A few years after Ridge's loss of remuneration, he discovers the plagiarism of his book by the *California Police Gazette* and publicly expresses his outrage at the injustice in several venues, including in his editorial for the *Daily National Democrat* and in his preface to the 1871 edition of *Murieta*.[23] The *Gazette* ran his story as a serial in their periodical for ten consecutive issues, from September 3 to November 5, 1859, and then published it in book form that same year.[24] The similarities between the two texts clearly demonstrate the plagiarism of Ridge's earlier edition: for comparison, the first sentence of Ridge's first edition reads,

> I sit down to write somewhat concerning the life and character of *Joaquin Murieta*, a man as remarkable in the annals of crime as any of the renowned robbers of the Old or New World, who have preceded him; and I do this, not for the purpose of ministering to any depraved taste for the dark and horrible in human action, but rather to contribute my mite to those materials out of which the early history of California shall one day be composed.

while the first sentence of the *Gazette* text reads,

> In portraying the life and character of Joaquin Murieta, a man as remarkable in the calendar of crime, as any of the celebrated marauders of the old or new world, it is not for the purpose of ministering to a taste for the horrible, but rather to contribute to those materials out of which the criminal history of this State, shall at some future day be composed.

The plagiarism of the writing, down to the sentence structure and the synonyms, is obvious here and throughout the narrative. The *Gazette* plagiarism, however, does make a number of its own textual edits: it changes the name of Murrieta's lover from Rosita to Carmela (later variants include Carmen, Clarina, and Clarita), omits Ridge's insertion of his 1852 "Mount Shasta" poem, and overall drops and adds several paragraphs while keeping Ridge's main narrative intact.[25] In particular, the omission of Ridge's "Mount Shasta" poem here again connects land rights and property rights—the removal of the "Mount Shasta" poem symbolically mimics the removal of Mount Shasta, a *site* of spiritual significance, from the sovereign rights of California Native nations, and at the same time it removes the author's *cite* of the poem, his self-citation of authorship with an asterisk and a footnote to the poem, in order to plagiarize his novel more completely.

Although some of the *Gazette*'s changes do polish Ridge's prose and add further details to Murrieta's life, they nevertheless work to disguise the theft of Ridge's literary labor. They also undermine the original narrative's call for racial justice, most notably in the changes made to the ending. As Joe Goeke documents, the *Gazette* radically alters Ridge's ending lament of injustice for people of color by cutting out two of the original text's most often quoted passages: "[Joaquín] also leaves behind him the most important lesson, that there is nothing so dangerous in its consequences as *injustice to individuals*—whether it arise from prejudice of color or from any other source; that a wrong done to one man, is a wrong done to society and to the world" and, the final line, "Alas, how happy might [Rosita] not have been, had man never learned to wrong his fellow-man!" The *Gazette* ends instead with an assertion of Americans, and implicitly white American women, as the victims of Murrieta, with no mention of the wrongs done to anyone else: in the plagiarism, the last sentence reads, "But little doubt exists in the writer's mind that many persons who are mentioned in the advertisements headed 'Information Wanted,' and emanating, perhaps, from a mother enquiring for her son, or a wife for her husband, have been the victims of the bandit Joaquin." Not only do the textual changes, therefore, sever Ridge from his text, but they also sever what Irwin identifies as Ridge's attempt to put "American racism at the root of the violence."[26]

The editorial dismemberments of the *Gazette* plagiarism also appear in the paratext. In addition to erasing Ridge's byline and copyright from the opening pages, the *Gazette* cuts out the first edition's two prefaces that address Ridge's identity and intentions for the text while also replacing the original Anthony and Baker lithographs with several illustrations by Charles Christian Nahl, a well-established artist whose work embellished many San Francisco periodicals during the 1850s.[27] The Nahl illustrations would later predominate nearly all major reprints of Ridge's *Murieta*, appearing in both plagiarisms and bylined editions from the nineteenth century to the most recent twenty-first-century Penguin reprint. Even as these modern editions restore Ridge's byline to his literary work, the Nahl illustrations continue to haunt the book and its paratext with the undead *Gazette* plagiarism.

No known records exist of any attempt by Ridge to pursue legal action against the *Gazette*, but neither did he give up his claims to his book. A few years after his unexpected death in October 1867, Frederick MacCrellish and Company published what they labeled as a "third edition" of Ridge's *Murieta* that includes his byline, a new preface by the author, and a text that the cover page announces to be "revised and enlarged" by Ridge.[28] Calling itself a "third" edition possibly signals the bibliographical loss of a second edition, as Ridge does write of an edition that he mentions sending off for publication in the Atlantic states because of the greater stability of their publishing houses.[29] Most likely, however, Ridge uses "third" bitterly as a jab against the *Gazette's* plagiarized "second" volume of his book.[30] His enraged author's preface indicates as much, as it calls out the unjust plagiarism of his book and claims this 1871 third edition as "a matter of justice both to the author and the public, inasmuch as a spurious edition has been foisted upon unsuspecting publishers and by them circulated, to the infringement of the author's copyright and the damage of his literary credit."[31] Already aware that other writers were trying to detach text from author, Ridge attempts to use the paratextual elements available to him to combat his book's theft and restore his byline to his book.

Instead, Ridge becomes further alienated from his novel and the potential profits of its copyright in the posthumous 1871 edition, in which the publisher himself registers the copyright in his own name and states in his preface that he has purchased it from the late John Rollin Ridge.[32] It is legally possible to sell one's copyright, and on the one hand, for Ridge to do so would have made a strong statement as a Native author about his ownership over his intellectual property and the exercise of his property rights. On the other hand, however, one might also maintain a healthy skepticism given the suspicious circumstances Ridge previously experienced in regard to his book's profits and copyright, and whether or not this was a legal sale authorized by Ridge or his widow has not been substantiated.[33]

While the judicial system and publishing industry denied Ridge as a Native author the full property rights to his book except when those rights became available for purchase, so the Cherokee Nation in Ridge's youth had experienced the same alienation from property rights. In *Johnson v. McIntosh* (1823), the first of the "Marshall trilogy" rulings by Supreme Court Chief Justice John Marshall that centered around the Cherokee Nation and became the precedent for federal Indian law, questioned not whether Indians had the right to convey title, but to whom they could confer such title. As Harris argues, "In *Johnson* and similar cases, courts established whiteness as a prerequisite to the exercise of enforceable property rights. Not all first possession or labor gave rise to property rights; rather, the rules of first possession and labor as a basis for property rights were qualified by race." The Grabhorn Press, who republished the *Gazette* plagiarism several times for their own profit throughout the twentieth century, repeated an eerily similar justification: because Ridge did not have "first" possession, either in an extant and acknowledged first edition or in the creation of the Murrieta legend, he did not have possession of, nor an economic right to, the written story. For both land rights and literary rights, in Ridge's experience, "Indian forms of possession were perceived to be too ambiguous and unclear" to have an impact on property and profit.[34] Under an unjust American legal system, for Native authors and Native nations alike, one did not have an unchallenged legal right to own property (or have the full protection of the law over one's property) unless one was white, had access to white privilege, or was willing to sell.

When the MacCrellish publishing house reprinted *Murieta* again in 1874, it fought for the continued association of Ridge's byline with his novel despite the overwhelming dispossession of author from text. However, the 1874 MaCrellish reprint also perpetuates the alienation of the book by aligning it more recognizably with Mexican American and Californian literary history rather than Native literary history. This later publication repackages *Murieta* by binding it together with a brief fourteen-page narrative of the *Career of Tiburcio Vasquez, the Bandit of Soledad, Salinas and Tres Pinos, with Some Account of His Capture by Sheriff Rowland of Los Angeles* (1874), as a clear attempt to capitalize on *Murieta*'s popularity with what it deemed to be a companion text. While the *Career of Tiburcio Vasquez* appears second in the MacCrellish reprint, a later 1927 edition by the Evening Free Lance press reverses this order and places the *Vasquez* text first, along with a prominent frontispiece of Tiburcio Vasquez.

The shift in canonicity here became so effective that Blake Hausman mentions the novel as inspiration for a number of Latinx writers (rather than Native writers)—Pablo Neruda, Rodolfo "Corky" Gonzales, and Isabel Allende. Hausman also mentions that the Murrieta character "became the basis for Zorro and therefore the progenitor of Batman," popular figures who arguably have clearer connections to Latinx cultures than Indigenous. In fact, by the time of Hausman's twentieth-first century reflection on teaching Ridge's novel, no doubt he shares the sentiment of many Native studies scholars when he considers the novel to be "problematic" for its derogatory portrayal of Native peoples in California and, by implication, for its place in the Indigenous literary canon.[35] Such a bibliographical alignment, along with the primacy of Mexican American characters in the novel's content, worked so successfully that although *Murieta* continues to be recognized as the first known Native novel, it remains largely overlooked in Native literary scholarship. Phillip Round's otherwise comprehensive overview of over two centuries of Native book history in *Removable Type* (2010) never mentions *Murieta*, nor does Daniel Heath Justice's Cherokee-specific literary history, *Our Fire Survives the Storm* (2005). Only a few critics housed within Native literary studies have taken up an extended analysis of the novel despite its milestone status, while others have expressed doubt as to whether it should be considered Native literature at all. Instead, most *Murieta* criticism has come from those working within Latinx literary studies or more broadly within the nineteenth century, as demonstrated by the 1999 Arte Público reproduction which places the narrative within its "Recovering the U.S. Hispanic Literary Heritage" series and by the 2018 Penguin edition by Hsuan Hsu, who works primarily as a nineteenth-century scholar rather than a Native literary studies scholar.[36] The 1874 MacCrellish reprinting, then, initiates a trajectory of alienation from Native literary history that corresponds to the overshadowing popularity of the *Gazette* plagiarism during the twentieth century.

Twentieth-Century Appropriations: The Grabhorn's Fine Press Edition

After the *Gazette*'s appropriation of Ridge's text, other publishing houses followed suit and republished the plagiarism without crediting or acknowledging Ridge. In 1932 the Grabhorn Press reprinted the book in an attempt to capitalize on the continuing popular and commercial success of the Murrieta legend, reinvigorated in that same year by the publication of Walter Noble Burns's *The Robin Hood of El Dorado: The Saga of Joaquin Murrieta, Famous Outlaw of California's Age of Gold* and in the 1936 MGM film version. Grabhorn clearly sought to distinguish itself through its quality reproduction, as its fine press edition includes eight reproduced color illustrations by Charles Nahl, an aesthetic attention to typeface and font on quality paper, a series of introductory paratexts that celebrate the edition as the first in Grabhorn's Series of Rare Americana Reprints, a "comprehensive" introduction and bibliography by Francis P. Farquhar, a brief editor's preface, and a large fold-out reproduction of the 1853 broadside advertisement for the exhibition of Murrieta's head. The publisher's preface unabashedly claims the *Gazette* "version" to be "considered by most critics to be the best of the early stories," and in keeping with the book's appropriation, the book lists no author and claims the copyright for itself.[37]

The plagiarism, however, does not seem to be a matter of concern to the edition's introduction by Farquhar. Instead he joins in the dismemberment of Ridge from his literary product: rather than acknowledge Ridge as the text's literary source, Farquhar instead calls Ridge's novel a "prototype" and identifies "two principal versions of the story,

distinguished by the name of the heroine." These claims might be partially mitigated by the fact that until approximately 1937, no first edition of Ridge's 1854 novel could be found, yet Ridge's preface, readily
available in the 1871 edition, clearly accuses another source of producing a "spurious edition" that infringes on the author's copyright and
attempts to obfuscate the original edition. Farquhar, however, further
disassociates Ridge's original and implicitly disavows any wrongdoing by claiming, "All subsequent Murieta narratives . . . appear to be
derived from one or the other of these versions," in an attempt to establish two textual "versions," rather than a first edition and a badly disguised plagiarism.[38]

In addition, Farquhar tries to convince the *Murieta* reader that such
accusations of plagiarism should not matter. "After all," he writes, "what
difference does it make whether he [Murrieta] was born in Sonora or in
Chile, or whether his *querida* was named Carmela or Rosita?" despite the
fact that he establishes on the same page the significance of tracing the
Carmela versus Rosita names to "two" original versions. He once more
repeats his disavowal of the plagiarism by the end of his introduction
with a more direct address of Ridge's claim, writing, "In default of a
copy of Ridge's first edition, and lacking positive assurance as to its date,
the question of plagiarism cannot be conclusively settled; but, after all
these years, we need not concern ourselves very seriously with matter
of infringement."[39] In other words, prior Indigenous claims should not
infringe the press's right to continue make a profit off a popular story,
even if the profit comes from stolen property.

When Valley Publishers reprinted the Grabhorn Press appropriation
in 1969, it added the "supplementary notes" of Raymund F. Wood and
Charles W. Clough immediately after the notes of Farquhar. Although
by 1969 the existence of Ridge's 1854 first edition had been widely pub-
licized and Franklin Walker's 1937 published collation "substantiates
beyond question Ridge's charge of plagiarism," both Wood and Clough
continue to discredit Ridge. Wood does credit Ridge for "the first 'fic-
tionalized' account" of Murrieta's life, but then speculates, based on
dubious guesswork, that Ridge wrote the *Gazette* piracy as well as his own
bylined editions. In doing so, Wood actually proposes that Ridge was
guilty of plagiarizing himself, perhaps as another way to deflect the plagiarism and Ridge's dispossession. Wood ends his preface by claiming,
"The true author will probably never be known, however, in the long
run the authenticity of the authorship is not a matter of great importance. What is of importance is that this story of Murrieta is a first-class

tale, founded on historical fact, but embellished with imaginative fiction. What more could a reader want?"[40] Here Wood repeats Farquhar's claims, thirty years later and certainly after the discovery of Ridge's original, that copyrighted authorship is not important—in the preface for a plagiarized text. While Wood is correct in referring to the legend of Murrieta that a single origin for the folk figure is not possible, his words disavow Ridge's legal authorship of his text and its continual appropriation.

Clough's notes conspire with Farquhar and Wood. He implicitly acknowledges the widespread appropriation of Ridge's text by claiming that most international editions have been taken from the *Gazette* publication, but he attempts to justify the appropriations by maintaining that none "will more dramatically tell the story" than the plagiarized version.[41] With this stance, Clough implies that although Ridge may have written it first, the *Gazette* wrote it best and in doing so may be excused for its plagiarism. His arguments sound eerily similar to settler colonial justifications of land theft, accusing Native peoples of not using the land or not using it correctly in order to rationalize their "better" use. In all, despite its bibliographic beauty, the Grabhorn Press appropriations disavow, discredit, and dismember Ridge from his text and continue to make a profit off the plagiarized text.

One hundred years after the 1854 publication of Ridge's novel, the University of Oklahoma Press reproduced the text as part of its Western Frontier Library Series to make the original volume widely available to the public for the first time since its original publication. With a lengthy introduction by *Murieta* scholar Joseph Henry Jackson, the 1955 University of Oklahoma Press edition works to reattach the first known Native novelist with his book. It acknowledges Ridge as the author and returns the authorial byline to its original attribution of "Yellow Bird," placing "John Rollin Ridge" below the byline in brackets. Yet the scars of editorial dismemberment and appropriation remain: the Press itself owns the copyright and mentions no other copyright ownership on the page, signifying in absentia the severance of Ridge from his original copyright and his family's literary and financial inheritance.

Moreover, the cover chosen for the Oklahoma edition reproduces a Charles Nahl illustration from the *Gazette* plagiarism, haunting and conflating the book's appropriated legacy. The fifty-page introduction by Jackson as a white male scholar, despite his advocacy for Ridge's novel, dominates the slim text that follows and repeats the moves of previous editions by aligning Ridge and his text predominantly with Mexican

American history and cultural production, which continues to alienate the book from the Indigenous literary canon. In addition, the press describes the novel's importance as a "classic tale of Western Americana," to fit its inclusion in their Western Frontier Library series, and it exploits Indigenous and Mexican stereotypes with the Nahl cover image of a wide-eyed Mexican and a series imprint that features a bear claw design encompassing feathered and war-painted Indians. The image of the series imprint leans in on the "charm" of racist stereotypes while its label within the American West sends a dominating message of colonization and new ownership.[42] Additionally, in contrast to the stereotypical images included elsewhere, the book oddly does not include an image of the author, despite several available photographs used by his biographers and the common appearance of such frontispieces in other works of Indigenous literature. Although this University of Oklahoma Press edition restores Ridge's byline (Yellow Bird as well as John Rollin Ridge) to *Murieta* and allows it to be widely available for the first time in over one hundred years, its paratextual elements also include discursive acts of violence and contribute to the perpetual reinscription of Indigenous property rights as white American property.

Conclusion: Hauntings and Re-Memberings

At the conclusion of the novel, the narrative follows Murrieta's head past its decapitation to its exhibition across the state of California. It reports the surprise of "superstitious" onlookers who "were seized with a kind of terror to observe that the moustache of the fearful robber had grown longer since his head was cut off, and that the nails of Three-Fingered Jack's hand had lengthened almost an inch." Three-Fingered Jack's hand also invoked in the morbid sightseers "a strange, haunting dread over the mind, as if it had been a conscious, voluntary agent of evil." David Drysdale reads the gruesome conclusion as a grim reminder of the "violence of incorporation and the containment of resistance" under the nation-state, and he invokes the novel itself as another type of decapitated exhibit, one through which Americans can similarly "read" the history of California conquest and participate in the circulation of the outlaw's head. As a reminder of the foremost theft and dispossession of California tribal nations, one might also recall here the similarly disturbing and exhibitionist circumstances surrounding the death of Ishi, perhaps the most well-known citizen of a Native California nation, who received an autopsy against his explicit personal and cultural wishes and whose dismembered brain was preserved in a jar at the Smithsonian Institution for nearly one hundred years until recently repatriated. Drysdale's words regarding the novel as exhibiting another type of state violence match McGill's description of reprinting as a process by which "authors are detached and reattached to their texts."[43] Their words provoke a sobering reflection on the production of editions as not only the rebirth of a bibliographical body, but also potentially the disfigurement or even decapitation of a previous corpus.

The latest 2018 edition of Ridge's *Murieta* exhibits such a troubled tension within editing and reprinting as it hauntingly traces the novel's continuance even after the paratextual decapitation of author and copyright and the disfigurement of the book's textual body. Its appendix gathers for display several excerpts from the "unsigned, plagiarized version" of the novel by the *California Police Gazette*, followed by Ridge's rebuttal in his preface to the "third" 1874 edition and several of its revised passages. It then includes two excerpts from texts inspired by Ridge's novel, including Johnston McCulley's *The Curse of Capistrano*, later republished as *The Mark of Zorro* (1919, 1924). Yet despite its attempts to reunite *Murieta*'s textual body with Ridge as the author, the new edition brokers an uneasy relationship between the authorized and unauthorized additions by stitching together the dismembered parts to create a type of new body for Ridge's text. It perpetuates the violence of the original plagiarism by showcasing a Nahl illustration from the *California Police Gazette* plagiarism on its cover, invoking the history of Ridge's dismemberment from his text. The illustration, titled "Joaquin Murieta: The Vaquero," has noticeably darker skin than previous illustrations but still sits astride a wild and wide-eyed horse, reinforcing the text's exoticized American West. The new edition boldly features the author's byline in orange ink, but it matches the orange ink prominently on the back cover with the description, "The first novel to feature a Mexican American hero, based on the real-life bandit who inspired the creation of Zorro, the Lone Ranger, and Batman." Taken together, the paratextual elements of the latest edition serve to obfuscate the novel's connection to Indigenous book history, highlighting instead its connection to Mexican American and Western literary history.

As further evidence of discursive violence, the Library of Congress cataloging-in-publication data then attempts to remove any bibliographical trace of race and ethnicity by listing only the following subject headings for classification: "Fiction. Frontier and pioneer life—Fiction. Revolutionaries—Fiction. Outlaws—Fiction. California—Fiction.

Biographical Fiction. Western stories." By way of contrast, the 1998 reprint of the less well-known Mohawk writer E. Pauline Johnson's 1913 short story collection lists "Indians of North America" as its primary subject heading. Though the 2018 edition takes steps forward to re-member original ownership, even in the contemporary moment the publication data of Ridge's novel continues to alienate Indigenous propriety and sever Indigenous relationships to their land and literary history.

In *The Unfinished Book*, Alexandra Gillespie writes, "books, like decapitated heads, are uncanny objects; they signify in the absence of their author's capacity to speak." The book history of Ridge's *Murieta* troubles our assumptions of new editions, even scholarly editions, as primarily in service of the text and its author. Like the continued growth of hair on Murrieta's severed head, the unsettling bibliographical body lives on after its dismemberment as both a "continuing presence that destabilizes the state's narrative of closure" and as a haunting testament to the racialized inheritance of book history. The bibliographical bodies of Indigenous book history continue to gesture toward the "expansive dispossession" that extends from property rights to copyright for Indigenous people, while simultaneously refusing to accept their bibliographical severance by growing, reanimating, and unsettling.[44] Every reading of the text, every reprint and new edition, participates in the reattachment and decapitation of Murrieta's head, exhibiting the ongoing tension between the membership and dismemberment in this country.

CHAPTER TWO

Whiteness, Blank Space, and Gendered Embodiment in Winnemucca's *Life among the Piutes* and Callahan's *Wynema*

I feel most colored when I am thrown against a sharp white background.
—Zora Neale Hurston, "How It Feels to Be Colored Me"

There is a tendency to imagine the Indians as virtual blanks—wild, unformed creatures, as naked in culture as they are in body.
—Stephen Greenblatt, *Marvelous Possessions*

Monte said our blank books made more sense to him than anything he had ever read. This guy was really cracked. Our books were blank except on one page there was an original tribal pictomyth painted by me in green ink, a different pictomyth on a different page in every blank book. Yes, pictomyths, stories that are imagined about a picture, about memories. So, even our blank books had a story.
—Gerald Vizenor, "Almost Browne"

FAR FROM BEING neutral, passive, or insignificant, the blank spaces within books impact not only what we read but also how we read. Space on the page makes words legible: it invites the eye and organizes the layout of text, it signals the beginning and end of book and chapter, and it sets the boundaries between text and page. Blank space gives an added emphasis to the words it sets apart, such as a title or a line of dialogue, and it invites the reader to place an added value on such words. In typographical language, it is white space, not solely words, that creates a "composition." Due to its vital function, therefore, blank space serves as a profound driving force in our relationship with print. Yet because of its paratextual nature, relatively few literary scholars turn their attention to the blank spaces of prose and the relationships they establish between text and page. For example, Genette's foundational *Paratexts* does not address, as Jerome McGann points out, "such matters as ink, typeface, paper, and various other phenomena which are crucial to the understanding of textuality" because they often fall outside of a linguistic purview. Yet as McGann asserts, "all texts, like all other things human, are embodied phenomena, and the body of the text is not exclusively linguistic."[1]

From some of their earliest colonial encounters, Indigenous peoples engaged with the blank paratextual spaces of European documents by inserting complex declarations of identity, agency, and Indigenous presence into the margins of ethnographies, Bibles, treaties, and other texts. Coll Thrush, for example, documents the indelible Roanoke presence in London from as early as 1584 when Thomas Harriot returned to Europe and provided to the English-speaking world one of the first detailed accounts of the Indigenous peoples of Virginia. As part of his "brief and true report" of his journey, Harriot attempted to write an Ossomocomuck orthography with the help of the Indigenous peoples he encountered, whose names he never credited as translators or coauthors on the title page but one of whom, nonetheless, inserted his name as what Thrush describes as a "material footprint" in the margins of the text: "King Manteo did this." In another instance, Hilary Wyss documents the creation of an "alternative text" by Native owners in the margins of the 1663 Algonquian Bible, which was translated, composed, and printed by John Eliot and, without accreditation, tribal citizens John Sassomon (Massachusett), Job Nesuton (Massachusett), and James Printer (Nipmuc). Yet Indigenous-authored marginal insertions, "scrawling sideways, upside down, on any bare space," stressed ownership over their Algonquian Bibles and their literacy, writing, "I, Nathan Francis, this is my writing at this time," "I, Mantooekit, (x) [*sic*] This is my hand," and "I am Matthew Seiknout, this is my Bible, clearly."[2] Although the paratextual absence of the Indigenous contributors' printed names obscures their role in the text, Indigenous assertions of ownership and agency into the book's blank spaces refuses to permit Indigenous erasure. In the face of the rising onslaught of colonization, their marginal, handwritten marks assert the continuing presence of Native peoples, bodies, and communities embedded within the book object.

By connecting the blank spaces of bibliography with the spatial embodiment of Native women, I extend the current scholarship on gender, writing, and space to underscore the spatial agency of early

Indigenous women's book history. Indigenous female authors entered the mainstream literary marketplace significantly later than their male counterparts, with over one hundred years between the first book published by a Native man and a Native woman, fifty years between the first male and the first female autobiography, and nearly forty years between the first novels.[3] Early book history for Indigenous women reflects their struggles, under the double bind of race and gender, to enter into and control the dominant literary discourses representing their bodies, and the genres they chose tellingly reflect a close association with the body: autobiography and sentimental fiction. Yet early Indigenous women's writing extends further than their choice of genre into the blank spaces of their books, as they repurposed the margins and entered into a textual and paratextual battle for control over their stories. By taking up Sarah Winnemucca Hopkins's *Life among the Piutes* (1883) and S. Alice Callahan's *Wynema* (1891) as the first known books published by Native women, I analyze three types of blank space—strategic rhetorical omissions, paragraph and chapter breaks, and the invitation of the margins—to argue that their books re-envision blank space not as erasure but as an opportunity to form relationships and provoke advocacy from their readers on behalf of Native peoples.

Bodies, Land, and Blank Space

In addition to Indigenous ways of knowing, perceiving, and being in relation to the land, the process of colonization initiated another type of association between Native peoples, bodies, and space. In *Mark My Words: Native Women Mapping Our Nations* (2013), Mishuana Goeman writes extensively on the spatialization of Native bodies, and especially the bodies of Native women, under colonization. Colonization remaps sovereign Native space, Goeman explains, by incorporating it under colonial control yet simultaneously pressuring it to exist outside of continually encroaching settler boundaries. Meanwhile, the settler colonial imaginary reconstructs Native bodies as abnormal and relegates them to existence only within specific physical and social boundaries, criminalizing them if they step outside their assigned, degenerate spaces. Such actions work together, Goeman concludes, as colonialism does not confine itself solely to "conquering Native lands through mapping new ownerships, but it is also about the conquest of bodies, particularly women's bodies through sexual violence, and about recreating gendered relationships."[4]

Blank spaces on colonial maps remain one of the most poignant visualizations of these settler colonial processes, as they materialize the attempted erasure of Native peoples—both their bodies and the sovereignty of their political bodies over the land—while representationally preparing settler colonials to encounter an empty and "virgin" space. So well aware were Indigenous peoples of the colonial strategy of blank space that John Ridge, father to John Rollin Ridge, wrote bitterly in the era of Indian Removal, "These treaties are valid and constitutional when an Indian sells dirt; but when he calls for protection from the encroachment of the white men, these treaties are immediately held up to the world as blank paper."[5] The respatialization of settler colonialism specifically targeted Native women, as immediately evident in the Euroamerican terminology of "virgin" land open to conquest, a conceptual violence that promoted a targeted sexual violence.[6] Black women and other women of color, however, also experienced the conceptual and physical sexual violence of blank space: speaking in another context, Faith Barter examines a scene from Hannah Crafts's *A Bondwoman's Narrative* (c. 1853–1861, 2002) in which a white female enslaver considers an enslaved Black woman not as a human being, but as "a space to fill," a phrase that points to the inhumanity of the systemic processes of slavery and its sanctioned rape of Black women.[7] The blank space of colonial maps, then, extends to other manifestations of blank space in a link between text and page, space and displacement, and bodies in relation.

Yet writing offers one way to respatialize, both materially and socially, the blank spaces of colonization and other systemic processes of inequality. Of her own book, and under a subtitle that claims "The Map and the Book Are the Same Thing," Lisa Brooks writes,

> This book, then, is at once an activity in which we participate, an instrument, and a map. It is a map of a network of writers and texts, as well as a process of mapping the historical space they inhabit. It is a mapping of how Native people in the northeast used writing as an instrument to reclaim lands and reconstruct communities, but also a mapping of the *instrumental* activity of writing, its role in the rememberment of a fragmented world."

Brooks's claims reinforce other current scholarship on gender, space, and writing, which stress both gender and space as social constructs that not only share much in common but are also used to reinforce each other. Feminist scholarship in spatial studies, for example, has highlighted the links between patriarchal power and the coding of both public and private spaces that enables agency for one gender while restricting it for another. Yet scholars also emphasize unjust spatial practices not as a natural, fixed, or permanent state, but rather as a working system under constant negotiation. For example, Goeman writes of an awareness from her childhood of her embodiment in space, reflecting, "Unlike the maps that designate Indian land as existing only in certain places, wherever we went there were Natives and Native spaces, and if there weren't, we carved them out." Women writers act in that negotiation, reclaiming and repurposing blank space in what Goeman calls the "spatial configuration in Native women's writing" and what Kinohi Nishikawa describes for Black women as black or embodied pagecraft, a Black feminist tradition of typographical experimentation and especially the use of blank space on the page to communicate trauma and vulnerability.[8] The activism of Indigenous women writers, then, extends into the realm of blank space to challenge its colonial uses as erasure and instead to reframe blank space as an arena for advocacy.

Petitioning Blank Space: Winnemucca's *Life among the Piutes*

Winnemucca's *Life among the Piutes: Their Wrongs and Claims* (1883) stages a political autobiography aimed at exposing the injustices of colonization and rectifying the theft of Northern Paiute land.[9] Her book begins in an autobiographical style with her birth, yet instead of recording the details of her personal life, Winnemucca titles the first chapter "First Meeting of Piutes and Whites" and immediately redirects most of her narrative to first contact and the resulting warfare, in essence developing her autobiography into a war memoir.[10] Aside from a short chapter on "Domestic and Social Moralities" designed to contradict racist stereotypes of Indigenous women, the remaining chapters document Winnemucca's diplomacy in Paiute relations with the United States. She describes the constant persecution and fear inflicted by settlers on her people, including sexual violence, acts of genocide, and duplicitous politics of land theft: nearly every chapter includes the horrific sexual exploitation of Indigenous women and emphasizes the physical violence of contact with Western culture.

Early in her narrative Winnemucca relays the proximity to her people of the Donner party cannibalism, an implicit counterpoint to the supposedly superior and beneficial coming of white "civilization." From her childhood she relates the relentless sexual harassment endured by her sister Mary and, while lying in the same bed, hearing her sister's heart beat in fear as men approached the house during the night. In another instance, Winnemucca tells the horrific story of two Paiute girls found gagged and tied to a bed in the basement of a trading post belonging to two white brothers, which "[w]hen my people saw their condition," killed the two brothers and started a war. Winnemucca relates several of her own instances of fighting off attempted rape and summarizes the overall climate of sexual persecution of Indigenous women early in the book when she testifies, "The mothers are afraid to have more children, for fear they shall have daughters, who are not safe even in their mother's presence."[11] As she relays her unflinching account of colonial relations, Winnemucca positions her adult life as being in dedicated service to the Paiute, which often entailed acting as an intermediary between them and the United States. For a large portion of her life she acted as a translator and mediator in conflict zones between government agents, the military, and the Paiute, as she details in her book, and later in her life she turned her activism into lobbying, drawing from previous experiences in theatrical public performances with her family to give hundreds speeches on behalf of her people.[12] She published only one book in her lifetime and died eight years after its publication, yet her autobiography stands as a boldly worded defense of her reputation, Indigenous women and their bodily sovereignty, and Paiute land rights.

Winnemucca's autobiography distinguishes itself in Indigenous literary history not only as the first known book published by a Native woman with her byline, but also in its departure from the autobiographical style of earlier Indigenous male authors. While William Apess and George Copway, for example, structured their autobiographies around religious conversion, Winnemucca mentions religion only to point out Christian hypocrisy among the white people she encounters.[13] Instead, she composes her book diplomatically around Native and white relationships, navigating the fine line between exposing white hypocrisy and racism while building alliances with her white readership. Winnemucca also centers gender as an important aspect of her autobiography, a choice that allows her to confront sexual violence and push back against gender stereotypes.[14] Autobiography asserts the value of women's lives in an American society that historically devalues them, and it documents what Sidonie Smith calls a "history of the body" and a material reclamation of the "I" of autobiography that "dramatically marks the white page."[15] Native literary critics similarly recognize the body politics at stake in early Indigenous women's writing: in reading the narratives of Cherokee citizen Catharine Brown, for example, Theresa Strouth Gaul identifies Brown's body as "a site where the struggles of empire were played out, both physically and textually." Specifically to Winnemucca, Cheryl Walker sees *Life among the Piutes* as foregrounding the problem of the body politic, which she defines as "the refusal of raced, classed, and gendered bodies to stay in their places in the national narrative."[16] Their analyses point out the pressures Native women face while speaking out for their own bodies, as well as for the body politics of their nations. The female authorial struggle over corporeal narratives renders a fraught, complex, and ongoing process that becomes manifest in social and literary struggles of Winnemucca's autobiography. *Life among the Piutes*, then, records not only Winnemucca's embodiment within the autobiographical genre but also the numerous ways in which she puts her body on the line, risking her life as a diplomatic messenger between parties, defending herself against rape, and defying gendered and racial stereotypes.

While Winnemucca published for decades in numerous periodicals, as Cari Carpenter and Carolyn Sorisio have documented, her entry into book production began with her determination to share her story in a more detailed and extended format than she could offer with either her newspapers articles or her lectures.[17] She found support and encouragement in her endeavors from a white philanthropist named Elizabeth Palmer Peabody, who sponsored the publication of *Life among the Piutes* with the editorial assistance of Peabody's sister, Mary Mann. Winnemucca met the sisters in Boston where they, well known in elite Boston circles for their political activism and social work, used their connections to organize a lecture circuit along the East Coast for Winnemucca, as well as an audience with Ralph Waldo Emerson, John Greenleaf Whittier, and Senator Henry L. Dawes. Winnemucca then produced a manuscript based in part on her public lectures with the goal of extending both her story and her reach. The social connections of the two sisters helped pave the way: Peabody and Mann supported Winnemucca's efforts with their limited resources, and they initiated a subscription to her book to help cover the publication costs and Winnemucca's expenses. Both John Greenleaf Whittier and Lydia Emerson, wife of Ralph Waldo Emerson, each subscribed for ten dollars, and Peabody found another five underwriters to cover the total publication expenses of $600, which allowed the profit from every copy sold to benefit Winnemucca directly.[18]

Together, the three labored to produce the book and to time its publication intentionally before the next session of Congress in order to sway the legislative session in support of Native peoples. Indian Agent

William V. Rinehart, however, attempted to block the book's publication as part of a larger Bureau of Indian Affairs campaign to discredit Winnemucca and her public accusations of corruption against the agency and its agents.[19] Winnemucca later excoriated Rinehart specifically in her testimony before the House Subcommittee on Indian Affairs in 1884, in which she mentions his attempts to block her publication and triumphantly remarks,

> I thank [Rinehart] for his kindness because instead of doing me an injury he has done me a favor. He tried to choke that book out of press in Boston, but my friends, whom I made, would not let it be done, and they got up a subscription and presented me with $600 and had my book published which I am not ashamed to give every man in the world to read[,] and if I knew where Major Rinehart was I would send him a copy of my book.[20]

Despite Rinehart's attempts, *Life among the Piutes* entered the literary marketplace in 1883, electrotyped by the Boston Stereotype Foundry and sold by Cupples, Upham & Co. in Boston; G. P. Putnam's Sons in New York; and by Winnemucca herself. The initial run of 600 books appears to be the only edition produced in her lifetime, however, and not until nearly one hundred years later did Chalfant Press produce a facsimile reproduction in 1969, followed by another facsimile released by the University of Nevada Press in 1994.[21]

While thus far I have discussed blank space as a geographical symbol, a key visual component of the printed page, and a contested space of erasure and violence, I also understand blank space as a rhetorical device. If we recognize the impact of blank space on the visual layout and thus interpretation of a text, then we can also recognize the social and contextual forces that, like blank space, profoundly shape what appears or does not appear on the printed page. In other words, I read blank space as a rhetorical strategy as well as a visual and symbolic paratextual element that influences the narrative's impact. Many scholars read *Life among the Piutes* as a deft rhetorical negotiation of both speech and silence, and they speak of the book's rhetoric as making "space" for Indigenous women's voices to be heard within an American literary corpus that has often represented their bodies as present in its narratives but given them no words or dialogue.[22] Rosalyn Collings Eves, for example, assesses how Winnemucca navigated each physical space of her performances, from lecture halls to military forts, in order to create a space of rhetorical persuasion for her audiences. Similarly, Danielle Tisinger argues for the ways in which Winnemucca carefully considered her image within her texts and during her physical performances in order to best craft "a space in the contact zone in which to open and maintain a dialogue between two disparate populations."[23] Winnemucca's technique, like the text on a page, arises from a white context that influences what she says in her narrative, yet she also negotiates profound moments of empowerment from within a predominantly white literary marketplace and bibliographical framework.

One of the most immediate ways in which *Life among the Piutes* negotiates space occurs from within the book's paratext. Existing scholarship on *Life among the Piutes* often focuses on the rhetorical strategies and impact of its paratextual elements, often noting them as implicit responses to the politically motivated slander leveled against Winnemucca. For example, on both her title page and her copyright, Winnemucca uses her married name, Sarah Winnemucca Hopkins, to reinforce her respectability within the social mores of nineteenth-century American culture. The title page similarly names her editor as "Mrs. Horace Mann," establishing the book as a product of respectable married women, and Mann's "Editor's Preface" reaffirms Winnemucca's status by referring to her formally as "Mrs. Hopkins."[24] Although such moves come problematically from within a politics of respectability, they also implicitly respond to the attacks on Winnemucca's morality due to her multiple marriages, her deviance from gender norms, and racist stereotypes of her "savagery" and perceived sexual promiscuity. Though Winnemucca did have multiple marriages and she indeed deviated from idealized white female gender norms through her role as a military translator, wartime diplomat, and political activist, the racist slander on her personal appearance and moral character were particularly vitriolic and offensive. After one of her successful lectures, for example, two regional newspapers targeted her personal appearance by pretending to judge her age by the "number of scales of greasy dirt" on her face, mocking her "unbound, unwashed, and uncombed" hair and muddy toes, and comparing her clothes to a horse blanket.[25] *Life among the Piutes* refutes such slander against Winnemucca's body and reputation by refusing to give such rhetoric any space in her narrative, yet its paratextual elements remain shaped, influenced by, and directed at the accusations made against her.

Winnemucca bookends her autobiography with additional paratextual matter that defends her personhood and morality, speaking back to the rhetorically silenced slander. While the title page, the copyright, and the editor's preface affirm Winnemucca's literary authority, no less than thirty-eight letters in a twenty-page appendix reinforce the veracity of Winnemucca's autobiography and her moral character. The affidavits range from "her conduct was always good" to affirming Winnemucca's "most valuable services during the operations of this year against the hostile Bannock and Piute Indians" to "She is entirely trustworthy and reliable." These paratextual elements reveal the tensions as well as collaborations embedded within *Life among the Piutes* as the letters problematically draw upon white testimonials to vouch for a Native woman's integrity. However, they also reinforce Winnemucca's authority and align the reputation of the individuals with hers to further promote the creation of white allies. In effect, the affidavits attempt to repurpose paratextual space as an invitation from the margins, so to speak, for white allies to join in what Sara Monahan identifies as the book's creation of a "web of Paiute relationships and textuality."[26] Siobhan Senier further points out that the documents "instruct us how to read her," as Winnemucca was "acutely conscious of being read and re-read."[27] By opening up her life experiences as a text, Winnemucca added to the pressures she faced as a gendered and representative embodiment of the Paiute, yet she also manages to redirect the readings of her person through a careful framing of paratextual space.

In addition to the paratextual elements that work to shape the book's reception, Winnemucca's book utilizes strategic omissions within her narrative storytelling. In her biography of Winnemucca, Sally Zanjani quickly notes that anything that might reflect badly on the Paiutes or Winnemucca herself has been omitted from her autobiography, and Malea Powell further claims, "what Winnemucca left out of *Life among the Piutes* was as important as what she put in." Zanjani's biography repeatedly highlights such textual omissions within Winnemucca's autobiography, including an odd absence of place-based descriptions, her multiple marriages, her father's death, her Christian conversion, and large chunks of her life. Mark Rifkin also remarks upon her glaring omission of the Ghost Dances of 1870 and 1890. In each case, Winnemucca's narrative silence plays to her white audience as a means of obtaining and maintaining their political sympathy. For example, Winnemucca mentions her marriage to Lewis Hopkins only in a brief sidenote in the last sentence of her autobiography, saying, "After my marriage to Mr. Hopkins I visited my people once more at Pyramid Lake Reservation, and they urged me again to come to the East and talk for them, and so I have come." Yet Zanjani documents three total marriages as well as three other men that she possibly married or with whom she had serious liaisons.[28] Clearly Winnemucca omits the details of her love life to avoid judgment from her white readership and the accusations of sexual promiscuity leveled at her by her enemies. Instead, she employs blank space as a rhetorical silencing or erasure in order to maintain her authority with her readers, while at the same time framing her respectability in the earlier paratextual spaces of her book.

While the byline, copyright, appendix, and strategic narrative omissions certainly play a rhetorical role in *Life among the Piutes*, the literal blank spaces of the book, such as its paragraph and chapter breaks, receive less scholarly attention for the critical role they play in creating relationships and inducing sympathy. Winnemucca's original manuscript is not extant, and no records remain to document the extent of Winnemucca's authorial control over the layout of her text. Yet what does remain is a printed text in which Winnemucca certainly expressed pride and felt represented her story. The blank spaces of her book align with her goals and function in Winnemucca's narrative as rhetorical devices in line with the other strategies of text and paratext. Therefore, one may read the chapter and paragraph breaks in Winnemucca's narrative as rhetorical strategies that communicate the injustices experienced by the Paiutes at the hands of white settler colonials without alienating its white readership.

For instance, the first few paragraph breaks within the fifth chapter invite its readers to reflect over white wrongdoing. Winnemucca titles the chapter "Reservation of Pyramid and Muddy Lakes" and she begins with an idyllic description of the two lakes and the large mountain trout there that sustained her people. She ends the paragraph, however, by stating, "Since the railroad ran through in 1867, the white people have taken all the best part of the reservation from us, and one of the lakes also" (Figure 2).[29] By inserting the reader into an picturesque description and ending abruptly with a flat statement of white land theft, *Life among the Piutes* employs the blank space of a paragraph break as a rhetorical pause from the reader, bringing an affective emphasis to her understated accusation. Rather than utilize inflammatory language, emotion, or grammar, the invocation of blank space allows Winnemucca to engage critically and reflectively with her white audience without ostracizing them.

Winnemucca repeatedly calls upon blank space in tandem with restrained emotions in order to secure her white audience. In the same chapter, Winnemucca continues to end her paragraphs with flatly stated accusations emphasized by the rhetorical pause of blank space. After a conflict with soldiers in which old men, women, and children, including Winnemucca's

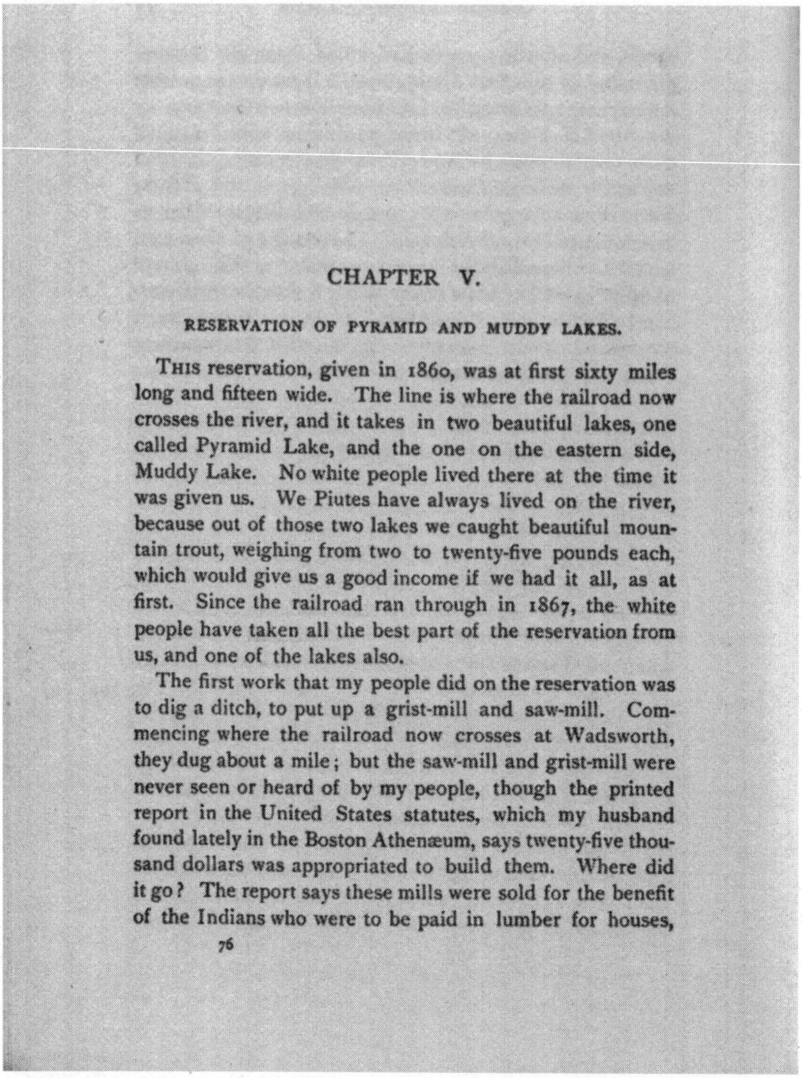

> ### CHAPTER V.
>
> #### RESERVATION OF PYRAMID AND MUDDY LAKES.
>
> THIS reservation, given in 1860, was at first sixty miles long and fifteen wide. The line is where the railroad now crosses the river, and it takes in two beautiful lakes, one called Pyramid Lake, and the one on the eastern side, Muddy Lake. No white people lived there at the time it was given us. We Piutes have always lived on the river, because out of those two lakes we caught beautiful mountain trout, weighing from two to twenty-five pounds each, which would give us a good income if we had it all, as at first. Since the railroad ran through in 1867, the white people have taken all the best part of the reservation from us, and one of the lakes also.
>
> The first work that my people did on the reservation was to dig a ditch, to put up a grist-mill and saw-mill. Commencing where the railroad now crosses at Wadsworth, they dug about a mile; but the saw-mill and grist-mill were never seen or heard of by my people, though the printed report in the United States statutes, which my husband found lately in the Boston Athenæum, says twenty-five thousand dollars was appropriated to build them. Where did it go? The report says these mills were sold for the benefit of the Indians who were to be paid in lumber for houses,
>
> 76

FIGURE 2. Paragraph break on page 76 of the 1994 facsimile edition of *Life among the Piutes*. Author's collection.

baby brother, were killed, Winnemucca tells a harrowing tale of the narrow escape of her sister while being pursued by the soldiers. The event, she relates at the end of the paragraph, "almost killed my poor papa. Yet my people kept peaceful" (Figure 3).[30] Despite the emotions inherent in relating an instance of genocide in which soldiers burnt babies alive, including

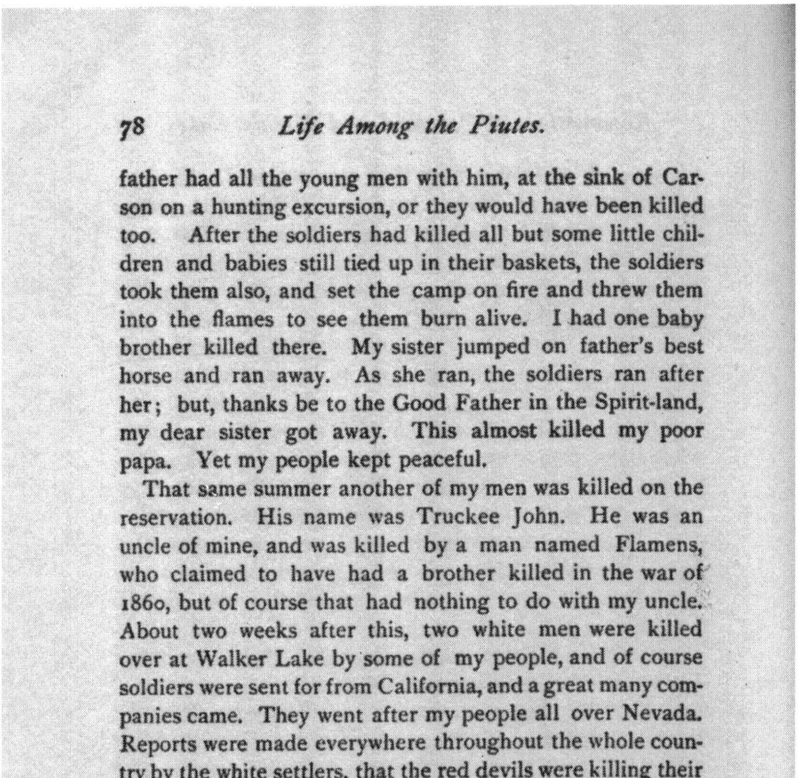

father had all the young men with him, at the sink of Car-
son on a hunting excursion, or they would have been killed
too.   After the soldiers had killed all but some little children and babies still tied up in their baskets, the soldiers
took them also, and set the camp on fire and threw them
into the flames to see them burn alive. I had one baby
brother killed there. My sister jumped on father's best
horse and ran away. As she ran, the soldiers ran after
her; but, thanks be to the Good Father in the Spirit-land,
my dear sister got away. This almost killed my poor
papa. Yet my people kept peaceful.

That same summer another of my men was killed on the
reservation. His name was Truckee John. He was an
uncle of mine, and was killed by a man named Flamens,
who claimed to have had a brother killed in the war of
1860, but of course that had nothing to do with my uncle.
About two weeks after this, two white men were killed
over at Walker Lake by some of my people, and of course
soldiers were sent for from California, and a great many com-
panies came. They went after my people all over Nevada.
Reports were made everywhere throughout the whole country by the white settlers, that the red devils were killing their
cattle, and by this lying of the white settlers the trail began
which is marked by the blood of my people from hill to
hill and from valley to valley. The soldiers followed after
my people in this way for one year, and the Queen's River
Piutes were brought into Fort Churchill, Nevada, and in
that campaign poor General McDermit was killed. These
reports were only made by those white settlers so that they
could sell their grain, which they could not get rid of in any
other way. The only way the cattle-men and farmers get
to make money is to start an Indian war, so that the troops
may come and buy their beef, cattle, horses, and grain.
The settlers get fat by it.

FIGURE 3. Paragraph break on page 78 of the 1994 facsimile edition of *Life among the Piutes*. Author's collection.

her baby brother, and nearly murdered her sister, Winnemucca ends with a short declarative sentence of restraint, followed by the blank space of a paragraph break. Both narrative text and the blank space of the paratext work in tandem to impress upon the readers an emphatic pause, asking them to absorb the inexpressible emotions evoked.

Rather than emphasize her own outrage, Winnemucca repeatedly transfers the emotion to the readers, whom she invites from the margins to react by offering the rhetorical and typographical *space* for such outrage. Winnemucca continues on the same page in another paragraph that documents the killing of her uncle, Truckee John, as part of a retaliatory killing spree by soldiers who "went after my people all over Nevada." The root of the killing, she claims, came from white settlers who made false accusations to instigate a war in order to profit off of selling beef, cattle, horses, and grain to the soldiers. She ends the paragraph with another short, declarative statement: "The settlers get fat by it," again invoking an inexpressible outrage and inviting the reader to absorb her emotions within the following blank space (review Figure 3).[31] D. Jan Mennell offers one way to interpret the management of blank space in *Life among the Piutes* as the transmission of understated rage from author to reader, as readers must "construct meaning out of the text" through being "incessantly forced to listen to, read and interpret not only what is actually articulated, but also the silent spaces between and behind the utterances." Blank space therefore functions not only as a visual component of the page, but a rhetorical and emotional component intended, in Simon Sibelman's words, to "jolt a reader from complacent attitudes of reading as a purely mechanical operation."[32] In the process, readers find the space to pause and reflect while finding themselves encouraged into an active engagement with the textual narrative.

The blank space in *Life among the Piutes* functions not only to induce an active emotional engagement from the reader, but also to solicit social action, as Winnemucca's petition demonstrates. Immediately following the end of Winnemucca's narrative, Mann includes a "Note" on the next page saying, "Mrs. Hopkins has met with so much intelligent sympathy and furtherance that she has been encouraged to make the following petition to the next Congress, which a Massachusetts representative will present in the hope that it will help to shape aright the new Indian policy, by means of the discussion it will receive:—." The note introduces a one-page petition below it, requesting the restoration of the Malheur Reservation to the Paiute, and the petition ends with a place for "[Signatures]" surrounded by blank space (Figure 4). Mann

NOTE. — Mrs. Hopkins has met with so much intelligent sympathy and furtherance that she has been encouraged to make the following petition to the next Congress, which a Massachusetts representative will present in the hope that it will help to shape aright the new Indian policy, by means of the discussion it will receive : —

"Whereas, the tribe of Piute Indians that formerly occupied the greater part of Nevada, and now diminished by its sufferings and wrongs to one-third of its original number, has always kept its promise of peace and friendliness to the whites since they first entered their country, and has of late been deprived of the Malheur Reservation decreed to them by President Grant : —

" I, SARAH WINNEMUCCA HOPKINS, grand-daughter of Captain Truckee, who promised friendship for his tribe to General Fremont, whom he guided into California, and served through the Mexican war, — together with the undersigned friends who sympathize in the cause of my people, — do petition the Honorable Congress of the United States to restore to them said Malheur Reservation, which is well watered and timbered, and large enough to afford homes and support for them all, where they can enjoy lands in severalty without losing their tribal relations, so essential to their happiness and good character, and where their citizenship, implied in this distribution of land, will defend them from the encroachments of the white settlers, so detrimental to their interests and their virtues. And especially do we petition for the return of that portion of the tribe arbitrarily removed from the Malheur Reservation, after the Bannock war, to the Yakima Reservation on Columbia River, in which removal families were ruthlessly separated, and have never ceased to pine for husbands, wives, and children, which restoration was pledged to them by the Secretary of the Interior in 1880, but has not been fulfilled."

[Signatures.]

Whoever shall be interested by this little book or by Mrs. Hopkins's living word, will help to the end by copying the petition and getting signatures to it, and sending the lists before the first of December to my care, 54 Bowdoin street, Boston. For the weight of a petition is generally measured by its length. Several hundred names have already been sent in.

FIGURE 4. Note and petition of the 1994 facsimile edition of *Life among the Piutes*. Author's collection.

then includes instructions for the reader and mentions the several hundred other names that have already been sent in.[33] In a culmination of the use of blank space throughout the narrative to elicit sympathy and active engagement, the petition now encourages its readers to transfer their sentiment into their own written word, transforming emotions into social activism.

Here both Winnemucca and Mann call upon the ubiquitous practice of signing one's name in blank space, on a petition and in the margins, in order to enact political change. Women had long been writing their signatures within the blank spaces of a book's margins: according to Cathy Davidson's *Revolution and the Word* (2004), during the nineteenth century male and female relatives often fought over the possession of a book by competitively signing their names as owners in its blank spaces. Apparently, women often won, as Davison notes that within the more than one thousand extant copies of early American novels she surveyed, women's signatures outnumbered men's nearly two to one.[34] The predominance of women's signatures can be read in many ways—a defiant assertion of ownership during nineteenth-century laws of coverture, a means of appropriation, or the attempt to leave an inheritance or legacy.[35] The act of signing one's name in the margins, however, ultimately speaks to a personal act of human agency. The individual impresses the page with her existence, marking her life and individuality within a social sphere, if not also a political one. She also creates a record for future readers, connecting with them from within the material space of a book likely to outlast her own physical body. Joseph Rezek reads this materiality as an important aspect of a signature's legacy in his analysis of Phillis Wheatley's autographs in her *Poems on Various Subjects, Religious and Moral* (1773), the first known book of poetry published in English by a person of African descent. By autographing her book on the copyright page, Rezek argues that Wheatley claimed her authority over her own book while emphasizing her humanity; furthermore, her signature ensures that her reader "felt her presence as part of their experience."[36] As Wheatley autographs her book's copyright page, then, she makes a powerful claim to ownership and to making a space for a material record of her body and her voice where there was no space, so to speak, from within oppressive regimes of slavery and sexism. Within *Life among the Piutes*, then, the petition's request for signatures in blank space not only affirms the support of Winnemucca's authority but also serves as an invitation for readers to contribute directly to the text, instigating a further collaborative alliance.[37]

Winnemucca and Mann's bid met with success, for a year later, on January 4, 1884, Winnemucca appeared before the House of Representatives, presented her petition containing thousands of signatures, and pled for the restoration of the Malheur Reservation on behalf of the Paiute.[38] Of the signatures listed in the petition, a significant number are women, whose signatures as well as the petition itself speak to the greater public and political voice women fought for during the nineteenth century. Historically the petition stood as one of the most readily available means for disenfranchised groups to protest the legal systems in place that controlled their bodies and their lives. As early as 1783, an African American woman known only as "Belinda" filed a petition with the Massachusetts legislature, seeking financial restitution from her enslaver for her fifty years of labor, and throughout the nineteenth century, the petition became a ubiquitous tool for social reform. Women found it empowering for gaining their political voice on a number of political issues, including temperance, antislavery, suffrage, and treaty rights, and in some cases their signatures omitted, perhaps for the first time, the gendered nineteenth-century honorifics of "Mrs." or "Miss." As Lori Ginzberg summarizes, female petitioners "simply confronted their exclusion as full citizens and objected to it" by enlisting both the written word and blank space as an invitation to assert their own individual identities and bodily autonomy.[39]

Many Native leaders also utilized the petition as a means of publicly claiming political power. From at least the eighteenth century, working on behalf of other tribal nations as well as their own, community leaders such as Oweneco, Mahomet, Samson Occom, William Apess, Henry Quaquaquid, and Samuel Ashpo brought forth petitions as a means of protecting Native spaces and recognized the form, in Joanna Brooks's words, as a way to "assert their authority and interject their own voices, perspectives, and beliefs into an often unfair and imbalanced legal process."[40] In *The Common Pot*, Lisa Brooks addresses the numerous Native petitions happening throughout the latter half of the eighteenth and early nineteenth centuries, and she describes them as a request to one political body from another within the relational dynamics of "mutual obligatory reciprocity."[41] Petitions harnessed the power of the collective "we," already ingrained within Indigenous social and political life, and they appealed from a position of power, as their collective body of signatures reminded government agents of their strength in numbers.

Yet Winnemucca's petition also expresses remarkable faith in the beneficial power of signatures in blank space given the history of treaty relationships between the United States and Native nations. While women and Native nations may have found a growing political power in putting their signatures, as well as their printed words, into the blank space of petitions, Indigenous men often faced coercion and gross injustice when putting their marks into the blank space of treaties. The Northern Paiutes did not have any formal treaties with the federal government, as the United States had ended treaty relationships in 1871, but the narrative of *Life among the Piutes* retains a healthy skepticism toward signing papers.[42] All her life, Winnemucca had seen her father treat a letter, his "rag friend," as an agent of power, yet she had also seen through military and federal government correspondence how the power of the page could be utilized as a tool both for peaceful negotiations and for violence.[43] Repeatedly through her autobiography, Winnemucca relates the deception her people encountered through paper, which in one instance was used to briefly sentence her brother to prison when a group of Paiute people were tricked into signing him away. As a result, Winnemucca often gives voice to Paiute refusal to sign through scenes in which individuals speak out and say, "'I am sick and tired of lies, and I won't sign any paper'" and "'I am going to quit signing any paper, for I don't know what I have been signing all these twenty-two years.'"[44] Meanwhile, however, Winnemucca chooses to make her pleas with print—in diplomatic correspondence, newspapers, and her book—as well as orally in her lectures and translations. She clearly retains hope in her father's "rag friends" and their potential as a space of possibility, despite her full awareness of their equal potential for deceit and social injustice.[45] Nevertheless, she creatively calls upon the petition, in a reversal of the historical relations of treaties, when she persuades her *white* audience to make their mark on blank space to *restore* land. Despite everything then, Winnemucca recognizes paper, its written words as well its blank spaces, as a tool that can be used to benefit her people, and she equally recognizes herself as capable of utilizing that tool in creating a space of potential empowerment.

Blank Space and White Space in
S. Alice Callahan's *Wynema*

When S. Alice Callahan takes up sentimental fiction eight years later in *Wynema: A Child of the Forest* (1891), she attempts to elicit empathy from her white audience for her Indigenous characters as they grapple with war, allotment, ethnocentrism, and assimilation. In addition to being the first known novel published by a Native woman, *Wynema* also marks an important moment in Indigenous literary history for addressing the genocide at Wounded Knee only months after it happened, ostensibly adding the novel's last few chapters in haste to an almost finished novel. *Wynema* had been picked up by H.J. Smith & Co., a publishing house in Chicago that predominantly sold subscription books; however, *Wynema* received few notices, and newspapers largely ignored Callahan's debut novel. After poor sales, the book was acquired by a Chicago-based new-comer to the subscription book business, the E. A. Weeks and Company, which reprinted *Wynema* in June 1893 with its Melbourne Series.[46] Yet after these initial runs and sparse critical reviews, the novel faded from public attention and became largely forgotten for most of the twentieth century. With less than a handful of surviving copies, *Wynema* nearly disappeared from the literary record, if not for the efforts of librarians and researchers such as Carolyn Thomas Foreman, who kept the novel alive in the historical record during the 1950s, and A. LaVonne Brown Ruoff, who recovered the novel in the 1990s and published a new edition with the University of Nebraska Press over one hundred years after its initial publication.

The novel opens with Wynema, a Mvskoke child living happily as a "child of the forest," who begs for a white education first from Method-ist missionary Gerald Keithly and then from the genteel Genevieve Weir, who comes to the Mvskoke community as a teacher.[47] Wynema thrives under Genevieve's tutelage and quickly learns Shakespeare and Dickens alongside her English language skills to become a star pupil. As Wynema grows up, she also educates Genevieve, who initially expresses ethnocentrism and balks at Mvskoke food, religious practices, and other cultural traditions. Though Wynema notices her teacher's prejudices, such as when Genevieve rejects the blue dumpling that Wynema devours eagerly, it is the white missionary Gerald who directly addresses Genevieve's ethnocentrism and reprimands her.[48] Rather than sow discord, however, the gentle confrontations between Genevieve and Gerald cause them to fall in love. In the meantime, Wynema meets and falls in love with Genevieve's brother Robin, and the novel likely would have ended with their marriages if not for the addition of the last several chapters in response to Wounded Knee.

By allowing the white characters to correct and educate each other, *Wynema* models a Native–white alliance that invites its readers into a similar political advocacy. However, one of the major critiques of the novel comes from the consequences of centering the conversations of the white characters while sidelining its Native characters. Leading such criticism, Womack reads the novel as a "document of Christian supremacism and assimilation" and opines that "total whitewashing seems to be the book's highest aim."[49] Although Womack rightly problematizes the novel, more than a dozen female scholars have since offered interpretations that situate the novel within the sentimental genre and cite its narrative strategies as a political appeal to white female readers.[50] Beth Piatote, for example, considers Callahan's choice of the sentimental genre as an effective vehicle for reaching a white readership, citing the genre's capacity to make space for "experiences of love and connection within Indian families" while simultaneously depicting the horror that colonial genocide enacts on those families. Cheryl Walker also counters Womack's reading of the novel's whiteness by pointing out that "the text itself is outspokenly critical of the assumption that white culture is superior to the culture of the Indians, and it is far from delicate in its condemnation of professing Christians." Melissa Ryan reads the novel as directed toward the "(re)education of white women reformers" rather than a culturally accurate representation of the Mvskoke Nation. She argues for the centering of white characters as a means to correct the reader's own ethnocentrism and prejudices, redirecting the "self-congratulatory rhetoric of Indian reform to present her readers with a reconstructed image of themselves."[51] Instead of promoting whiteness and white supremacy, then, *Wynema*'s narrative seeks to reform it by working from within a white literary and bibliographical framework, though with admittedly uneven success.

Wynema does not have to contend with the personal slander and attacks of immorality that shape the text and paratext of *Life among the Piutes*. Nowhere in the paratext does there appear a "Mrs." or a "Miss," and Callahan's book contains no petition or lengthy appendix of letters testifying to her character. The book does open, however, with a publisher's preface and a dedication that situate the book uneasily as an Indigenous representation to a white audience. In *Wynema*'s first edition, the reader first encounters a lengthy paratextual space occupied by a publisher's preface that attempts to build sympathy for Native peoples. It reaches out to the fellow white reader to listen to "an Indian, one of the oppressed," and it praises the novel for representing "the Indians' side of the Indian question told by an Indian born and bred." However supportive it tries to be, though, the preface continually undermines itself with its own racism: it labels the novel as "worthy of respectful consideration even though they be [*sic*] the opinions of an Indian" and diminutively describes "this little volume" as the offering a "picture of the home life of this simple people." Thus, though the preface positions itself as advocating on behalf of Callahan's plea for political justice, the presumably white publishers mediate Callahan's text by highlighting first their own authority to vouch for her and then undermining Native opinions and intelligence. It also distances the white reader's investment and complicity in white supremacy, locating "white greed" as outside of the reader's experience and aligning the readers instead with "our Red brothers." Like *Life among the Piutes*, then, the paratextual framing presented here fights for the rhetorical space to mediate, control, and interpret the narratives of Indigenous literature in what Watts describes as a bibliographical staging of the colonial drama.[52]

While the preface comes before Callahan's dedication in the first edition, the order is reversed in the contemporary University of Nebraska Press edition, prioritizing Callahan's words in space before those of her white publisher.[53] Callahan's dedication, however, remains troubled by how best to facilitate a sympathetic alliance between Native and non-Native peoples while also calling out white supremacy. The opening paratextual dedication reads, "To the Indian tribes of North America who have felt the wrongs and oppression of their pale-faced brothers, I lovingly dedicated this work, praying that it may serve to open the eyes and heart of the world to our afflictions, and thus speedily issue into existence an era of good feeling and just dealing toward us and our more oppressed brothers." Like *Life among the Piutes*, however, such paratextual spaces exhibit a rhetorical tension in their political stance: though the book is lovingly dedicated "to the Indian tribes," such language distances the author from an immediate racial or tribal affiliation, in contrast to a dedication such as "To my people," or "To my Mvskoke people," for instance. Though later in the sentence the author does claim a stake in "our afflictions," she then asks for more "just dealing toward us and our more oppressed brothers," ambiguously deflecting the sentence's earlier declaration of Indigenous "wrongs and oppression" toward an unknown, more oppressed peoples. Furthermore, the dedication also deflects its declaration of "wrongs and oppression" by attributing it to "*their* pale-faced brothers" rather than "*our* pale-faced brothers," again reinforcing a distance between the author and her tribal nation. Lisa Tatonetti describe the complex and ambivalent positionality of Callahan's paratextual framing here succinctly: "Indians are a 'they' and 'them' of which Callahan herself is sometimes a part and sometimes not."[54] Finally, the language of "pale-faced brothers" assigns blame to white men, leaving white women unaccounted for in the workings of social injustice. Winnemucca's *Life among the Piutes* exhibited a similar rhetorical tension in the paratextual space of its subtitle when it announces that Winnemucca will speak of "their," not "our," wrongs and claims. Overall, the language of Callahan's dedication intends to create the paratextual space for a political statement without alienating its white readership, yet it ends up with ambivalent shifts in possessive pronouns that successfully build sympathy but unsuccessfully communicate the political intentions present.

More so than *Life among the Piutes*, Callahan's novel struggles to find its rhetorical footing. While sentimental fiction dominated the literary marketplace for women writers and readers during the nineteenth century and thus offered an appealing vehicle for social reform, it could also be a conservative genre, guiding its readers toward not only "proper" feelings but also whose bodies could appropriately display sentiment and citizenship.[55] Sentimental fiction also tended to privilege models of white domesticity, as Beth Piatote warns. *Wynema*, however, embraces the genre as one way to reconfigure literary whiteness and invoke a corporeal sympathy from her white audience.[56] Sentimental genres aim to elicit emotions and sympathy from their readers: Sánchez-Eppler describes the particular success of sentimental fiction as its ability to connect physically as well as emotionally, "to translate words into pulse beats and sobs." Rather than other genres that may hold the body in suspense or fear, sentimental fiction invites a physical response of intimacy and connection that nevertheless performs cultural and political work. Most scholars, in fact, point to Callahan's use of sentimentalism as the primary achievement of her text: as Bernardin asserts, sentimentality offered one of the few meeting grounds for nineteenth-century women from different and often antagonistic positions, and it provided them with a set of shared vocabulary and affective values with which to address "socially unspeakable issues of race and sexuality—often through a narrative focus on miscegenation—and their implications for national self-definition." Not only does the sentimental genre seek to connect physically with the body of the reader, then, but it also takes up the body as a central concern. Positioning the body as what Sánchez-Eppler calls a "privileged structure for communicating meaning," sentimental fiction links the textual body, the readerly body, and national bodies in ways that trouble boundaries and fixed categories.[57]

The first chapter begins with a full paragraph describing the birth and happy childhood of Wynema. Although the paragraph caters to the racist and culturally erroneous language of Wynema as a "little savage" who lived in a "teepee," the narrative nevertheless communicates the deep love Wynema's parents have for her and the peaceful, not war-mongering, life they lived.[58] The narrative also uses vivid descriptions that immediately appeal to the reader's senses, such as the "dark, cool forest" and the river that "flowed peacefully" around their homes.[59] Such language invokes the genre conventions of sentimental fiction as it appeals to the reader's senses, both physically and emotionally, and invites them to build an emotional connection with Wynema and her family. Picking up on the subtitle, the narrative then asks the reader to relive or imagine their own happy feelings as a child with charming descriptions of Wynema as a little girl, "quite small, and barely able to hold a rifle," learning how to hunt with her father. The idyllic depictions quickly disintegrate over the next two paragraphs, however, into choppy, short, emotional descriptions of colonization that speak of the "rough, white hand that will soon shatter your dream and scatter the dreams" and the white man's destruction of Indigenous "quiet habitations into places of business and strife."[60] The paragraph breaks imitate the cultural breaks described, and the typographical white space of the one- and two-sentence paragraphs reinforces the repetition of "white hand" and "white man." Here blank space takes on a symbolic "white" space, working in relation with the textual narrative to put race and racism at the forefront. Yet the narrative also calls up the emotional and physical sensations of sentimentality to reconfigure Indigenous humanity (even while utilizing stereotypes) as peaceful, loving family members.

The first chapter ends with a similar use of blank space to underscore the complicated and conflicted political stance of *Wynema*. After initiating a movement to build a school in her community, Wynema pleads for the white missionary Gerald Keithly to send for a female schoolteacher. When one agrees to come, the narrative ends abruptly with a single sentence, "Thus came civilization among the Tepee Indians," followed by the white space of a chapter break. While Wynema begged to receive a Western education, only a few paragraphs before the narrative had lamented the coming of settler colonialism and the "rough, white hand that will soon shatter your dream" followed by the accentuation of blank white space. With this chapter break, however, preceded by the abrupt declarative sentence, the reader is left unsure and conflicted. Does the abruptness and blank space together signal an understated irony about whether it is really "civilization" coming? Does the blank space hint of the "whitewashing" that follows assimilation similar to the ways in which

Susan Bernardin, in another context, considers the temptation to read white space in California literary and aesthetic arts as a "visual nod to the whitewashing of California history, especially mission history"?[61] Or, does it match the ambivalent political position revealed in other paratextual spaces such as the dedication?

The blank space here offers a number of interpretations for the reader, interpretations made richer by an attention to the relationship between text and space. Barbara Postema's analysis of the use of space between comic panels yields a similar understanding of the possibilities that space generates when she claims, "Unlike the spaces between words, the space between panels does not always signify the same thing. We are faced with the necessity to *read* the spaces, as the space itself generates meaning." Callahan wrote her debut novel when she was twenty-three years old, and without an extant manuscript we do not know her authorial intentions in regard to her novel's layout and the placement of its paragraph and chapter breaks. Yet since the material conditions of print production already trouble any claims to an unmediated and uninfluenced book, attending to the paratext allows us to redirect our considerations from whose intent to whose voices the book puts in conversation and in relationship. In sentimental fiction, the relationships built with "pulse beats and sobs" in the narrative become additionally affective with the pause of blank space that invites the reader to absorb, reflect, and even write down their responses. Bonnie Mak pinpoints its rhetorical power when she claims, "By leaving space on the page unfilled, designers provide openings for readers to pause and consider the thoughts that they have encountered. Readers are given the opportunity in these zones to contemplate, consider, and question ideas, and may even be encouraged by the empty spaces to add their own thoughts to the page."[62] Although the genre conventions of sentimental literature may seek to influence its readers with physical and emotional sensations, *Wynema*'s blank space invites the reader from the margins into an additionally affective moment of critical reflection when considering the impact of "civilization" and settler colonialism.

As the novel's plot progresses, the narrative becomes more politically direct but still retains the reflective assistance of blank space. While the main characters listen in, a minor character named Chikena tells of the wrongdoing by the U.S. government toward her people, identified in the novel as the Sioux. After a long paragraph of injustices such as starvation that led them to the Ghost Dance, Chikena stops her reflection with the sentences, "'Many of our men died dancing, for they had become so weak with fasting that they could not stand the exertion. Then the great Government heard of our dances, and fearing trouble, sent out troops to stop us.'" While the reader pauses to reflect on the injustice surrounding the Ghost Dances, a sentence set off with dialogue spacing ensures that the reader did not miss the point: "'Strange the great Government did not hear of your starving too, and send troops to stop *that*,' remarked Robin, per parenthesis."[63] Nearly a full line of blank space follows Robin's short statement, meant to invite further reflection and empathy from the reader. Working in conjunction with the text, blank space reinforces the act of reading as a political act, shaped by the forces of sympathy and emotion as well as critical pauses.

Like Winnemucca's autobiography, *Wynema* struggles to re-create the white space of white supremacy into a white alliance, and moreover, to express women's stories from within an oppressive silencing, or in Tatonetti's words, "telling the very tale that is ostensibly lost to the world."[64] The rhetorical omissions within *Life among the Piutes* come from a place of protection, as Winnemucca silently omits any information that may damage her authority with her audience. Callahan's novel, however, struggles with its own elisions and absences of representation and is in fact "shadowed by omissions," including the absence of African American characters, mention of the Mvskoke internal conflict named the Green Peach War, and the Battle of the Little Bighorn.[65] I argue elsewhere for the political significance of such absences and narrative gaps, citing the immense social pressure Callahan faced from the racist stereotypes of print culture, prominently included in the text, as well as the psychological trauma induced by the racism and genocide Indigenous peoples lived through during the late nineteenth century. Callahan's novel nearly breaks against the conventions of sentimental fiction in its effort to communicate genocide and horror within a generic space of domesticity and romance. In his biography of William Apess, Drew Lopenzina articulates similar narrative gaps as Apess runs against the emotional and literary limits of his experience, trying to convey "a shattered emotional state difficult if not impossible to articulate, and experiences beyond the pale of what Western audiences were capable of hearing and what he himself was capable of telling."[66] Both authors claimed the blank spaces of rhetorical omission as a place in which they could inscribe Indigenous experiences, yet such space also remained fraught and contested as they struggled to speak within the predominantly white space of the literary marketplace.

Blank space, therefore, plays a meaningful role not only in a book's paratextual and rhetorical spaces but also within its materiality as "white" space. Drawing from the foundational work of archaeologist James Deetz, Bridget Heneghan points out the increasing whiteness of material objects, including ceramics, house paint, gravestones, women's clothing, and interior design, emerging in America during the late eighteenth century and spreading over the course of the nineteenth century. She argues that the increasing whiteness of such objects coincided not only with the increased technologies of mass production but also with the social solidification of race based on one's possession, or nonpossession, of whiteness. Paralleling Cheryl Harris's foundational essay on whiteness as property, Heneghan claims that whiteness in America came not only from one's claim to racialized whiteness based on the color of one's skin but also from one's ownership over white objects, such as the book. Put simply, Heneghan states, "White things radiated refinement, order, discipline: but in doing so, they also radiated race." Anne McClintock makes a similar argument in drawing connections between white commodities and white imperialism in her chapter on "Soft-Soaping Empire: Commodity Racism and Imperial Advertising," in which she connects a "middle class Victorian fascination with clean, white bodies and clean, white clothing" with white supremacy and its imperial economy.[67] The ownership of the more expensive white objects, then, became material proof of one's racialized whiteness as well as the evidence of whiteness as a property to be owned. Applied to the whiteness of the book's blank space, its racialized connotations structure, shape, and attempt to control the reader's encounter with the narrative. In other words, the material whiteness of the page reflects not only the white dominance of the publishing industry but also the racialized white power structure embedded and embodied in bibliographical spaces.

Lest such arguments seem overwrought in connection to paper, many bibliographers have remarked on the increasing whiteness of paper from the late nineteenth century to the early twentieth century, not coincidentally the time during which Indigenous women writers first published their books and writers of color joined the literary marketplace in exponentially increasing numbers. In his *A History of Paper-Manufacturing in the United States*, Lyman Weeks notes that many papermakers during the late eighteenth century set aside white rags for a higher quality product, while the more common papermaking practice generated a dirty white or brownish-colored pulp that produced a typically brown, gray, or mottled hue of paper. Papermakers then reserved white paper for writing and printing, while brown paper went to more utilitarian purposes such as wrapping paper or butcher paper. Such sorting practices, even to the point of segregated white mills for white paper and brown mills for brown paper, required significantly greater labor and cost. Yet as the industrialization of the nineteenth century continued, paper manufacturing made an even greater investment in the whiteness of printing paper, so much so that by the beginning of the twentieth century, Jan Tschichold laments the loss of paper's ecru tone and attacks the modern "detergent white offset paper which was never meant to be used for books," while derogatorily comparing its stark white to refrigerators, sanitary appliances, and the dentist's office.[68] The starkly printed contrast between white page and black ink, therefore, had less to do with its readability than with a continuing investment in white ideology.

Race and gender became deeply embedded into the page as "white" paper and the language surrounding its value. Whiteness, Jonathan Senchyne claims, had become a common expectation of paper by the middle of the nineteenth century, and its blank, white sheets signified a variety of social formations such as white femininity, virginity, purity, and, not least of all, racialized whiteness. The blank white page symbolized the "virginal," white, and receptively feminized body upon which one could write one's name, disseminate and reproduce a text, and procreate one's own immortality. Megan Benton also analyzes the modern implementation of more white space around and within text blocks as a nineteenth-century development in "feminine" type and typography, which later nineteenth- and early twentieth-century designers such as William Morris would deride using gendered terms. Furthermore, as racialized whiteness worked to establish itself throughout the nineteenth century as the normal, invisible background against which other hyper-visualized bodies should be judged and evaluated, the blank white page also works to establish the "black" text and other nonwhite bodies as highly visible and meant to be read. In this way, whiteness attempted to control the power of bodies in space: as one of the tenets of the "racial contract," Charles Mills explains, "The norming of space is partially done in terms of the *racing* of space, the depiction of space as dominated by individuals (whether persons or subpersons) of a certain race. At the same time, the norming of the individual is partially achieved by *spacing* it, that is, representing it as imprinted with the characteristics of a certain kind of space."[69] In other words, bodies and spaces become mutually constitutive in a circular process—we learn to read and define the body in terms of the spaces it occupies, and we characterize spaces by the bodies which inhabit it.

Callahan's *Wynema*, therefore, treads carefully in the midst of such underlying connotations for blank white space and deserves attention not only for its rhetorical strategies toward a white audience, but also for its negotiations of material whiteness and cultural power. In *The White Possessive: Property, Power, and Indigenous Sovereignty*, Moreton-Robinson notes the dearth of Indigenous studies scholarship on whiteness and argues for whiteness as a category of analysis as central to understanding "how white possession and power in its discursive and material forms operate in tandem through identity, institutions, and practices in everyday life." Both Winnemucca and Callahan constantly engage in the rewriting of white space: Carpenter, for example, points out Winnemucca's persistent calling out of whiteness in *Life among the Piutes* as a visible, racialized identifier as well as a politically potent signifier. Rather than work within a racialized binary, however, Winnemucca "rewrites racial language so that a word like 'white' refers not to skin color but to one's betrayal of family or, by extension, one's nation."[70] The consciousness and high visibility of a white readership shapes Callahan's novel, and as a result, its paratextual elements walk the line between the creation of white alliances and the constrictions of the bibliographically embedded manifestations of white supremacy. Taken together, *Wynema*'s aesthetic shortcomings, as well as its rhetorical strengths, both point us to the ways in which the first known novel published by a Native woman must negotiate the predominate social and material whiteness of the literary marketplace.

Conclusion: Indigenous Female Corporeality and Book Production

Later editions of both *Life among the Piutes* and *Wynema* place a greater emphasis on representations of the bodies of its Indigenous female authors. While the 1891 and 1893 publications of *Wynema* do contain generically drawn illustrations of Native women in wooded scenery, no image of Callahan herself appears until the 1997 edition, in which Ruoff provides two images of Callahan, one as a frontispiece and the other as a very enlarged portrait of Callahan's face, centered on the cover with the title in a large, white text.[71] For *Life among the Piutes*, neither the 1969 Chaffant Press nor the 1994 University of Nevada facsimile editions change very many paratextual elements. They each provide only short introductions to the text that situate it more as a historical document than as an autobiography; instead, their paratextual changes seem directed more toward representations of Winnemucca's body. Although the first edition includes no images or illustrations at all, the 1969 reproduction includes five photographs of Winnemucca and her family, the first two of which feature Winnemucca in a portrait image and then in a full-body-length image. The 1994 reproduction then showcases a cover image that consists almost entirely of blank space, with a reproduced head shot of Winnemucca hanging over the edge of the cover and taking up only about one-third of the space (Figure 5). Yet here the blank space that composes the main aesthetic body of the book's cover features red, rather than white, blank space.[72] As the first Indigenous female authors of the book, Callahan and Winnemucca fought to create space for "red" writers within the material and ideological whiteness of print culture. Their focus on a white readership performs a response to the social and material conditions of race and gender in nineteenth-century America, conditions which they simultaneously chose to work within and to challenge. As a financial and political venture, the success of their books depended on, in Senchyne's words, their literal "ability to present ideas in black and white," and yet their political content seeks to create a "red" space in which to rewrite genre conventions, racial stereotypes, and gendered constraints.[73]

Blank space prompts us to recall the multi-faceted nature of reading: it does not simply consist of a sequential or linear decoding of letters, but a broader conceptual activity of meaning-making that takes into account every aspect of the page and includes "learning how to let books speak to us in ways other than through the words they contain." As a result, a critical awareness of the impact of space upon textual narratives reminds us of the material impact of stories upon bodies and the physical and geographical spaces which bodies occupy. The paratextual reader must work not to see any bibliographical space as passive, but rather to recognize the active role bibliographical space plays in shaping the text, its aesthetics, its interpretation, and its politics, especially for marginalized writers. These marginalized subjects, and especially female subjects, bear the unjust burden of marked corporeality, yet Callahan and Winnemucca manage to re-create Indigenous female corporeality from "at the edge of visibility, troubling the space from which it has been banished."[74] Though their texts confront dismissal or a diminutive status for cultural misrepresentation, perceived assimilationist politics,

FIGURE 5. Cover image of the 1994 University of Nevada Press edition of *Life among the Piutes*. Author's collection.

and aesthetic shortcomings, yet they also speak to the revisionist ways in which Indigenous female writers find expression within constraint and reach toward empowerment from within disenfranchisement. The Indigenous woman writer's engagement with the blank page, then, reappears as the struggle for agency, authorship, and the paratextual embodiment of women's stories.

CHAPTER THREE

Pretty Shield's Thumbprint

Body Politics in Paratextual Territory

> Stories are corporeal acts; the body gives rise to narratives. And bodies are themselves narrated, discursive, inscribed; stories give rise to the body.
> —Katharine Young, *Presence in the Flesh*

O VER SEVERAL COLD March days in Montana, three people gathered around a wood stove in a vacant school building on the Crow reservation. They met for more than pleasant conversation: from the start, all three considered their words as an important means of cultural preservation for the Crow/Apsáalooke Nation. Frank B. Linderman, who had spent the last forty-six years of his life living in Montana and building relationships with Native peoples, took careful notes while he watched the hands of a Crow elder, Pretty Shield, as she shared her life's story through sign language.[1] Linderman conversed fluently with Pretty Shield in Plains Indian Sign Language, yet to ward off any misinterpretation, Pretty Shield also spoke simultaneously in the Crow language while another Crow woman, Goes Together, translated into English for Linderman's added benefit. Although Linderman had spent a lifetime in Montana and had just published the memoir of another important Crow leader, Plenty Coups, he recorded this as the first extended conversation he had ever had with Native women. In the resulting text, *Red Mother: The Life Story of Pretty-Shield, a Medicine Woman of the Crows* (1932), later republished as *Pretty-shield: Medicine Woman of the Crows*, he wrote of his desire to document "a woman's story," a perspective that he regarded as underrepresented and undervalued in Native American autobiography.[2] To correct the trend, Linderman directly and repeatedly requested a Native woman's perspective in his interview questions. As a result, the book draws continual attention to the race and gender of Pretty Shield, not only throughout the text but within the book's paratextual elements as well.

As an ethnographic collaboration, *Pretty-shield* presents a two-body problem: as the non-Native recorder of a Native informant, to what extent did Linderman control, limit, or misrepresent Pretty Shield's life narrative? On the one hand, critics such as Stephanie Sellers question Linderman's qualifications, as a white male author, to chronicle the life of a Crow woman. She devotes a chapter of her book to addressing her numerous critiques of the text, including instances of Linderman's ethnocentrism, his questionable qualifications as a cultural outsider to write Pretty Shield's story, the absence of the Crow creation story, and Linderman's missed opportunities to "ask the right questions" about Crow culture. On the other hand, Gretchen Bataille and Kathleen Sands compliment Linderman for embedding within the text "explanatory notes that another anthropologist might have relegated to notes or an appendix" and for the fact that Linderman "does little restructuring of the text, allowing Pretty Shield's childhood stories to be included at the place she remembered them rather than at the chronological moment." Overall, they claim, *Pretty-shield* offers an example of "recorders who knew their subjects well" and conveyed their life stories with "sensitivity and insight."[3]

The body politics of racial and gender identity and the role they play in Native autobiography lead one into an intellectual hot spot in Native studies. Yet a shift in the field promoted by Michelle Raheja, Stephanie Fitzgerald, and David Carlson proposes a reexamination of Native American autobiography and as-told-to narrative that centers the Native subject rather than the non-Native ethnographer. As Raheja and Fitzgerald argue in "Literary Sovereignties: New Directions in American Indian Autobiography" (2006), previous focus on the ethnographer's mediation "often obscured the Indian voice of the text and shifted the focus of the scholarship away from indigenous lived experience to that of the non-Indian editor." Similarly, Carlson protests readings of Native American autobiography that center on how "authentic" they may or not be. He calls such approaches, following Robert Warrior, a "critical dead-end" and instead suggests readings of "how individual autobiographical acts can reveal a *process* of self-definition whose engine was engagement with legal models of Indianness in a highly charged communicative context." Such a reframing, he suggests, considers Native autobiographies as "something more complex than capitulation to colonial power; they produced a vibrant tradition of Native American literary and political discourse that should be better appreciated today."[4]

While I join the contemporary critical reframing of Native autobiographies, I advance current autobiographical criticism as well as spatial theories of the American West by conceiving of the paratextual elements in Pretty Shield's life narrative as contested and negotiated bibliographical territory. If, as Hertha D. Wong states, Native life narratives might be described as "miniatures of those treaty conferences . . . an attempt to negotiate between one's individual/tribal identity and a new dominant culture," then the paratextual framework of a text best reveals its legal, bibliographical, corporeal, and cultural negotiations.[5] As such, I offer a theoretical framework that connects spatial theories of the American West to the materiality of the book across the four extant editions of *Pretty-shield* (1932, 1972, 2003, and 2021).[6] I argue that the paratextual elements of the *Pretty-shield* editions shine new light on debates over the text's production when examined as a bibliographical territory in which bodies collaborate, battle for agency, and forge new relationships. Highlighting the unique paratextual insertion of Pretty Shield's thumbprint, I address a number of collaborative negotiations within the narrative's paratextual territory to reframe *Pretty-shield* as a feminist project involving Linderman, Pretty Shield, and their descendants; as an ethnographic collaboration rather than an exploitation; and as an assertion of corporeal agency in Western space through the material book.

Contested Space: Bodies and the Paratextual Frontier

Self-consciously concerned with "pre-contact Indians" in the nineteenth and early twentieth centuries, *Pretty-shield* calls one's attention to the space of the American West, which imaginatively unfolds before its readers as Linderman describes the "wide plains, screened by the giant cottonwoods, that surround Crow Agency" and Pretty Shield vividly remembers "long strings of travois and pack-horses . . . raising dust on the plains."[7] Yet the West exists not only in the descriptive spaces of the narrative, but also in the material and paratextual spaces of the book itself. While the majority of Western literary criticism connects narrative descriptions of the American West to the cultural work of nation-building by theorizing Western space as variously closed, regenerative, or rhizomatic, I argue that not only the textual and imaginative content but also the materiality of the book conjures up conceptions of Western space.[8] The material size and shape of a book communicate its narrative boundaries, similar to the ways in which the physical geography and land-scape of the American West shapes the stories created about its regions and boundaries. Like the American West, the spatial boundaries of the book may shift throughout history as additions, subtractions, and ownerships adjust to new legal, political, and social circumstances. The changing legal landscape of the American West also finds a parallel in the changing legal boundaries of the modern book's paratextual copyright page, as Ridge's *Murieta* demonstrates so poignantly. Furthermore, and at times problematically, books also tend to establish an expectation of the bodies to be found within the territory of region and genre. Summarizing Maurice Merleau-Ponty's 1962 *Phenomenology of Perception*, Jessica Johnston stresses that the idea of external space can be understood "only through its relationship to the body."[9] Any conceptualizations of the American West, therefore, come from the body's lived or imagined experience in that geographical space, an experience in turn reproduced within the material embodiment of the written word.

Within the materiality of the book, the paratext functions as another space of the frontier, a combat zone of colonization in which Indigenous authors fight for recognition, respect, and power, or, in Louis Owens's frontier definition, "a space of extreme contestation. . . . a shimmering, always changing zone of multifaceted contact within which every utterance is challenged and interrogated, all referents put into question."[10] History teaches us that the "margins" of America, its frontiers and denigrated spaces, often reveal its most intense racial conflicts and power struggles. Literature of the largely rural and often marginalized American West especially rehearses and reimagines these uneven power struggles through textual encounters: from tourists or Eastern transplants writing of their life-altering contact with the American West to racially marked authors offering alternative perspectives on the relationships of place, history, and cultures often romanticized as exotic or primitive. Writing specifically in regard to Native American life narratives, Arnold Krupat calls such texts the "ground on which two cultures meet" and "the textual equivalent of the frontier." Referencing another early twentieth-century Native narrative, Linda Karell considers the Native and non-Native collaboration between Mourning Dove and Lucullus Virgil McWhorter in the writing of *Cogewea* (1927) to be a "textual frontier, a historical moment of meeting, clashing, and cooperating multicultural encounters."[11] The paratext of *Pretty-shield* embodies the contested frontier not only in a figurative sense—the struggle for control over pictorial and narrative representations of Indigenous bodies in Western place—but also in a material and spatial sense within the cultural negotiations of the book.

While the textual content of Western regional literature most often receives consideration as a representation of the frontier, the liminal paratext may be even more suited for such a discussion. As Genette puts it, "More than a boundary or a sealed border, the paratext is, rather, a *threshold*, or . . . a 'vestibule' that offers the world at large the possibility of either stepping inside or turning back . . . or, as Philippe Lejeune put it, 'a fringe of the printed text which in reality controls one's whole reading of the text.'" The language here of boundaries, thresholds, and fringe of course parallel closely with "territory" and "frontier," foundational terms in Western literary scholarship. Building upon Genette's readings, scholars Beth McCoy and Richard Macksey directly utilize these Western terms. In his foreword to Gennette's work, Macksey declares that the "interrogation of the frontiers between the text and its public demands a dedicated reader, in the senses both of one widely read and of one alert to every artful disruption, intrusion, and lacuna." In addition, McCoy contradicts Genette's proposal of the paratext as "undisputed territory" to claim,

> Texts and paratexts emerging from the African American freedom struggle, however, suggest that the paratext is territory neither subordinate nor undisputed. Rather, tangled throughout books (and other printed texts) as well as around the images that are the stock in trade of an increasingly visual culture, the paratext is territory important, fraught, and contested. More specifically, its marginal spaces and places have functioned centrally as a zone transacting ever-changing modes of white domination and of resistance to that domination.[12]

Pretty-shield reveals the paratextual politics at play with unusual clarity, asking readers to consider the body politics that envelope the both the imaginary and material spaces of the book.

Book Faces: The Editions of *Pretty-shield*

While the narrative content of *Pretty-shield* does not change across editions, significant changes do occur between each of the four extant editions that repackage the same text for a new generation in a new historical context. The cover images differ dramatically, as do the publishers, illustrations, title, type, and introductory matter, and each change demonstrates the shifting dynamics in the book's paratextual politics: while the 1932 edition reflects a driving social interest in ethnography, exoticism, and primitivism within the context of modernism, the 1972 University of Nebraska Press facsimile edition reflects a renewed scholarly interest in Indigenous texts as a result of the incorporation of Native studies into academia. The later 2003 edition brings to fruition the promise of that inclusion: it removes all the primitivist illustrations; modernizes the type; includes a collaborative preface written by Becky Matthews and Pretty Shield's granddaughter Alma Snell; and for the first time includes a photograph of Pretty Shield, given courtesy of Snell and used as the cover image. The 2021 edition returns the book to a popular audience, picked up by HarperCollins and featuring as the cover image what appears to be Pretty Shield's likeness modernized into a brightly colored acrylic illustration. Each of these changes speak to the collaborative negotiations across time and at work within paratextual territory.

The John Day Company in New York first published *Red Mother* as yet another installment in the works of Linderman, who published the majority of his books with this press. The company advertised his works alongside a number of their other significant texts during the early twentieth century, including two Pulitzer Prize-wining books: Pearl S. Buck's *The Good Earth* (1931) and poet Audrey Wurdemann's *Bright Ambush* (1934). From the first edition, the title draws attention to Indigenous women's bodies: the title of *Red Mother* uses the "red" color of her skin to imply her race and uses "mother" to imply her gender and to connote the popular association of the Indigenous body with the land, as in the stereotypical "Mother Earth." As one of the reader's earliest impressions of the book, the book's title acts not only as a "liminal frame," but a "cognitive frame" as well, setting up the reader for a racialized and gendered encounter.[13]

The cover image and textual illustrations of *Red Mother* continue to draw attention Pretty Shield's body and identity. The first edition, and the later 1972 reprint, includes illustrations by Herbert Morton Stoops, a famous Western illustrator whose artwork appears prominently throughout the text, including on the original dust jacket, the full title page, preceding the foreword and appendix, and accompanying a majority of the chapter headings. On the dust jacket, a Stoops illustration of an Indigenous woman appears centered and astride a horse attached to a travois (Figure 6). Her straight posture leans slightly back in her saddle and portrays a comfortable confidence as she holds the reins high. The image reveals her full face, yet the direction of her gaze appears to scan the horizon to the right of the reader. Both her head and that of her horse are held high,

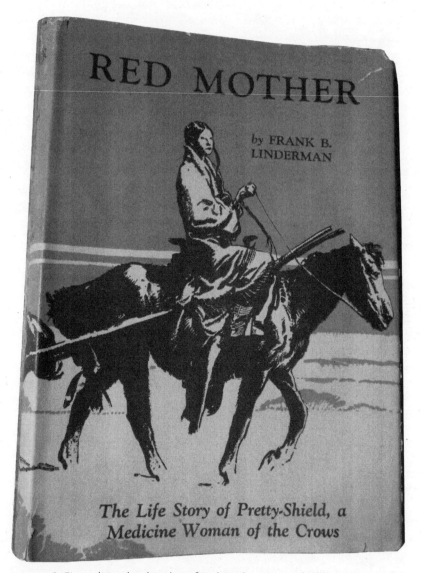

FIGURE 6. First edition book jacket of *Red Mother* (*Pretty-shield*). Courtesy of the Merrill G. Burlingame Special Collections, Montana State University.

in distinct contrast to the James Earle Fraser "End of the Trail" sculpture already famous at the time of the book's publication. On the book's full title page, a bust portrait of Pretty Shield appears centered under the title of *Red Mother* and gives readers a rather generic-looking image of her body. The next illustration in the text depicts a topless Indian woman holding a baby in a cradleboard with teepees and a big Montana sky in the background. Nearly all of the illustrations follow in this vein, portraying Indigenous women's bodies engaged in traditional activities. These illustrations augmented the fame of Idaho native and World War I veteran Herbert Morton Stoops, who was commissioned to illustrate many of Linderman's books. While the illustrations do reflect a certain romanticized or primitive aesthetic of Indians during this era, they also portray Native peoples with sympathy, confidence, and humanity in the midst of other representations, like the Fraser sculpture, that projected less positive associations into the public eye.

The prominence of Indigenous women's bodies remains consistent throughout later editions. The 1972 facsimile edition maintains the Stoops illustrations throughout the text, but for its paperback reproduction it replaces the original dust jacket image with an illustration from the Appendix of a mother and her child in a cradleboard, now colored with an olive-green background and Old West-style decorative typeface. The image reinforces the "mother" of the original title, despite the new title of *Pretty-shield*, and it recalls the decoration on the first edition's binding, which might be interpreted as red moccasin footprints of a mother and child standing in contrast against the lightly-colored cloth binding.[14] Later printings of the same 1972 edition soon replace this cover design, however, with a painting by Evelyn Teton, identified as a Shoshone-Bannock artist, whose accreditation is announced on the back cover under a brief biography of Linderman. This cover image evokes the original dust jacket image as it depicts what seems to be an Indigenous woman riding a horse attached to a travois with all heads held high, although the aesthetic style blurs the faces and most details of the scene. In yet another visual shift, a photograph of Pretty Shield appears on the cover of the 2003 edition from the University of Nebraska Press, courtesy of her granddaughter Alma Snell, and this edition chooses to remove all of the previously mentioned Herbert Morton Stoops illustrations. Finally, the cover image of the most recent 2021 edition, also commissioned by a female artist but not identified as Native, again features Pretty Shield's body with a bust image wrapped in a shawl or blanket with plaited hair, all rendered in modernized and nearly fluorescent colors of pink, green, orange, and yellow.

My purpose here in drawing attention to the changing cover images and illustrations in *Pretty-shield's* paratext is not to discuss the long history of Native representations in art and photography, but to underscore the centrality of Indigenous women's bodies generally and Pretty

Shield's body specifically in the book's paratextual territory. Moving from a romanticized "red mother" to a fluorescent portrait, the nearly one-hundred-year span of *Pretty-shield*'s editions documents the book's increasing empowerment of Native women in the American literary marketplace but also the capitalization of Indigenous bodies as cultural commodities and marketing devices. In "Book Faces," Jacqueline Goldsby connects the frontispieces and dust jackets of African American literary history to Black personhood and humanity, and Joseph Rezek identifies shifts between editions as the "racialization of print," an "uneven and contested" process that occur within the book's "changing associations with such other unstable and developing social and ideological categories as class, gender, religion, and nation."[15] Each edition puts Pretty Shield's body—her Indigeneity, gender, and personhood—at center stage, and each faces anew the contestation of narrative and material space in Indigenous literary production.

Making Her Mark: Feminist Collaboration and Pretty Shield's Thumbprint

Paratextual territory contains collaborative negotiations as well as contestations, and the paratextual changes made across the four editions also reveal a complicated but constructive feminist project involving Linderman, Pretty Shield, and their descendants. In the first edition, the copyright page reserves all rights to Linderman alone and appears next to his dedication to his granddaughter. A full title page lists Linderman and Stoops as contributors and highlights Linderman specifically by listing ten of his other publications with the John Day Company. Pretty Shield's name appears only within the subtitle, following the original title of *Red Mother*, without any copyrights. These early paratextual pages depict Linderman rather than Pretty Shield as the headliner, legal owner of the narrative, and main attraction to potential readers. Linderman does, however, wield his considerable literary influence to bring attention to Native women and to Pretty Shield's life story in particular, and in addition to the subtitle, Linderman embeds her name immediately into the first paragraph of his foreword.

The paratextual framing of the 1972 edition begins to move Pretty Shield forward as a main focus of the text. Because of a title change from *Red Mother* to *Pretty-shield*, her name appears larger than Linderman's toward the top of the full title page and as the sole name on the preceding half title page. A more complex copyright page now lists the book's multiple publishing houses and a renewed copyright by Linderman's descendants, all female. Placed next to Linderman's dedication to his granddaughter Sarah Jane Waller, these pages now reveal a fulfillment of Linderman and Pretty Shield's dedication to future generations who they implicitly hoped would value the narrative of a Crow woman's life.

While the 1936 edition focuses on contributing an Indigenous woman's story to the corpus of Native American autobiography and the 1972 edition begins to feature the feminist collaboration between the Crow women Pretty Shield and Goes Together, along with Linderman, in the telling of that story, the 2003 edition places an added emphasis on the feminist nature of the project. In this edition, the Sarah Jane Waller dedication now appears side by side with Pretty Shield's thumbprint, implicitly referring to the lasting friendship of the authors and those of their descendants. The preface more explicitly documents the flourishing "family bonds that span seventy years" as Linderman's descendants host a reunion celebration with Pretty Shield's descendants in the Linderman family home shortly before the release of the new edition.[16] The preface also includes a more prominent integration of Pretty Shield's legacy, as Snell speaks of the significance of her grandmother's activism and leadership in tribal politics. In fact, Snell's collaboration with a non-Native scholar, Becky Matthews, in the writing of the 2003 preface as well as their continued collaboration after writing Snell's own autobiography, *Grandmother's Grandchild: My Crow Indian Life* (2000), speaks to the positive collaboration modeled in Snell's life between Linderman and her grandmother Pretty Shield. The predominant presence of Pretty Shield's name and image, the female copyright holders, and the opening preface co-authored by Snell and Matthews bring to fulfillment Linderman and Pretty Shield's valuing of "a woman's story" and also point to their intentions for the book to be the cultural inheritance of future generations who would live together on western soil.

Pretty-shield's most unique feature, however, comes from the paratextual insertion of Pretty Shield's thumbprint as part of the opening matter of the book (review Figure 1). The thumbprint, along with a caption, stands apart on an otherwise blank page, and it consistently appears across all four editions after the dedication but before any of the textual content.[17] Because of its predominance and its proximity to the copyright page, Pretty Shield's thumbprint acts as her copyright, albeit a non-legal copyright, that nevertheless pushes against the social and literary constraints of her situation, including the constraint of the first edition's paratextual predominance of Linderman's name as its selling point.

Pretty Shield uses her thumb as a marker of authority over her own story, despite its publication by someone else. Unlike Winnemucca and Callahan, Pretty Shield never owned the copyright to her narrative, but here she similarly inserts her agency over paratextual blank space with a thumbprint in place of a signature. Additionally, in the first two editions, her thumbprint appears only after the full stop of a preceding blank page which, as discussed in the previous chapter, itself acts as a powerful paratextual device to force the reader to pay special attention to the significance of her thumbprint and her words. In each case, the thumbprint precedes Linderman's foreword and, aside from the few words of dedication, seats Pretty Shield's words as the first sentence that the reader encounters.

Although the insertion of a thumbprint stands as a singular feature across all Native American literature, Pretty Shield's thumbprint did not occur first in Linderman's oeuvre. Published two years before his *Pretty-shield* collaboration, Linderman also produced *Plenty-coups: Chief of the Crows* (1930) as the life narrative of another Crow tribal member. Like *Red Mother/Pretty-shield*, Linderman originally titled the book *American: The Life Story of a Great Indian*, and it also features the paratextual insertion of Plenty Coups's thumbprint. Because of their many similarities, most scholars discuss the two Crow texts as companion pieces. Yet while each includes a thumbprint of authority from the Native authors, each thumbprint receives notably different treatment throughout the bibliographical history of Linderman's books. In the original edition of *American*, Plenty Coups's thumbprint appears after Linderman's dedication, this time "To My Grandson, James Beale Waller." Here Linderman's dedication sets up the reader for gendered differences in the texts as he dedicates his work to his grandson and yet dedicates his work in *Pretty-shield's* text to his granddaughter. While the grandson's dedication appears opposite Linderman's copyright page, a blank page precedes Plenty Coups's thumbprint and its much lengthier caption in quotations: "'I am glad I have told you these things, Sign-Talker. You have felt my heart, and I have felt yours. I know you will tell only what I have said, that your writing will be straight like your tongue, and I sign your paper with my thumb so that your people and mine will know I told you the things you have written down.' . . . Thumb-print of Plenty-coups, Chief of the Crows."

While both Plenty Coups and Pretty Shield's captions appear with an "I" narrative, the paratext places Plenty Coups's words in quotes to signal their culling from the last paragraph of the text and to give a lengthier explanation for his thumbprint. Plenty Coups's thumbprint also receives a clear identification as such in a caption under the image, while in contrast Pretty Shield's shorter statement, "I told Sign-talker the things that are in this book, and have signed the paper with my thumb," does not receive quotation marks, and her thumbprint receives no clarifying explanation. Both statements, however, do use the words "I sign your paper" or "I signed the paper" in order to construct the thumbprint as a sign of agency. To use their mark in order to "sign the paper" problematically invokes a long history of treaty signatures and fingerprinting which I will address shortly, yet here no land changes hands: instead, both thumbprints serve to validate Native claims and Native testimony, not far removed from other legal documents such as depositions or affidavits.[18]

After the first editions of their books, the treatment of Plenty Coups and Pretty Shield's thumbprints starts to vary. The University of Nebraska Press also reproduced *American*, reprinting the text as *Plenty-coups: Chief of the Crows* in 1969. Like their first reproduction of *Pretty-shield*, the press retains the original illustrations by Stoops, and overall the book remains largely unchanged except for the radical replacement of Plenty Coups's thumbprint into an inconspicuous bottom right corner in the back cover of the paperback. While items appearing on the back cover might imply a paratextual importance as a potential early encounter with the perusing reader of the twentieth century, the placement significantly undercuts Plenty Coups's statement as a preface to the text and instead positions it as a potential afterthought to the textual body. The most recent "new edition" of the text in 2002, also from the University of Nebraska Press, moves to omit the thumbprint completely despite a number of paratextual improvements, including an introduction by Crow tribal leaders Barney Old Coyote Jr. and Phenocia Bauerle and an afterword, map, and glossary by Timothy McCleary. Although the differences between the Pretty Shield and Plenty Coups texts provide fertile ground for a host of critical interpretations, at its most basic comparison the multiple editions of *Pretty-shield* treat her thumbprint with prominence, invariably appearing immediately before Linderman's foreword. In contrast, the thumbprint of Plenty Coups appears less and less significant with each reproduction. Due to this paratextual emphasis, the predominance of Pretty Shield's Indigenous female body to the text remains central to the reader's experience.

The paratext, then, acts a contested territory not only for the author, the text, and the mainstream market into which both seek to enter, but also for the reader, who is directed toward particular emphases and interpretations. The paratextual reader must work to see bibliographical space not as passive, but rather to recognize the active role bibliographical territory plays in shaping the text, its aesthetics, its interpretation, and its politics, especially for marginalized writers. For this reason, Michele Moylan and Lane Stiles argue for an increased attention to editions and reprints of a single text as an essential step in both literary and bibliographical analysis, claiming, "In fact, we would argue that every edition of a text, every printing that adopts a different set of advertisements, every version with a different cover is a different literary object—a different configuration of the forces that shape meaning."[19] As one can see through the different editions of *Pretty-shield*, each reiteration reflects a changing emphasis that reveals the bodily, cultural, and bibliographic negotiations within the book's paratextual territory.

Fingerprints, X-Marks, and Body Language

As the American West continues to be linked with liminal spaces such as the frontier, the liminal spaces of the book—its paratextual elements—can mirror the ideological forces at work in the spaces of book "geographies." From this perspective, Pretty Shield's thumbprint can be compared to an "x-mark" in the Western space of the book, a mark that Scott Richard Lyons revives from its typical use as a coercive Native signature upon treaties and redefines as "a commitment to living in new and perhaps unfamiliar ways, yet without promising to give up one's people, values, or sense of community." Pretty Shield's own words support Lyons's remarks when she sadly reflects, "I am trying to live a life that I do not understand." Lyons's reconceptualization of the x-mark offers readings of it as a sign of coercion, but not of capitulation. In his words, "I use the x-mark to symbolize Native assent to things (concepts, policies, technologies, ideas) that, while not necessarily traditional in origin, can sometimes turn out all right and occasionally even good." His nuance of the x-mark redirects interpretations of Native signatures of assent as void of agency toward a more complex understanding of Indigenous agency under colonization, in line with current critical approaches to Native autobiographies. Lyons does not seek to frame the x-mark in rose-colored glasses; he cautions that the x-mark "is the agreement one makes when there seems to be little choice in the matter." Yet he offers that, for the x-mark, "To the extent that little choice isn't the quite [*sic*] same thing as no choice, it signifies Indian agency."[20]

Although the history of Native thumbprints during colonization and in government documents calls for further study, references to the practice appear frequently: in Deborah Miranda's *Bad Indians* (2013), she mentions an ancestral relative who often vouched for the "Indian blood" of many relatives on their Bureau of Indian Affairs applications, using her thumbprint as a signature. In Louise Erdrich's *Tracks* (1988), the fictional character Nanapush despairs at the number of tribal citizens who "signed their land away with thumbs and cross" and shares with the reader how as a young man he had lost his job as a government interpreter when he told a Native negotiator, "'Don't put your thumb in the ink.'" In Zitkala-Šá's 1921 short story regarding government bureaucracy and legalized land theft, the narrator mentions both an x-mark and a thumbprint, the latter of which the narrator identifies as a signature.[21] Yet the life stories of Pretty Shield and Plenty Coups remain the only known books in Native literary history to include the mark of a thumbprint itself.

Fingerprints and x-marks share a similarity in their history as a means of individual identification, especially on official government documents, and both appear in often-contested circumstances of duress, inequality, and legality. While only x-marks appear on treaties, both thumbprints and fingerprints do make their way onto other government documents: in addition to the literary references mentioned previously, additional nonfiction sources also mention Native peoples using their thumbprints in government records, such as the endorsement of government checks at trading posts or on a deed of sale.[22] Yet while x-marks have a long history in U.S.–Native treaty relations, the official use of fingerprints did not come into common practice in America until the early twentieth century, where the practice migrated after its colonial uses in Europe and gained authority in the literal policing of bodies due in part to the perceived homogeneity of Native Americans and racialized minorities in all other physically visible and identifiable ways. Sir Frances Galton, the creator of today's fingerprint classification system of whorls, loops, and arches, approached his study of fingerprints with the express intent of finding racial hierarchal differences, although he failed to do so in his substantial tome *Finger Prints* (1892). Undeterred, Galton continued to pursue a quantification of racial differences throughout his career. The first legal uses of fingerprinting in the United States both involved Black men—in the 1903 case of William West, who police and later pro-fingerprinting campaigners believed to be indistinguishable in both body and face from another unrelated Black male prisoner except for his fingerprints, and in the 1910 trial of Thomas Jennings, whose murder conviction came after the first use of fingerprinting as evidence in a criminal trial in the United States.[23] The U.S. government and eventually the private sector would employ fingerprints in a number of ways by the twenty-first century, but the specter of race continues to haunt the origins and practice of fingerprinting. Yet as Galton realized to his chagrin, fingerprints themselves defy racial characteristics and, in contradiction to a racist homogeneity, they assert a uniquely individual and insistently physical presence. Like Mary Jemison's subversive use of her as-told-to autobiography in order to establish her land claims, Pretty Shield's thumbprint testifies to her personal authority and reinforces the ongoing physical presence of Native peoples in Western and bibliographical space.[24]

Like Scott Richard Lyons who reads the x-mark as a sign of coercion but not of capitulation, I read Pretty Shield's thumbprint as the product of agency under ethnographic pressure. As mentioned previously, Pretty Shield never owned her book's copyright, and she had limited control over her text's production. Neither herself nor her descendants received royalties from the book's sales, but both Linderman and Alma Snell do mention payments or gifts from Linderman toward Pretty Shield; however, that seem to intimate an ongoing friendship and mutual respect. Snell also receives credit and compensation as a coauthor of the book's preface. The thumbprint is not a standard part of ethnographic autobiography, but it testifies to Pretty Shield's agency and assertion of ownership, albeit from within the forces of a Western academic enterprise. Her thumbprint impresses upon the reader that she did not act as a dupe in an ethnographic scheme or a naïve informant to the larger social context of her storytelling. As Lyons argues, the x-mark "assumes that indigenous communities are and have always been composed of human beings who possess reason, rationality, individuality, an ability to think and to question, a suspicion toward religious dogma or political authoritarianism, a desire to improve their lot and the futures of their progeny, and a wish to play some part in the larger world."[25] Pretty Shield's thumbprint casts her as a socially astute individual who consciously agreed to participate in the literary production of her life story.

The narrative content of *Pretty-shield* reinforces the agency preemptively asserted with Pretty Shield's paratextual thumbprint. From the first paragraph of the text, Linderman uses the word "consent" when describing the nature of his collaboration with Pretty Shield, saying that she "delighted me by consenting to tell me her story." He does not give the reason for her consent, nor does he imply any pressure or coercion on his part, but simply mentions her choice from the start. By recording her physical gestures and her thumbprint, he also works to record, as Jeffrey Glover advocates, "a boarder world of political communication that includes oral and gestural politics as well as the written word." He chooses to write the book in his voice, rather than co-opting Pretty Shield's voice as his own, a choice that Christine Colasurdo praises as a more honest depiction of their collaboration. Finally, Linderman also mentions her "willingness to talk to me without restraint," although he shortly corrects himself by mentioning that Pretty Shield refused to talk of colonization. In her first words quoted by Linderman in the text, she says only of that time, "'There is nothing to tell, because we did nothing. There were no buffalo. We stayed in one place, and grew lazy," words that signal both her disgust over the impact of colonization and her assertion of narrative boundaries.[26]

Mullen Sands points to Pretty Shield's reluctance to speak of colonization later in her life story as a flaw in Linderman's ethnography, claiming that it reveals Linderman as "a product of his times" and suggesting that "he chose not to probe the latter part of her life experience because of the prevailing 'salvage' mode of ethnography that dominated the period, an anthropological attitude that was more concerned with recovery of traditional culture than the study of the dynamics of changing culture." Yet her critique elides Pretty Shield's agency and focuses instead on Linderman's actions and motives. While the cultural dynamics that Mullen Sands points out are an important context for the narrative, Pretty Shield's silence may also be read as an empowered and intentional choice that may offer insight into her motives as well as Linderman's. Susan Kollin argues for this interpretation when, citing a number of critics, she writes that Pretty Shield's "refusal to recount life in the postcontact period might operate as an active form of resistance," functioning as a narrative strategy that "refuses to allow Euro-Americans to define Montana or the West." Such a strategic silence, she claims, "positions Indians at the center of Montana literature and refuses to allow the Anglo West to serve as the only version remembered or recorded." In other words, Pretty Shield elides Euro-American invasion almost completely, asserting her right to end her narrative when she chooses and at all times centering the past and present Crow Nation. Additionally, while Annette Portillo calls out Pretty Shield's thumbprint as "problematic," Portillo also emphasizes Pretty's Shield agency in redirecting or "manipulating" Linderman's questions in order to tell the stories she wants to tell. Pretty Shield's refusal to tell certain parts of her story asserts her control over the narrative (placed under her thumb, so to speak) and remind us that even the silences of a story must be taken into account.[27] She offers silence for the parts of her life that are most painful for her, and she sets the boundaries for her book. Linderman does not intervene in these choices, and while there are moments of cultural relations or descriptive choices that do date Linderman and the book as a product of its times, there are also many moments of respectful collaboration.

In addition to her thumbprint, Pretty Shield continues to use her body to assert authority over her life narrative and her place in Western space. Corporeal language operates as an important link between the material book and the contested space of the American West. As Annette Kolodny, Anne McClintock, and other scholars have argued, a woman's body functions as a significant metaphorical figure in literary representations of the frontier. In particular, Indigenous women's bodies often become intimately linked to the frontier in order that both may be subjected to the dual oppression of patriarchy and colonization. Jacqueline Fear-Segal and Rebecca Tillett's *Indigenous Bodies* (2013) points out early images representing the American continent as a vulnerable, supine, and yielding Native woman. A woman's body becomes a symbolic territory, meaning a physically and ideologically contested space. As discussed earlier, the cover images of the four *Pretty-shield* editions point us to this contestation, as both Native and non-Native media artists offer various representations of Indigenous women's bodies generally and Pretty Shield's body specifically as the reader's first encounter with the book.

Throughout her narrative, Pretty Shield's story is told, like all stories are told, through her body. She speaks, signs, and reenacts scenes from her memory, and her stories invite or instigate bodily reactions from the audience to her story—listening, laughter, tension, surprise, and so on. Her awareness of her body as the medium through which to tell her story occurs from the very beginning of the text, when Linderman directs her to talk to him through signs and in Crow to Goes Together, their interpreter. At this directive, Pretty Shield immediately signals her agreement and comfort level with Linderman as "instantly her blanket fell from her shoulders. 'Yes,' she signed, her eyes telling me that she perfectly understood the reason for this request. She never forgot it. Her sign-language told her story as well as her spoken words."[28] Linderman's encouragement signals not only his appreciation and knowledge of Plains Indian

Sign Language (PISL) as a Native form of communication that had been socially denigrated within his lifetime, but also his cultural awareness of signing and orality as an interwoven means of expression for many Plains tribes. In her research on Plains Sign Talk within another Montana tribal nation, the Assiniboine, Brenda Farnell's teachers called Plains Sign Talk "part of the language," which indicated for Farnell that historical understandings of PISL as a distinct and primarily intertribal language is "grossly misleading." She further explains,

> In the context of storytelling performances, both speech and manual gestures provide an integral part of the narrative sense, and the latter are not simply dramatic enhancement nor a repetition of the spoken narrative. In view of this, it seemed appropriate to explore storytelling performances not as multimedia events in which two languages go on at the same time but as crossmedia events, where action signs and speech integrate.[29]

From the thumbprint to its embrace of PISL, the *Pretty-shield* collaboration makes space in unprecedented ways for language as a fully embodied, "crossmedia event," pushing for its fuller representation in bibliographical space.

Communicating in sign language as well as spoken language allows for a direct conversation between Pretty Shield and Linderman and gives Pretty Shield more agency and control in the telling of her story. In addition, by using both, Pretty Shield labors to pass down a knowledge of PISL which, while an endangered and historically denigrated language, currently remains in use across tribal nations and may have served as a base for American Sign Language. According to Martin Heavy Head, elders still utilize the language while speaking to serve as an emphasis, "signs to really get the point across." In fact, just two years prior to the publication of *Pretty-shield*, the Blackfeet Nation of Montana hosted a historic Indian Sign Language Grand Council, which gathered leaders from across a dozen tribal nations with an awareness of the importance of preserving PISL. Their conversations were documented by General Hugh L. Scott, who received federal funding to document the event and produce a film dictionary but who unfortunately died before he could finish the project.[30] Today, preservations efforts continue as PISL teachers, including Ron Garritson and Lenny Real Bird, offer workshops and classes at Crow Nation's Little Big Horn College and across Montana.

Certainly Pretty Shield's simultaneous use of PISL emphasizes both the content of her life story and her gifted storytelling techniques that refuse to let her audience disregard the physical presence of all involved. Her communicative style emphasizes the physical presence and its expected interaction from her listeners when at one point, while telling a story involving a snake, she teasingly pinches her interpreter's leg to make her jump in reaction to her story. At other times, she enthralls her listeners with vivid reenactments of her memories, such as the scene in which she grabs one of Linderman's pencils and raps it against the table to drum out an antelope song. Her gestures range from "brushing her eyes with both hands, as though wiping away the years" to mimicking the attitude of a bear pouting and often causing Linderman and Goes Together to catch her contagious laughter.[31]

Because of the framing paratextual thumbprint, these everyday responses take on additional significance. Pretty Shield puts her body on the line in order to tell her story, beginning with the use of her thumb as a marker of authority over her own narrative. As Katharine Young articulates, "Bodies can be invoked as both source and site of discourses of the self. Stories are corporeal acts; the body gives rise to narratives. And bodies are themselves narrated, discursive, inscribed; stories give rise to the body." A connection between bodies and stories holds additional significance in Pretty Shield's case. Summarizing Farnell in her description of PISL, Yandell emphasizes the importance of storytelling not only with the hands, but with one's entire body: "regular speech patterns of nineteenth-century Plains people incorporated sign talk to the extent that they often spoke their tales with their voices and their hands at the same time, even when speaking to others with the same first language; for this reason, they often make no distinction in their autobiographies between things spoken with the voice and things communicated with the hands."[32] Here Yandell reminds us that sign language acts as both an intra- and interlinguistic tool, enabling communication between speakers of the same language and between speakers of different languages in instances of cultural contact in the liminal spaces of the "frontier."

Yet the thumbprint and corporeal gestures embedded in the text reinforce the book's paratextual frontier, as Pretty Shield still struggles against corporeal stereotypes in her portrayals while drawing upon the expressive power and agency of her own body's storytelling. Pretty Shield repeatedly expresses her awareness of gender stereotypes, for example, as she teases Linderman for attempting to single out only a woman's story. When he asks her for more information about Long-hair, a famous Crow chief, she pretends to be shocked and exclaims, "'In the beginning you said that you wished me to tell only a woman's story. Do you

now want me to tell you a *man's* story? Long-hair was a man, you know.'"
While Pretty Shield then proceeds to tell his story eagerly, she uses her
body language as well as her words to underscore the false distinction
between a woman's narrative realm and a man's. She also defies gender
stereotypes that restrict her to stories of tribal domestics rather than tribal
history, as she relays to Linderman the Battle of the Little Bighorn from
a Crow woman's perspective and includes the story of a woman warrior in
the battle, a story that Plenty Coups and his companions had neglected
to share with Linderman.[33]

Linderman acts in collaboration with Pretty Shield's storytelling
techniques with her emphasis on physical presence. Linderman carefully records the physical presence of their conversation, noting in the
first pages of the narrative the women's footfall as they enter the room,
their body language, and their facial gestures. He keeps up a constant
running commentary on her body language, implicitly considering it
as essential information to aid in interpreting her meaning, personality,
and narrative style. For example, he notes her responses to his questions
such as "Now she smiled, her eyes full of fun"; her unpleasant memories such as "She stopped short, her lips pressed tightly together"; and
her storytelling techniques such as "She leaned forward, her fine eyes
softened." In an additional attempt at accuracy and transparency,
Linderman crafted their conversation into an interview-style narrative
that gives the reader a vivid impression of their conversation and enables
direct quotations of Pretty Shield's words. Linderman inserts himself into
the text as a character who poses questions and guides the direction of the
narrative while placing quotation marks around Pretty Shield's words and
describing her expressions, her audience's reactions, and even outside
interruptions. In her foundational study of Native American autobiography, Hertha Wong marks these narrative interruptions as a significant
choice by a non-Native ethnographer: "This editorial decision gives the
reader a flavor of the actual experience of the interviews; it highlights
the oral nature of the stories, reveals the interrelations among the members of the group, and provides a sense of daily life and surroundings
that is often edited out of such accounts."[34]

Linderman's editorial choices represent a culturally responsive practice
to well-documented features of Indigenous storytelling—the importance
of place and audience, the ongoing presence of the past, and the relationships between storyteller and audience that shape the telling and
interpretation of the story. Crow intellectual Phenocia Bauerle confirms this perspective when she states that Linderman "modified the

European genre to be more accepting of Crow traditions by incorporating oral story-telling presentations." She notes that Linderman point-
edly mentions the communal storytelling enacted in the compilation of
Plenty Coups's life narrative and documents this act as significant:

> In noting the manner in which Plenty Coups recounts his stories,
> Linderman does what many writers do not in their autobiographies
> and biographies of Crow people: he keeps the story as true as possible by
> acknowledging the multiple accounts he hears. Whether or not Linderman
> actually recognized the process that he was witnessing as an integral com-
> ponent of the oral tradition, he did acknowledge it.[35]

While Linderman's account of Pretty Shield's storytelling does not exactly
replicate Plenty Coups's communal storytelling method, Goes Together
does accompany Pretty Shield and serves as more than an interpreter:
Pretty Shield includes Goes Together as a personal presence in addition
to her professional capacity as an interpreter, sharing private asides with
her in Crow and at times teasing her.

Linderman also retained an awareness of reciprocity to Crow tribal
members who told their life stories. Wong mentions that Linderman
paid Pretty Shield four dollars and then sent her "numerous deer skins"
after he went home to write her story.[36] Although some might interpret
this act as Linderman's financial manipulation of Pretty Shield and
his treatment of her story as a commodity, equal consideration should
be given to Linderman's awareness of her financial difficulty in supporting her grandchildren, an acknowledgement of the value of her
story, and a culturally respectful act of reciprocal gift-giving. Concerns
over Linderman's sole copyright and financial profit remains; yet to say
that Linderman had only financial aspirations of literary acclaim would
be a gross oversimplification equivalent to claiming that Pretty Shield only
told her life story for financial gain. As Pretty Shield remembered the
past with a sense of loss and nostalgia while Linderman listened and
recorded with an ethnographical lens, both authors were also motivated
by an interest in cultural preservation and the inheritance of the future.

Indigenous and non-Indigenous collaboration, then, may be viewed
as what Thorell Tsomondo calls "a kind of boundary negotiation and/
or border dispute producing colloquies in which an endless play of
intertexts and power relations make visible and comment on the rules
and terms of the narrative construction." These boundary negotiations
connect to the material spaces of the book as well as to the geographical

spaces of the American West, and productively redirect the current "authenticity" debates regarding Native American autobiography. In other words, as William Andrews redirects scholars in "Editing 'Minority' Texts," how might critics veer away from asking the ultimately unanswerable question of "Whose book is this?" and instead follow more productive inquiries into how this book (and all books) represents a collaborative venture? Such an approach enables one to gaze unflinchingly at the multifaceted interests that may perhaps inevitably be represented in conflicting ways, yet it may also provide an opportunity to teach one about the historical moment in which it was produced as a literary and material object. As an intellectual leader of the Crow Nation, Phenocia Bauerle's words are worth quoting at length here as she reflects upon the perils of ethnographic yet collaborative life narratives in general and Linderman's publications in specific:

> While some critics might point out that Linderman's lack of complete cultural understanding inhibits the full potential of the book, it nevertheless is an effective and useful tool in the understanding and preservation of Crow culture. After studying the Native American oral tradition during a good portion of my undergraduate career, I can recognize that certain components of this story suggest that whether or not Linderman recognized it, he was becoming part of the oral tradition. The presence of another man while Plenty Coups related the stories of his life is true to the Crow tradition of having someone verify your words to make sure you were telling the truth. For me, details such as this, existing within the text, validate the importance of Linderman's book to contemporary Crow people. While there are inaccuracies or misrepresentations existing in this book, they are few and may serve as a tool for Native people. By understanding where there is confusion about our ways and cultures we are left to correct it, which means we must also understand the culture that we are to explain it to. As we search for a way to negotiate the gap between different cultures and lifeways it is important to have a model that reminds us that change will happen; this book illustrates a courageous and dignified way to become part of that change.[37]

As Bauerle points out, Linderman's collaboration with Plenty Coups, Pretty Shield, and other Crow citizens falls short by a twenty-first century measure of an equally beneficial collaboration. It remains limited by the standard practices of its time and the gaps in Linderman's language and cultural knowledge. Yet as Bauerle also points out, certain details of the book become teaching tools in how to integrate an ethnographer's goal with the goals of community members, how to learn from ethnographic mistakes, and how to negotiate cultural change. The paratextual elements of Plenty Coups and Pretty Shield's texts testify to their corporeal mediation of their narratives in a book product that, though flawed, remains a model in hindsight to younger generations of the Crow Nation.

Clearly Linderman, without formal ethnographic training or ties to a university, had more in mind than academic accomplishments. While his autobiography does not attempt to hide his interest in a writing career, his lifelong devotion to the tribes of the American West and his political advocacy on their behalf conveys his best intentions, even if those intentions may fall short in some ways from a twenty-first century perspective. If, as Robert Warrior suggests in *The People and the Word*, recovering an Indigenous literary heritage means re-evaluating an essentialism that undervalues the difficult political leadership of Indigenous writers within the context of their times, then the collaborative nature of Linderman and Pretty Shield's work also deserves reconsideration in light of the paratextual elements my argument brings to the fore.

Conclusion

Acknowledgment of the collaborative nature of writing and producing a book helps to shift expectations of authenticity to a more holistic picture of Indigenous agency, even within as-told-to narratives. The paratext reminds us of this collaborative nature in the text, and it offers more complex political readings rather than a simple capitulation of agency to hegemony. To view the production of a text as a process involving multiple bodies is to acknowledge the multiple, overlapping, and even contradictory influences upon our own bodies and identity. Paratextual elements allow us to see all texts as a collaborative venture, one with various political, social, and economic agendas and with multiple instances of unequal power structures.

The benefit of this complexity within Indigenous literary criticism is the greater incorporation of texts formerly considered inauthentic or compromised when produced with a white editor or under an unequal power dynamic, a pigeonhole that elides Indigenous agency and conscious contribution to such texts. Instead, acknowledging that a text, any text, exists as a contested territory allows us to see assertions, moments of agency, and control of corporeal and geographical space that had previously been ignored, silenced, or denigrated. Pretty Shield negotiates the difficult cultural space of the paratext, from her physical storytelling through voice and hands to an invocation of her body as a marker of ownership. Her thumbprint invokes the danger of dismemberment and potential displacement of bodies in the contact zone, bringing attention to the bodies on the line, so to speak, in the colonial battle. By inserting her body, Pretty Shield reminds us of the material impact of stories upon our bodies, the physical and geographical places which our bodies occupy, and the spaces in which stories may be told, heard, shared, and preserved.

CHAPTER FOUR

Citational Relations and the Paratextual Vision of D'Arcy McNickle's *The Surrounded*

What Indigenous texts do is make visible what's so often unseen.
—Daniel Heath Justice, *Why Indigenous Literatures Matters*

At the university of New Mexico (UNM), a series of four large paintings stand prominently in the elegant West Wing of the Zimmerman Library. Titled "Three Peoples," the paintings would originally have greeted library patrons within the front entrance, whose doors had opened two years before the installation of the paintings in 1940 by Kenneth Adams.[1] As specifically instructed by then UNM President James Zimmerman, the paintings feature the "three cultures" of the state, identified by Zimmerman as "Indian, Spanish, and Anglo."[2] The first of the four paintings offers a representation of the state's "Indian culture" with five figures—three women weaving a rug, painting pottery, and making a basket, and two men wrapped in a blanket and leaning against the wooden weaving frame. The second painting attempts to showcase the state's Hispanic culture by depicting one male figure hunched over a farming implement and two women building an adobe structure. The third painting chooses to symbolize Anglo culture by depicting three people who occupy themselves in modern and scientific occupations in a laboratory setting, one of whom uses a microscope. In the final panel of the series, three figures hold hands, with a blond, blue-eyed white man in the center staring back hypnotically at the viewer and two faceless brown men standing in profile next to him (Figure 7).

FIGURE 7. Kenneth Adams, *Three Peoples*, 1940. Oil on canvas, fourth of four panels. Photograph by Amy Gore.

The "Three Peoples" paintings have provoked campus controversy for decades. Speaking out publicly since the 1970s, Chicana/o and Native students have objected to their stereotypical representation as primitive craftspeople or manual laborers, divorced from a participation in science and modernity. Student activists also point out the white supremacy that the paintings enforce, with an Aryan-looking white man at the center. Additionally, the "tricultural myth" of New Mexico perpetuates a cultural erasure by limiting state history to only three cultures while undervaluing and largely omitting other cultural groups, especially the ongoing Black history of the state. The tricultural myth also homogenizes nearly two dozen distinct tribal nations located within the state, as well as the plurality and complexities of ethnic cultures. While debates over what to do with the artwork raged on, the paintings were defaced on two occasions and became the subject of multiple student rallies, protests, and appeals to administration.[3]

At the center of the controversy, like the center of the fourth panel, lies the white gaze. While the "Three Peoples" paintings represent most of the racialized figures without eyes, it portrays the white male with wide-open and startingly blue eyes making uncomfortably assertive eye contact. Such representations of a racialized gaze prompted one of the earliest documented protests of the paintings, when Joann Santiago of the newly formed student organization "Las Chicanas" wrote to the campus newspaper and contested in a heated letter to the editor, "Basta! As [C]hicanas we would like to inform you our eyes are open."[4] The painting's clear emphasis on the eyes of the white male differentiates him in the panel as the only one capable of seeing, as well as being seen, and it asserts his positionality as the agent rather than the object of the gaze. Additionally, his positionality echoes the long-standing art market and cultural tourism made famous in New Mexico and the greater Southwest since the late nineteenth and early twentieth centuries: encouraged by marketing strategies from the Fred Harvey Company and the Santa Fe, Atchison, and Topeka (AT&SF) railroads, middle-class white Americans could take affordable domestic sight-seeing excursions such as the "Indian Detour" to states like New Mexico. As part of their promotions for the Indian Detour, the AT&SF hired ethnographers, artists, and photographers to portray Indian life in the region, which resulted in more than simply a "collection of images, but a social relation among people, mediated by images." Writing specifically of New Mexico tourism and racial spectacle, Sylvia Rodriguez points out the paradox of the all-seeing yet invisible whiteness that such tourism hinges upon: "an Anglo-dominated racial hierarchy that must somehow be erased from touristic view."[5] The white subject remains invisible or "disembodied," capable of consuming images but rarely becoming the subject of one. As a result, Native peoples found themselves surrounded, both physically and commercially, by the tourists and anthropologists who overwhelmingly came to gawk, consume, appropriate, and project their own desires.[6]

During the same decade as the first student protests over the "Three Peoples" paintings, the University of New Mexico Press reprinted two of D'Arcy McNickle's novels, and in doing so it solidified McNickle's long-standing connections to the American Southwest and to New Mexico in particular. After multiple trips to the area over the course of his life to work with tribal nations, McNickle had retired to Albuquerque in 1971 and passed away in his home there in 1977. The UNM Press memorialized McNickle's legacy by immediately picking up and reprinting within the next year both *The Surrounded* (1936) and *Wind from an Enemy Sky* (1977), which had been published by Harper & Row just a few months before his death. *The Surrounded*, however, posed more of a financial risk: it had been out of print for over forty years. Although the novel had originally been published by the Dodd, Mead Company in the heyday of Southwestern ethnographic fiction, it had flopped in comparison to the Indian novels written by white authors such as Oliver La Farge, whose *Laughing Boy* (1929) won the Pulitzer Prize. McNickle struggled for seven years to find a publisher for his novel, undergoing extensive revisions from the original manuscript. Only once he changed the ending from positive and profitable to tragic and fatalistic for the Native protagonist did he find a publisher with the Dodd, Mead Company, and even then they required McNickle to share the book's financial risk in his contract.[7] Though the UNM Press reprint left the book largely unchanged from its original production, a notable change materialized on the novel's cover: while the original cover featured a simple outline sketch of a mountain range, the new paperback version portrays the bodies of three Native men. These three figures, out of focus but not featureless like the "Three Peoples" murals, lean against wooden poles and gaze back at the viewer.

In the midst of the visual and literary consumption of Native bodies and cultures perpetuated by the twentieth-century tourism of the American Southwest, *The Surrounded* challenges the white ethnographic gaze through its covers, footnotes, epigraph, and other paratextual elements. Establishing whiteness as the invisible norm, cultural tourism paints Native cultures as primitive and white subjects as the only figures capable of visual agency and consumption. In response, McNickle's novel holds a mirror to the white gaze and implicitly critiques the way readers expect to see Native literature and peoples. As an author of both fiction and nonfiction books, McNickle persistently wrote Native peoples into national dialogues about race and reframed the ethnographic subject as complex, mirroring, and modern. He sought trade presses for his books and published in other national literary venues, urging his mainstream audience of non-Native readers to revise their stereotypes of Indians and reminding them that their perceptions of Native peoples come almost exclusively from Euro-American rather than Native perspectives. In the words of his biographer Dorothy Parker, "he appealed to anthropologists to look beyond the image of Indians frozen in the ethnographic present and search instead for the dynamics of change within Native societies."[8] Reinforced by paratextual elements that situate the novel uneasily within ethnographic literature and revise ethnography's citational relations, the narrative of *The Surrounded* redirects the white ethnographic gaze by exposing its failures of vision.

Epigraphs and Ethnography

In her annotated bibliography of McNickle's oeuvre, Parker describes the author's legacy as the creation of a "vision of Native American identity," yet critics struggle with the vision he portrays in *The Surrounded*. As Louis Owens points out, in spite of "valiant attempts" on the part of scholars to plaster optimism onto a novel that ostensibly refutes it, McNickle's fiction frustrates the optimism and political advocacy that ring through so clearly in his nonfiction. The plot of *The Surrounded* does indeed appear grim, as it follows the Salish and Spanish protagonist, Archilde, as he returns to visit his parents on his home reservation after a year's absence. His visit becomes prolonged as tensions mount between the Native and non-Native characters, and by the end of the novel Archilde stands accused of a murder he did not commit. In response, Archilde meekly holds out his arms to accept the handcuffs of Indian Agent Mr. Parker, who sneers the final spoken words of the novel: "'It's too damn bad you people never learn that you can't run away. It's pathetic—.'"[9] Because McNickle remains an important political figure for Native rights during the twentieth century, such an ending for McNickle's debut novel troubles contemporary scholarship. Why does the novel parrot the fatalism aimed at Indigenous peoples through popular rhetoric such as the Vanishing Indian? Why would McNickle's novel send such a bleak political message while his nonfiction and political life worked relentlessly to promote Indigenous sovereignty?

By way of explanation, scholars such as Benjamin Balthaser, Kirby Brown, Alicia Kent, and Rita Keresztesi situate the novel in relation to American modernism. Kent, for instance, fights for *The Surrounded*'s inclusion in the modernist canon, citing its omission primarily as a result of the historical exclusion of minority writers from the "high" modernist literature that includes celebrated white authors such as Gertrude Stein, Ernest Hemingway, T. S. Eliot, and F. Scott Fitzgerald.[10] Certain milestones in McNickle's biography, in fact, do closely mirror those of high modernist authors: after selling his allotment on the Flathead reservation in Montana in order to fund his education at Oxford, McNickle spent years living in Paris and traveling across Europe, as did many of the expatriates of high modernism. The original manuscript title of *The Surrounded*, "The Hungry Generations," makes a nod to Stein's famous "lost generation," and in another similarity to the lives of some expatriates, he never again lived in the borders of his own (tribal) nation, instead choosing to live outside of the reservation for the remainder of his life.[11] Yet what readers expect to "see" from minority writers, according to Kent, reframes minority fiction as ethnographic rather than as contributing to a broad literary heritage and constrains it to "'real' accounts providing knowledge about the true nature of strange and different cultures." As Kent, Keresztesi, and others argue, such ethnographical readings miss the "genre signals" and experimentation in fiction such as *The Surrounded*, and they trap racialized fiction in the expectations of its readers.[12]

The ethnographic entrapment of multicultural fiction extends to other writers of color during the early twentieth century as well, many of whom pushed back against their billing as primarily cultural ethnographers and as a foil to modernity. In her reading of Richard Wright's *Native Son*, Becca Gercken argues that Wright "anticipates the power of the 'gaze'" to shape perceptions of identity, and his narrative techniques allow him to "control the way readers see his main characters and, by implication, how these characters see themselves." Like Gercken, Balthaser also reads Wright's *Native Son* as a modernist novel meant to heighten an awareness of the white gaze on minority bodies in what he calls "a pointed satire of the documentary aesthetic." Balthaser reminds his readers that Wright rephrased W. E. B. Du Bois's term "double consciousness" as "double *vision*," emphasizing the role that sight plays in modernity and its relations with marginalized peoples. Modernity, for instance, brought a heightened awareness to the function of gaze upon the body: as Alan Hyde claims in his research on the role of sight and the racialized body in U.S. law, "Race in American law is thus unthinkable without a body and an eye. The body displays race, but only as perceived by the eye of the chancellor, the figure of authority." Homi Bhabha puts it another way, saying, "The white man's eyes break up the black man's body and in that act of epistemic violence its own frame of reference is transgressed, its field of vision disturbed." Race, sight, and the body became inextricable in the history of racial formation, and the ultimate power over bodies—their visibility or invisibility, their relation to space and place, their actions, and their identities—became sought after within the construction of whiteness and its social vision.[13]

The U.S. literary marketplace was not immune to the promotion of white vision. As print became increasingly affordable and accessible, paper and the printed word reinforced the primacy of vision in modernity. As Brownlee reminds us in *The Commerce of Vision*,

> As something to be viewed, scanned, skimmed, or read, paper also functioned increasingly as a medium of perception, as a vehicle for a new kind

of seeing. . . . Amid this thriving print and visual culture, the eyes both saw and were seen. Eyes were considered the primary organ for visual experience and the accumulation of knowledge; yet, they were also, like so many other surfaces, to be scanned as one might gloss over a page of print."[14]

Print's emphasis on visuality, of course, did not guarantee a depth of perception or insight, and the literary marketplace often favored a single vision, an entrapment of expectations that Zola Neale Hurston ridiculed in 1950 by calling out publishers in her essay "What White Publishers Won't Print" for their lack of interest in stories that depict complex racial characters. Hurston challenged the reading public's comfort in the racial stereotypes of flat literary characters of whom "everybody knows all about . . . lay figures mounted in the museum where all may take them in at a glance. They are made of bent wires without insides at all. So how could anybody write a book about the non-existent?" About Indians in particular, she sarcastically writes, "Who is so dumb as not to know all about Indians, even if they have never seen one, nor talked with anyone who ever knew one?"[15] These racist expectations became so engrained in American culture that Philip Deloria writes of *Indians in Unexpected Places* (2004), the discordance of white cultural expectations that occurs when Native peoples "unexpectedly" drive cars, sit under a hair dryer at a beauty salon, play baseball, and otherwise engage in modernity. Hurston's essay not only confronted such systemic expectations in the content of mainstream books, but also the deep inequality of the publishing industry that continues today, as a recent study by Richard Jean So and Gus Wezereck made more visible: despite the notoriety of best-selling writers of color, white authors continue to dominate the literary marketplace and represented 89 percent of fiction books published in 2018. The heads of all major publishing houses in the United States are white, as are 85 percent of the people in the industry who acquire and edit books.[16]

The white gaze of modernism cultivated a symbiotic relationship with what it deemed as primitive and "exotic" or non-white literature, art, and culture. Although an imperial interest in supposedly primitive cultures extends far back into history, the era of modernism took a particular and renewed interest in primitivism, which came to signify modernity as its antithesis and be deemed "inseparable" from it.[17] Marianna Torgovnick describes primitivism as "the sign and symbol of desires the West has sought to repress," and although she points out its "rich history of alternative meanings, the term often carries a derogatory implication of "simple" or "crude" with an evolutionary inferiority. As a result, Indigenous bodies and cultures became a commodity to be seen and visually consumed during the advent of primitive modernism in the twentieth century. In the West generally and Southwest specifically, tourist phenomena such as the Indian Detour turned the primitivism of "foreign" culture into a consumer event. Visual tourism also extended to literary tourism, as amateur ethnographers such as Charles Lummis, Adolf Bandelier, and La Farge visited the Southwest in search of the primitive experience and wrote fictional and nonfictional literature that reported on such to the mainstream reading public. Ethnography, as Fatimah Tobing Rony puts it, comes from an anthropological tool in which an observer writes about or describes a people but is more often used as a "category which describes a relationship between a spectator posited as Western, white, and urbanized, and a subject people portrayed as being somewhere nearer to the beginning on the spectrum of human evolution."[18] Indigenous and ethnic writing became widely perceived during modernism as yet another commodity, used as a token and ethnographical insight into another culture.

The book history of McNickle's novel demonstrates the fetish of primitive modernism at work within the U.S. literary marketplace. In his archival research into the McNickle Papers housed in the D'Arcy McNickle Center of the Newberry Library, Chicago, Louis Owens uncovers an editor's manuscript report from 1934 that praises McNickle's work as "one of the best novels ever written about the American Indian, and the essential poignancy and beauty of its theme and background will find a wide audience. Moreover, it is becoming easier and easier as time goes on to put across books with the primitive American appeal."[19] Despite the enthusiasm, however, the unidentified publisher rejected the manuscript, as did nearly every major publishing house over the next several years before it finally found a home with Dodd, Mead, & Co. in 1935. Yet the press also had doubts of the novel's financial success during the Great Depression, and they hedged their bets by offering McNickle a contract that was, in his agent Ruth Rae's words, "in no sense of the word a flattering one," including a demand that McNickle share the financial risk. E. H. Dodd rationalized the cautious terms in a letter by explaining the difficulty of marketing an unknown author's first novel, especially one that he considered to be "serious fiction."[20] His caution lies in keeping with the typical business strategy of the company, which published Paul Laurence Dunbar and sponsored several literary prize competitions yet garnered their financial success, like most other publishing houses, primarily from their backlist of "sure sellers" including westerns, mysteries, and adventure tales.[21]

Once published, *The Surrounded* did indeed sell poorly: McNickle's first royalty statement from August 1936 itemizes that after his $50.00 advance and merchandising costs had been deducted, the author received $8.33 and his agent $0.93 for that period. E. H. Dodd contacted Ruth Rae with additionally disappointing news, writing, "'We all feel very partial to Mr. McNickle and his work but *The Surrounded*, in spite of its quality and excellent reviews, sold so few copies that the net result was a pretty bad loss to us'" and therefore he declined to offer an advance on the novel that McNickle already had underway.[22] The novel did find critical success from a number of reviewers, however, including Oliver La Farge himself, who wrote of it glowingly in the *Saturday Review of Literature*; Harold Merriam, who gave it an enthusiastic review in *Frontier and Midland*; and Constance Lindsay Skinner, an editor for Farrar and Rinehart, who wrote McNickle personally to tell him that she "smelled smoke-tanged buckskin suddenly somewhere in your book."[23] Most mentioned and praised his use of ethnography.

While I am less concerned about placing *The Surrounded* within the category of modernist literature, I argue that the paratextual elements of the novel shape and expose the ethnographical expectations of its non-Native readers during the early twentieth century. Modernism marked a surge toward visual culture: the rise of photography, film, commercialism, anthropology, and psychology during the era of modernism affected the way modernists viewed the world. As a significant method of these new perspectives, ethnography functioned as one of many ways to observe and understand the reality of the perceived world, emphasizing the importance of the gaze in participant-observer anthropology as well as technological mediums. Yet visual culture targeted Indigenous peoples and people of color within various forms of what Colleen Eils describes as "compulsory visibility," a form of colonial practice that involves "looking for differences between groups of people, objectifying otherness, and assuming the privilege of observing other cultures' bodies, sacred institutions, epistemologies, and stories." The practice of compulsory visibility extends to the practice of reading literature as well: echoing the words of Zora Neale Hurston and many others, Eils connects the compulsory visibility and dis/embodiment of the ethnographic gaze to the pressures writers of color face, explicitly from the publishing industry and implicitly from mainstream readers, to produce depoliticized, "authentic," ethnographic literature. This kind of literature should not make the readers aware of their white privilege or systemic inequalities but instead allow them "to experience difference passively" and "sate their curiosity by peering into characters' lives from the privileged, abstracted position of a curious reader looking down on a page."[24]

As a rejection of such expectations, *The Surrounded* critiques primitive modernism and its racial spectacles through a preoccupation with seeing and being seen in the novel, a trope that challenges the ethnographic gaze upon Indigenous bodies. The novel's central concern revolves around vision, from the mysterious ability of Archilde's mother Catherine to move without being seen to the attempt by several characters to disappear into the mountains. Even the novel's title of the "surrounded" speaks not only to physical confinement—Archilde's perceived inability to leave the reservation after the start of the novel and his eventual arrest—but also to a visual confinement, or surveillance. Modernism manifested a new way of seeing and being seen that impacted the Indian subject as well as the Native author, yet *The Surrounded* critiques the white ethnographic gaze by revealing only a limited internalization of the Native characters, as well as their motivations and cultural practices.

For example, the first chapter of *The Surrounded* begins with the sentence, "Archilde Leon had been away from his father's ranch for nearly a year, yet when he left the stage road and began the half-mile walk to the house he did not hurry." The narrator gives the protagonist's first and last name as if introducing him to a stranger, establishing the reader's outsider gaze and preventing a familiarity with Archilde. Instead, the narrative technique creates an emotional and narrative distance with the character. The narrator then addresses the power of vision directly in the second sentence of the novel: "When he emerged from behind a clump of thornbush and cottonwood and caught his first glimpse of the cluster of buildings before him, he looked once, and that was all."[25] Here the narrative constructs the act of seeing as an act of power, as Archilde chooses to look only once at his familiar but emotionally complicated childhood home. As he looks, he assumes that he already knows all there is to see, and while Archilde is not necessarily mistaken, his act of looking mimics the presumptions often found behind the ethnographic gaze.

When Archilde arrives home, he encounters his mother sitting in the shade, and the narrative immediately begins describing their relationship in terms of vision. As Archilde approaches his mother, the narrative informs the readers, "If she heard him she did not look up at once." As with Archilde, the narrative forces the readers to become conscious of vision as a display of power, one that might be potentially withheld as one processes emotions such as the homecoming of one's favorite son. Because the narrative then describes Catherine as "a little deaf and a little blind," Archilde seeks his mother's attention and creates a noise with his heavy suitcase. When Catherine finally looks up at the noise, she sighs and smiles at the sight of her son, and as they talk, she "looked at him quickly," and he calls her to "'Look!'" at the money he earned while in Portland. The homecoming scene incessantly draws the reader's attention to vision, as while they speak Archilde's "gaze returned to his mother. How did she look after a year? Her eyes, which were getting weaker each year, were watery slits in the brown skin. . . . Nothing was any different. He knew it without looking."[26] By emphasizing the interplay of vision between the characters, the novel not only draws the reader's attention to the power of the gaze but also to the reader's own role in envisioning the Native characters.

The power of the gaze intensifies as Archilde greets his father, Max Leon. As Archilde approaches the front porch of his father's house, Max stretches his hand out to his son. In response, the narrative writes, "Archilde looked down at it with some surprise. This was his father's hand." During their conversation, Archilde first looks at Max to size up his appearance and then "gazed steadily" at him while Max tries to bully and irritate him.[27] Here the nature of seeing and being seen changes with the relationship: between Archilde and his mother their visual connections contain deep emotions felt for each other, yet with Archilde and his father their eye contact becomes wrapped up in a power play for respect.

As the narrative sets up the reader to become acutely conscious of vision by repeatedly emphasizing the way vision shapes character interaction, it also emphasizes vision as the primary means of experiencing modern life. In doing so, it mirrors early twentieth-century expectations of a supposed dichotomy between primitive and modern races. When the fourth chapter takes the reader back in time to the opening of Flathead Reservation land to non-Natives after the Dawes Act, it describes the newcomers as taking "one look" at the impoverished town of St. Xavier and erecting their "neat clapboard bungalows" on the opposite side of town. The novel implies some incredulity at their snap judgment, and it highlights vision as the central interaction between a Native and non-Native population now occupying the same space. Simultaneously, the use of the word "primitive" occurs repeatedly in the novel as a means of contrasting visions of "primitive" life with modernity. In the beginning paragraph of the same chapter, the narrative opens with, "The mission town of St. Xavier belonged to two ages. A brief sixty years separated its primitive from its modern, but the division was deeper than years."[28] The use of the terms "primitive" and "modern" separates people according to race and class while uncomfortably reflecting the shortcomings of the white gaze for the reader.

Father Grepilloux, a life-long missionary on the Flathead Reservation and its Confederated Salish and Kootenai Tribes, serves to emphasize the ethnographical lens of the novel as he is the only character to repeat the characterization of Native peoples as primitive. As Grepilloux shares with Max excerpts from his personal journal, he reminisces about a story he heard in 1884, during a time in which the "primitive law still swayed them" and supposedly skewed their sense of justice in regard to murder among the tribal citizens. By the end of the same chapter, Father Grepilloux finishes his nostalgic conversation with Max but "his thoughts continued to move through the yellow pages in which he had recorded the lost life of a primitive world."[29] Crucially, the novel never places the word "primitive" in the mouth of any of the Native characters, only in the thoughts of the missionary and the narrative vision of the reader. Though the reader of the text might be drawn into feeling ethnographical nostalgia with Grepilloux, the narrative clearly communicates his perspective as skewed by an ethnographical lens that prohibits him from understanding his neighbors in the Flathead community. *The Surrounded* calls out the white gaze, here embodied by Grepilloux, by citing the limitations and ultimate failures of his vision that make him unable to see beyond his own stereotypes and ethnocentrism.

The paratextual elements of *The Surrounded* reinforce the narrative's emphasis on ethnographic vision and the fraught relationships it engenders. Once readers open the book, they encounter an epigraph facing the full title page that reads, in all caps, "The Surrounded—They called that place *Sniél-emen* (Mountains of the Surrounded) because there they had been set upon and destroyed." Like Callahan's dedication, the choice of the third person plural "they" distances both the writer and the reader from Salish peoples, and the use of past tense in "called" and "destroyed" seemingly reaffirms a primitivist stance in confining Native peoples to the past. Additionally, the passive voice of "had been set upon" obscures the perpetrators of the destruction and potentially depicts Native peoples as victims. Yet in contrast, the inclusion of the Salish place name, *Sniél-emen*, complicates the vision of the other language choices. Knowledge of the Salish language implies that although the translation creates a rhetorical distance from the Salish cultural knowledge, the narrative itself does have cultural knowledge and willingly shares a limited amount of it with the reader. Furthermore, in conversation with the title, the epigraph creates an ambiguity: who is surrounded, and who had been destroyed? Citing the use of the mountain range as a place for hunting, as a victorious place against Salish enemies, and as the site of the 1855 Treaty of Hellgate that established the boundaries of the Flathead reservations, Beth Piatote notes that the Salish history contextualizing the term *Si-ni-el-le-em* contains "both positive and negative connotations" and as such the epigraph acts as "a palimpsest of the ways in which the novel enters and builds upon Native narrations of history and the land."[30] Thus while the epigraph overtly sets up an ethnological lens for the reader, it simultaneously announces control over the amount and type of cultural knowledge the reader may gain from the novel. It also works to create uncertainty and a critical consciousness in the reader by complicating who exactly who is being seen and surrounded.

As the narrative keeps the primacy of vision and perspective in the forefront of the reader's mind, it also resists the penetration of the white gaze. Rather than confirm the white gaze as informed, knowledgeable, and intimate with the Native peoples being observed, the narrative prevents readers from feeling like cultural insiders and blocks their perceived ability to understand Native people and Native life. The two main Salish characters demonstrate this lack of access to the "Indian." Although the narrator describes the actions and characteristics of Archilde's mother, Catherine, from the beginning of the novel, the narrator does not provide the reader with access to her thoughts until briefly in the middle of *The Surrounded.* Even here this interiority does not amount to much access, as Catherine merely thinks to herself about the tastiness of the mountain fish and how it feels good to be out of her cabin.[31] The rest of the novel continues to give extremely brief and limited insights into her character, preventing the reader from capturing an understanding and a presumed intimacy of Catherine.

McNickle limits the narrative vision, in effect controlling what can be seen or understood by the reader about his novel's characters. His strategy stands in stark contrast to many during the era and beyond who falsely or naïvely claimed to have "insight" into Native cultures. Eils identifies this narrative strategy in contemporary multiethnic fiction as a strategy of "narrative privacy" and as a means of evading ethnographic surveillance, explaining, "By explicitly drawing attention to the ways they limit readers' access to characters' lives, these authors challenge the role of native informant so often expected of nonwhite and indigenous authors by US audiences, instead creating spaces of narrative privacy."[32] *The Surrounded* shares very little of any of the characters' emotions, thoughts, or motivations, blocking any surveillance inclinations to understand Indian people and distancing the reader from any sense of intimacy with a character. Instead, it creates a critical framework that aligns the reader with an ethnographic gaze but disallows for the reader's insight into the characters or full absorption into the story.

For example, despite being the protagonist, Archilde remains just as inaccessible as Catherine throughout the novel. His seeming lack of motivation and agency in his life concerns most readers and frustrates their understanding of his motivations, as the narrative's rhetorical style prevents their access to his thoughts. The novel allows its readers to see a Native character, but in the limited scope of an ethnographical lens Archilde becomes an enigma, leading Keresztesi to describe, "Archilde moves through the narrative in a dreamlike state, never really aware of his surroundings, never quite understanding what happens to him." McNickle remained well aware of the obfuscated vision society had of Native peoples and readers had of Native literary characters. In McNickle's own words, written as a short essay for *The Nation*, he protested, "Most attempts to write about Indians in American history turn out to be accounts of what happened after contact with whites—a history of Indian-white relations in which the Indian is *seen* only in reaction to an incoming society and usually at a disadvantage. His own society is only dimly *perceived*, his motives are guessed at, his destiny is under a cloud."[33] Similarly, Archilde maintains radio silence for most of his feelings, explanations, and motivations, frustrating the reader's tourist gaze into Salish culture and leaving one to wonder if Archilde's actions and characterization instead constitute a symbolic performance for experimental fiction, ultimately prompting a critical introspection for the novel's white audience.

The dance that occurs toward the end of the novel epitomizes the critical stance the textual and paratextual elements of the book create between the reader and the narrative. The dance begins by being introduced in an ethnographic style with the words, "In the old days the Salish people held a great dance in midsummer, just as the sun reached its highest point. . . . At night their camp fires would be like a host of stars fallen out of heaven. This dance was the expression of their exultation at being alive, it sang of their pride, their conquest, their joys." By choosing the third person plural pronoun, the narrative again reinforces the reader's status as a cultural outsider who gains only limited insight to Native cultures through Native literature. With such a position enforced, the dance itself begins in the next chapter with a great deal of description focusing on the eyes and seeing. One character, an "old woman," prepares a young man Mike for the dance by painting six white dots under each eye. As Mike receives this preparation, Archilde "watched him closely," noticing that Mike's "eyes were active. . . . At odd times, he looking guardedly at Modeste, revealing a shyness which expressed his awe of the old man and his excitement at the drama he was to have a part in." Mike's admiration for Modeste is revealed through an attention to his eyes, but throughout this scene, dialogue is completely absent; the characters do not speak, but their eyes reveal their relationships to each other. Such a technique excludes the reader from intimacy or insight and only steps in to give the reader limited and perhaps unreliable ethnographical information: "In the old days this would have signified that each eye was to have the strength of six; today it signified no more than an old woman's fancy."[34] Here the narrative mimics and potentially mocks tourist expectations that place cultural traditions in a static, primitive past, including expectations of cultural traditions as inevitably dying or already dead.

Archilde continues to observe the preparations for the dance without participation in the action. The narrative repetitively emphasizes that Archilde is "watching" and "sees" all this, especially watching his mother in order to "guess how she had lived." All of his observations set him up for the shock of the dance scene itself, which he describes as "a spectacle, a kind of low-class circus where people came to buy peanuts and look at freaks." Although the novel itself takes a critical stance on the spectacle of presumed white ethnographic insight into Native peoples, it is this scene that most directly unveils its criticism of the white gaze that views Native peoples as primitive "freaks." Archilde is disgusted by the commercialization of the dance and the degree to which his culture becomes a spectacle: "This pavilion [sheltering the dance] was *surrounded* by selling booths decorated with bunting, and the crowd was coaxed to buy 'ice col' pop' and 'strawb'ry ice cream' and to win a 'cute Frenchy doll' on the roulette wheel."[35] The narrative comments highlight the visual surveillance to which the novel's title refers, as Native culture becomes "surrounded" by the commercialization of the ethnographic, as well as the tourist, gaze.

The novel depicts the dance as a complicated display of Indigenous performance. The scene continues with "all that was part of the circus atmosphere. The dancers, meanwhile, enacted their parts and showed no concern because of the staring eyes and the distractions beyond the pavilion." While the dancers may have "no concern" for the tourists and their gaze, the novel also depicts them as acutely aware of their role as cultural actors, performing for the "staring eyes" of the tourists as they "went forward like actors in a play and lost themselves in their game." While Archilde watches the dance, he calls it "a sad spectacle to watch. It was like looking on while crude jokes were played on an old grandmother, who was too blind to see that the chair had been pulled away just before she went to sit down." Archilde feels disgust at both the commercialism of the dance and the spectacle it creates for tourists, although when he later thinks about it in comparison to a "white" dance, he finds more cultural meaning in the tribal performance. The narrative reserves no admiration for the white spectators, however, who at one point Archilde finds laughing and making fun of an elder who was too weak to dance in the circle. The narrative writes of the elder as "oblivious of the laughter at his expense" while his face shone with inner contentment, but at the sight of this interaction Archilde can stomach no more and he immediately leaves the dance.[36]

The repeated emphasis on the visual again occurs here, as Archilde mentions not only the "spectacle," but also uses the synonyms "watch," "looking," "blind," and "see." As Kent expresses in her reading of this scene, "For Archilde, the presence of white gawkers drains the celebration of meaning and turns the Indians into objects of a primitivizing gaze."[37] Through Archilde, the narrative poses the reader in a critical stance on the political work of tourism and the ethnographic gaze, potentially also redirecting the reader into a reflection on their own positionality and complicity in the "crude jokes" that primitivism invokes.

What Archilde, and the reader, do not see, however, is the Indigenous agency involved in performance. In catering to the gaze of primitive modernism, McNickle taps into a long history of Indigenous people "playing Indian" to meet, critique, and defy (sometimes simultaneously) the expectations of a mainstream audience.[38] While motivations for playing Indian vary widely, the temptation to do so was especially strong during modernism not only because of the rise of photography, cultural tourism and commodification, and ethnography, but also because there was a growing market for doing so, as the careers of Geronimo, Sitting Bull, Zitkala-Šá, and others can attest. In "Playing Ourselves," Peers describes a "Native performer's gaze," in which Native performers remain aware of the expectations of the outsider gaze and in return manipulate the expectations of their audience for their own purposes. Native performers "were forced to deal with externally imposed images and situations of unequal economic and financial power," but Peers points out their agency in taking "colonial contexts and audiences and turn[ing] them into meaningful events designed to educate: using stereotypes to make a living, to teach about the reality of Native cultures and lives, and to build bridges between cultures."[39] In other words, the ethnographic gaze of primitive modernism does not preclude the subject from gazing back. Even while engaging in performance and the complex interplay of primitivism and modernism, Native peoples retained agency in the process and did not stand by passively or as victims.

Over time, the changing cover images of *The Surrounded* work in tandem with the textual narrative to return the gaze and continue to unsettle and complicate the reader's vision. At first the dust jacket of the first edition situates the novel in geographical space: the front image emphasizes the mountains to which its title and subsequent epigraph refers, featuring a minimalist white outline of a sweeping mountain range in contrast with a beige background. Paired together with the title and epigraph, the novel's paratextual elements ground the book in geographical space and the homelands of the Salish peoples. Yet while the Dodd, Mead Company's first edition of *The Surrounded* chose to feature the mountains of the Flathead community, the subsequent UNM Press reprints most prominently feature Native bodies. The image on the first dozen printings of the UNM Press reprint of *The Surrounded* reproduces an out-of-focus photograph of three Flathead men, with all three seemingly returning the gaze of the camera and reader. Parker identifies the photograph used for the cover image of *The Surrounded* as a cropped 1909 U.S. Reclamation Service photograph in front of the St. Ignatius mission, used as a model for the mission in *The Surrounded*.[40] The image continues to tie the reader and the book's vision back to place, but since nowhere in the book does the paratext identify the image, the viewer is left in the dark and either does or does not have insider cultural knowledge about its location. Furthermore, while there are many diverse cultural mores about the social appropriateness or rudeness of eye contact, the stance of the men and their engaged vision assert Native agency, even though the image's lack of focus attempts to mediate it. With clear individuality and the modern glint of one man's suspender shining in the sun, the men look back at the reader and participate in an exchange of vision, as equally perceptive and fully embodied subjects rather than ethnographic objects. The most recent cover image by the UNM Press continues to depict Native bodies but now replaces the blurred image of the three men with five young Native girls, now in sharp focus and gazing directly back at the viewer (Figure 8).[41]

FIGURE 8. Cover of the 1993 UNM Press reprint of *The Surrounded*. Author's collection.

The continued representation of Native bodies on the newest cover could be read as the continuing objectification of Native bodies and peoples, replicating the tourist gaze onto what is now a canonical text in Native literary history. Yet it may also be read as an even more powerful return of the gaze, coming from the renewed and enduring sales of *The Surrounded*, the ever-growing strength and depth of the Indigenous canon, and a renewed era of Indigenous self-determination. Reading *The Surrounded* through the lens of its exposure of primitive modernism, then, makes sense of the novel not as a tragic, pessimistic aberrant in McNickle's oeuvre, but as fitting with the work he did to educate a mainstream Euro-American audience of their misreadings and miseducation. With McNickle's deployment and critique of the ethnographic lens of primitive modernism, his novel exposes the violence of the colonialist spectacle but also creates a powerful space of control for Indigenous and ethnic writers, one that in turn opens a dialogue within modernism, its practices, and contemporary criticism.

Footnotes and Citational Relations

While *The Surrounded*'s narrative, reinforced by the title, epigraph, and cover images, instructs its readers to maintain a critical awareness of the white ethnographic gaze with which it aligns them, two additional paratextual elements further nuance the novel's stance toward ethnographic literature. A "Note" and a series of footnotes annotate the novel, redirecting the reader's perception regarding sites of knowledge. In the first edition, a "Note" appears after the conclusion of the narrative: signed by McNickle, the Note's first sentence establishes the novel as a "story of the Salish people" and asserts elements of the story as "belonging to" tribal nations from Hudson Bay southward. As the Note continues, McNickle lists his sources for Salish history as coming from the journals and writings of a number of ethnographers, fur traders, Indian agents, Jesuit priests, and other settler colonials, seven of whom he mentions by name. The Note additionally credits two Salish citizens, Big Raven and Chief Charlot, and two ethnographers, Marius Barbeau and Helen Fitzgerald Sanders, for the Salish stories he retells in *The Surrounded*. McNickle even includes a recommendation for the last book of ethnography he mentions, *Trails through Western Woods* by Sanders, who transcribed the "Story of Flint" from Chief Charlot.

In some ways, the Note reinforces the ethnographic gaze of the reader. It affirms the reader's expectations of an insightful and authentic glimpse into Salish life and concludes the novel with a reference to other ethnographic literature. However, the Note modifies the ethnographic perspective by reframing ethnography as a network of exchange rather than a one-way exploitation, similar to what I argued *Pretty-shield* expresses with nonfiction. McNickle ensures that Salish oral storytellers receive at least equal accreditation and places them in a community of knowledge production, what Daniel Heath Justice describes as "citational relations." Writing within the twenty-first century, Justice joins Indigenous feminists and other scholars of color to advocate for "a more mindful and ethical consideration of our citational practices in academia," a practice that McNickle prefigures nearly one hundred years earlier with his Note. In doing so, McNickle contrasts what Eils identifies as one of the key tenets of colonialism, "in which people of color produce culture but the lack the capacity for intellectual engagement."[42] His Note demonstrates that not only can Native people produce culture in the form of oral stories, but they can also engage intellectually with them in a network of citational relations and creatively in the form of a modernist novel.

Although McNickle builds from and even recommends the work of non-Native ethnographers, McNickle's Note asserts his authority and his own place in knowledge production. He makes his authority clear when he inscribes his name to the Note, ensuring that the readers see him as both cultural informant and an intellectual capable of entering into conversation with the field of anthropology itself. Doing so makes way for a Native reclamation of ethnography and anthropology, a cause taken up by earlier Native writers such as George Copway, Jane Johnston Schoolcraft, David Cusick, and many others, and to which McNickle would devote the rest of his life. Kiara Vigil cites the reclamation of anthropology as one of McNickle's major intellectual contributions, writing,

> Like other leading Native intellectuals such as Vine Deloria Jr., McNickle responded to the work of professional anthropologists by using both fiction and nonfiction to offer counter-narratives for broader public consumption. . . . For McNickle, anthropology needed to be claimed by Native Americans for intellectual as well as political purposes. As practitioners in this field, Native people might revise the types of methods used for studying indigenous communities.[43]

Beyond his first novel, then, McNickle's dedication to the reclamation of anthropology would later influence all of his publications. Although he never earned a degree, he nevertheless established himself as a "nationally prominent authority both in the field of anthropology and in Indian affairs" despite being "completely self-taught."[44] Kent argues that both McNickle and another of his contemporaries, Mourning Dove, published novels that attempted to "resist the essentialist gaze of anthropology of the period," aware of their role as mediators between the gaze and the Indigenous subject.[45] The Note embeds *The Surrounded* in the citational relations and existing power structures at play within ethnography while also carving space for Indigenous assertions and revisionist practices in the field.

The citational relations of the Note work in tandem with the narrative as it weaves the Salish oral stories into the text. Laurent Mayali describes the relationship between annotation and the text as "less a relation of meaning than it is a relation of power," that reveal the political dynamics at work within the structural apparatus of a book. Furthermore, Mayali argues that annotations can serve as a bibliographic apparatus for "reproducing knowledge in a form that legitimates the annotator, the annotation, and the social structures within which they exist." Within *The Surrounded*, the narrative reinforces the political stance of the Note through the way in which it incorporates ethnography. For example, both William Brown and Alicia Kent underscore the revisionist power at work within McNickle's inclusion of the Salish oral stories. Brown conducts a detailed collation of Helen Sanders's version of "Coyote and Flint" as recorded in her book, *Trails through Western Woods*, and McNickle's revision of the story within *The Surrounded*. As a result of the comparison, Brown argues that McNickle expresses "actual storytelling experiences more closely." Kent expands on Brown's research by including an attention to the narrative setting as well, pointing out that McNickle's narrative "reinserts the stories into the context in which they might have been told," in contrast to common ethnographic practices of the modernist era that often recorded oral stories but "failed to include the setting and situation of their telling."[46] McNickle embeds the Salish stories in context and in community, further emphasizing the citational relations of the knowledge production.

In the contemporary reprints of *The Surrounded*, the Note moves from the back to the front of the novel in order to preface the text and continue the ethnographic work started by the epigraph. By moving the Note to the fore, the reprints intensify the reader's attention to the power dynamics at work within the book, its paratexts, and ethnography. Its position also reframes portions of the narrative, especially Grepilloux's personal, ethnographical journal, as a colonial chronicler and as a single, incomplete perspective on Salish experiences. As James Cox argues, the narrative's inclusion of Grepilloux's limited perspective "casts into doubt the ability of a colonial chronicler" and undermines a single perspective that "ends with the conversion, assimilation, and salvation of the Salish" instead of seeing and accounting for the complexities of Native perspectives and experiences. In fact, Cox maintains, Grepilloux's "devotion to a single spiritual and historical plot *blinds* him to the lives of his Native parishioners" and renders him as "incapable of seeing or unwilling to see his role in the disruption of the Flathead Reservation community."[47] Yet McNickle does not replace the single viewpoint of a European narrative with another single narrative, not even a Native one. Instead, he uses the multiple written and oral stories in his text to represent the importance of multiple perspectives in viewing history and culture. Through the Note, then, *The Surrounded* both acknowledges and then relegates the anthropological, colonial narrative to the margin while simultaneously representing the complexities and hetereogenity of historical accounts that must include multiple perspectives.

While the Note works to reveal the political relations in dialogue between text and paratext, the novel contains additional annotations that reinforce a critical awareness of the ethnographic gaze. Authorial footnotes appear in other works of modernist literature, perhaps most famously in T. S. Eliot's *The Wasteland*, and in addition to serving as an experimentation with form, the appearance of footnotes in a novel serves to reinforce the ethnographical lens of its readers by reminding them of their positionality. Moreover, by inserting a footnote in a fictional text, the author pulls the reader away from complete absorption in the narrative and persistently reminds the reader of the act of reading, disallowing the reader to forget the frame. Footnotes disrupt not only the conception of reading as a linear act, but they also disrupt the gaze, provoking the reader into breaking their visual stride, scanning to locate and read the footnote, and then scanning to return to one's previous place in the text. The act of disruption refuses to let the reader be "lost" in the story, unaware of the visual processes of reading; instead, annotations force the reader to remain cognizant of their visual consumption of the novel, which *The Surrounded* utilizes in its criticism of the white ethnographic gaze.

Only three footnotes appear in the novel, yet their presence speaks volumes in the struggle for paratextual mediation and meaning. Each of the footnotes appear within a memory or tribally specific story of a Salish elder, and each serves to translate a Salish word appearing in the text into English. The first appears with Catherine as she reflects back to her earliest memories of contact and colonization; in fact, she reflects with a hint of grief that her memories of the priests "did not go beyond them, it began with them." She remembers her father's words, which welcomed the priests as an answer to their prayers to "Kolinzuten," which is footnoted with the explanation, "This was God, the Maker." The unexpected appearance of this first footnote pulls the reader out of the narrative to listen to the authoritative commentary of the author, and it occurs just at the moment when Catherine admits that even though she converted many years ago, she feels "frightened and uncomfortable in the knowledge the priests had given her" of Jesus and hell.[48] Her challenge to religious authority in the text matches the primacy given to the Salish word, with the English translation for God in the footnote. Meanwhile, as the footnote offers ethnographic insight, it also establishes the Native author as the one in control of the information, rather than a non-Native ethnographer. It also reminds the reader of the paratextual frame and reaffirms the reader's status as an outsider in need of explanations.

The second and third footnotes also translate Salish words into English and place the Salish language prominently into the text rather than marginally into the footnotes. The second footnote occurs within a scene in which Archilde struggles to enjoy a feast until the elders start telling Salish stories. As the stories continue, Archilde begins to listen with wonder and a new-found respect, until he reflects, "A story like that, he realized, was full of meaning." Immediately after the narrative shares Archilde's thoughts, the group turns to the last elder, Modeste, to tell a story. Like Catherine, the narrative emphasizes Modeste's lack of sight, which functions ironically in the novel as both characters arguably see the plot's social situations most clearly and with the greatest amount of insight. When Modeste begins his story, he dedicates it to Archilde because Modeste wants him to "see better just what it was like back in those times." Although his words contain a return to the historical past, unlike primitivist modernism his story does not seek to set up nostalgia or a hierarchy of primitive and modern peoples, nor does it attempt to paint a false picture of another culture's lifeways. In Modeste's words, "This is no boast about something that never was." The second footnote occurs here as he begins his story, situating his audience in their traditional land base from the mountains of Sniél-emen to the "Snpoilshi" River, which receives a footnote to give readers the river's American name, the Columbia. Both footnotes, then, center the Salish language, the

Salish religion, and Salish place names while marginalizing their English translations. The third and last footnote of the novel also occurs within Modeste's story, during the point at which he recounts the colonization of the Salish and the dark times that the colonizers brought. As a result, Modeste narrates, "Our voices, they said, no longer reach Amotkan," another Salish word that the footnote explains as "The old word for God. It could be rendered the Old man, or the Venerable One."[49] Modeste's story embeds Archilde and his audience in a Salish worldview, distancing the reader as a cultural outsider but offering them an opportunity to learn and join in knowledge production.

Footnotes refer to bodies—a separation from the textual body, bodies of knowledge and of scholarship, but also an ethical responsibility to the bodies who produced that knowledge. Building from DuBois's theory of double consciousness and James Weldon Johnson's theory of the double audience for ethnic writers, Warner Sollors identifies for racialized writers "an actual or imagined double audience, composed of 'insiders' and of readers, listeners, or spectators who are not familiar with the writer's ethnic group." Paratextual elements such as footnotes function as "signposts" of racialized writers who feel forced to address this double audience and who use footnotes as a "shift in perspective" and an interruption in the reader's consumption of the narrative.[50] In response to the framework of the Note, the footnotes of *The Surrounded* "interrupt" salvage anthropology by forcing it to the paratextual margins and exposing the failure of anthropological and tourist perspectives, rather than an Indian failure to be modern. It demonstrates an accountability to bodies of knowledge, and it prevents the reader's body from fading from sight as an invisible observer.

Footnotes embody a long history of uneven structures of power for marginalized subjects. Sara Ahmed describes the politics of citation as "a rather successful reproductive technology, a way of reproducing the world around certain bodies," and a number of scholars point out the internal politics of citation as white male scholars frequently cite themselves and each other at a far greater rate, contributing to the continuing systemic inequality of female scholars and scholars of color in the academy.[51] As a result, citation practices contain tremendous power not only over an informant or a scholar's visibility but also over their financial compensation, their hiring and promotion, their career, and the credit and acknowledgment for their ideas. For example, a recent study by Molly King et al. found that "an academic's visibility, reflected in citation counts, has a significant, direct, positive effect on his or her salary."

Not only, then, can a lack of ethical and reflective citation practices mean perpetuating the disparities for women, BIPOC, and LGBTQ+ scholars in higher education and in other professions, but it can also contribute to the persistent devaluing of the social contributions made by disenfranchised communities and obfuscate their intellectual heritage and communal knowledge. In this way, the paratextual elements of the Note and footnotes bibliographically "surround" the narrative from the margins, but they also enclose and surround what Shari Benstock identifies as the "shifting line of critical discourse, a line that sometimes acknowledges and admits readers within its circumference but sometimes excludes them, fences them of from the closed space of the scholarly activity." Benstock continues, "It is essentially this closed circle of reasoned criticism that footnotes negotiate, clarifying hidden assumptions, pointing out referential pre-texts, insisting that the author engage readers in the critical process."[52]

Following the call of Ahmed and others, Justice's *Why Indigenous Literatures Matter* calls out to Indigenous literary studies to improve our "citational relations" and to advocate for "a more mindful and ethical consideration of our citational practices in academia."[53] Citations matter because they position a scholar in relation to others in a discipline and establish one's reputation as a scholar, in turn providing greater career and economic opportunities.[54] Yet they also matter as they establish one's authority over narratives, especially for Indigenous communities. Footnotes demonstrate one's inclusion into higher education, not easily gained by McNickle and not easily gained by other marginalized subjects. In an interview with Henry Louis Gates, Jr., Harry Belafonte relates that his introduction to higher education came from a realization that most Black intellectualism had been rendered invisible or marginalized in footnotes. When he went to the Chicago public library with a list of books, the librarian refused to help him borrow so many, and Belafonte recapped, "I said, 'I can make it very easy. Just give me everything you got by Ibid.' She said, 'There's no such writer.'" I called her a racist. I said, 'Are you trying to keep me in darkness?' And I walked out of there angry.'"[55] In a city that later celebrated McNickle's intellectual leadership by establishing the D'Arcy McNickle Center for American Indian and Indigenous Studies, Belafonte and many others found themselves denied access to the hidden and often blocked wellspring of marginalized intellectuals.[56] To correct these historic injustices, contemporary scholars advocate in a number of ways to make bodies of knowledge more visible, including recommendations toward better citational diversity for journal editors, for a citation diversity statement for scholarly writers, and social justice movements such as the Cite Black Women Collective.[57]

Embedded acknowledgments can provide some measure of citation for Indigenous communal knowledge, but a lack of a collective citation method still indicates a scholarly individualism that excludes other kinds of epistemologies. McNickle remained acutely aware of communal knowledge and resisted Euroamerican conceptions of copyright. In a letter, McNickle complained to his agent about the need to obtain permission from the authors of the sources in his Note, writing, "'It is difficult to see how a myth or folktale can be copyrighted, especially when it comes so close to yourself as this does to me.'" As Parker argues, "McNickle's complaint about intellectual property rights allows us to see his 'Note' not only as a submission to copyright rules but also as a protest against colonialist theft of property rights in the name of their preservation."[58] In contrast to the problems John Rollin Ridge faced in obtaining sole copyright and accreditation for his novel, McNickle pushes back against individual copyright as an ethnocentric conception that often does not fit all types of knowledge construction and may leave the collective rights of Native nations unacknowledged.[59] Kent also reads McNickle's note as an assertion of Salish ownership of the stories told within: "The stories 'belong' to the Indian peoples of the region, not to the folklorists he subsequently lists and who own the copyright under US law."[60]

From this perspective, the Note points out the structural challenges in citing communal or tribal knowledge, as the very system of academic knowledge favors an individual "expert" and often a cultural outsider, a problem that remains in academic scholarship today. Yet footnotes also contain the potential to insert the novel and the reader into a greater sense of community, to hold scholars accountable, and to impress upon the reader that the text does not stand alone but comes from communal knowledge and storytelling. The citational relations of footnotes and the other paratextual elements in *The Surrounded* acknowledge a heterogeneity of voices and perspectives, preventing one's interpretation of events to stand alone and critiquing a single vision of perspective. They re-create ethnography, scholarship, and cultural learning as a more inclusive conversation, and they insert Native voices into relationships of political power.[61] By including the Note, footnotes, and multiple storytellers in his novel, McNickle implicitly challenges the Western conception of the single author and instead privileges community and collaborative authorship.

Conclusion: *The Surrounded*'s Ending
and Paratextual Visions

After forty years of periodic but tenacious protest, on August 13, 2021, the University of New Mexico administration concealed the "Three Peoples" paintings with large white shades which can be retracted upon request for educational viewing and placed a small sign citing the controversial history underneath the paintings. Tao Pueblo and Diné professor and associate Glenabah Martinez commented on the decision with the response, "'The murals themselves present a very racialized perspective of who is in authority. It was about the portrayal of how the racial hierarchy works in New Mexico.'"[62] Her words continue to emphasize the role of vision in the "perspective" and "portrayal" of who wields power and authority, who and what receives citations, and what may or may not be shielded from view. The "Three Peoples" paintings also remain inextricably linked to visions of the future: as the paintings represent all of the brown figures without eyes, the blue-eyed white male is the only one capable of and positioned to look forward.

The ending of the novel also confronts its reader with the expectations they have for Indigenous futures. As mentioned previously, while many critics express concern with McNickle's vision for Archilde's future, and implicitly through the character McNickle's vision for Indigenous futures broadly, I counter that the narrative deploys the ending against its readers to test their own expectations and possible alignment with Agent Parker's racism at Native peoples' place in modernity. If, as the criticism continues to point out, Archilde and the other Native characters seem tragically but inevitably doomed to fail, then that vision matches not McNickle's lifelong political advocacy but the perspective of salvage anthropology and the white gaze.[63] In doing so, the narrative avoids any tinge of romanticism associated with the Vanishing Indian in the novel's ending; rather, the narrative recasts expectations of Indigenous deficiencies as racist, misplaced, and shortsighted.

In the last few pages of the novel, Archilde's lover Elise murders Sheriff Dave Quigley when he comes to arrest Archilde. Before the murder happens, Archilde had a sense of what Elise might do and tried to silently communicate to her, "'Keep your nerve. Let's see it through.'" Instead, Elise catches Quigley by surprise and fires three rounds into his chest. In the aftermath, the narrative continues to underscore the reader's attention to vision when Archilde exclaims in shock, "'Elise! Christ Almighty!

See what you've done!'" and Elise berates him for "staring" at her. Meanwhile, Indian Agent Parker bursts out of the surroundings and Archilde realizes that he had been "out of sight but probably looking on," which accounted for Sherriff Quigley's unusually mild behavior. Parker then pours out his frustrations with "you and all your kind" and utters the infamous last words of the novel, "'It's too damn bad you people never learn that you can't run away. It's pathetic—'"[64] While the novel ends with Archilde's silent submission to his arrest, the narrative's constant attention to vision compels the reader to pay attention to the gaze: what did Parker see? What do his words reveal about what he expects to see from Native peoples? In turn, by the end of the narrative, what do the readers of Native literature expect to "see" of Native characters and peoples?

By the end of the novel Archilde becomes a litmus test for the reader's vision as he acts out the foreseeable impact of the white gaze, or what Matthew Herman describes as the "outcome of the racial logic of colonial social relations."[65] Parker's vision and potentially the reader's own lacks the knowledge and insight that could see Archilde and Native peoples as possessing any agency of their own. Instead, such a vision potentially ensnares everyone, Native and non-Native alike, in the expectations of Indigenous deficiencies which manifest as the seemingly "inescapable determinism" at the ending of the novel.[66] For the Native characters, to be visually confined is to be painfully aware of the expectations that others have for one's actions and one's life, expectations that demean one's autonomy and which may feel inescapable. Within the white gaze, the reader becomes unable to view Indigenous peoples as participants and contributors to modernity and unable to see beyond tragedy to imagine Indigenous futures. The reader's gaze of Archilde's passive and wordless surrender fulfills the ethnographic gaze that expects Indian subjects to likewise surrender to modernity and progress. Ultimately, it is the shortsightedness of the white gaze that arrests not only Native bodies but all bodies in its prejudice.

Yet rather than running "afoul of the publisher's knife," as Paula Gunn Allen speculates, the novel accomplishes a critical moment of reflection for the reader, who can either sympathize with Parker's frustration and racist pity or choose instead to feel unsettled and misaligned with such a vision.[67] Through Parker's eyes, the narrative offers the readers an opportunity to question the "bankruptcy of the white idea" of the Indian and their role in the gaze that "surrounds" Indigenous cultures and perpetuates tragic expectations in the first place with myths like the Vanishing Race.[68] It is the white body, or more specifically the white gaze, that is the ultimate failure in the novel.

The work of the tragic, disappointing ending of *The Surrounded*, then, startles those of us interested in reading works that we hope speak to Indigenous power and agency into reflecting back upon our expectations for a Native novel and author. Do all Native stories have hopeful endings, and what are the constrictions of expecting such an ending? If scholars dismiss or avoid Native novels that have pessimism, what could we potentially be missing in the political or aesthetic work of the text? As Peers advocates in her analysis of Native interpreters at living history sites, not critiquing the dominant narrative "denies the agency of Native people, and misses the potential for this gaze to be interrupted or returned by those who are gazed upon." Rather than succumb to being a visual target with a tragic ending, then, *The Surrounded* instead accomplishes the possibility of reflection and relationship. The paratextual framework works alongside the narrative to revise the reader's relationship to the text, and it calls our attention to the social perceptions of Indians in modernity direct us, in Phil Deloria's words, to a "reimagining of the contours of modernity itself." McNickle critiques these "contours of modernity" from its outskirts, not seeking to redefine it but to expose its fallacies and misperceptions, at least in the eyes of his readers. As Andrew Piper puts it, "Books have never just been objects of reading. To understand books is to understand the act of looking that transpires between us and them. It is to ask how we face books and how they face us."[69] With a trust in the power of literature, both fiction and nonfiction, to be transformative in the eyes of its readers and in society, *The Surrounded* makes visible Indigenous contributions to modernity and the power of citational relations.

Paratextual Futures

There are no bodies on the Internet. There is no land.
—Leanne Betasamosake Simpson, *As We Have Always Done*

He wanted not to take refuge in a better library but to live in a better world.
—Robert Bringhurst on Jan Tschichold

WHEN WE READ a book for its narrative content only, we miss half the story. Indigenous book history and its paratexts matter not only for the ways in which they embody Native resilience through the horrors of genocide and colonization, for the ways in which they testify to the obstacles Native authors faced in the mainstream literary marketplace, and for the ways in which they document the complex perception and reception of readers in Indigenous literary history; they also matter in their materiality, as bibliography grapples with the groundswell of digitization. Since the advent of the internet, the future of the printed book has sparked countless debates, but most importantly it has inspired scholars to reconsider the value of the printed book in a digital age. As I have argued, the multiple reprints and editions of Indigenous books hold value in their material composition, as they leave bibliographic witness to Indigenous literary embodiment. Yet as *Book Anatomy* extends beyond pointing out the presence of bibliographical bodies, I end my discussion of Indigenous book history not only by revealing its under-examined past but also addressing why its materiality matters to the future.

Technology, too, impacts the body. As my previous chapters argue, book publication served as one means of fighting for the inherent bodily sovereignty and humanity of dehumanized subjects. As Indigenous authors embedded the lived experiences of their bodies into the storied and bibliographical pages of the book, they gained power and control over corporeal narratives within the literary marketplace and enlisted the printed word in struggles for justice. New book technologies impact bodies as well, as digital readers learn to guide a mouse, navigate a screen by touch, and adjust the brightness of a lit screen. Countless studies have taken up the ways in which digital reading interacts with our brains and bodies, including the ways in which digital reading can impact our relationships with our children, change our comprehension of a lecture or a text, disrupt linear reading patterns, and modify the processes of our brains.[1] In many ways, digitization promises a transformation of the human body itself—through unprecedented access to human knowledge and intellect, and through improvements or substitutions to the human body. Corporeal transformation and even disembodiment may even be said to fulfill the ultimate dream of humanity. In *Haunted Media*, for example, Jeffrey Sconce writes of humanity's persistent wish to transcend the body, first through religious experiences and more recently through the means of technology, dematerializing the body into eternity and perfection.[2]

Yet others worry about the dehumanizing aspects of the digital, its costs to human nature and even to humanity itself.[3] Upon reflection on the use of social media in the Idle No More movement, Leanne Betasamosake Simpson acknowledges the critical role technology played in building the movement, yet Simpson also considers that the connections formed and built on social media could have only been enabled by embodied kinship connections. In her words,

> [m]ovement building was relationship building, and it involved traveling large distances to create physical connection with other human and nonhuman beings. This privileged the power of human connection and intimacy and of being fully present in the moment. Walking a great distance to spend significant time with people and the land builds empathy, trust, and the ability to give each other the benefit of the doubt. It connects bodies to land, and bodies to Ancestors.

Simpson further ponders the "digital dispossession" of the internet and the ways in which the digital undermines Indigenous presence, connection, and the relations that can only be achieved in the hard work of face-to-face interactions. Ultimately, Simpson concludes, social media becomes the "antithesis of Indigenous life" and builds false communities of human connection.[4]

Simpson's need to assert the difference between a webpage and a person, an internet connection and a friend, speaks to the modern crisis over definitions of life, bodies, and human beings. From Bartolomé de las Casas to Black Lives Matter, the modern world remains in crisis over its inability to agree on the difference between a human being and a machine, a body and a nonbody, a subject and an object. At the heart of such conversations lies a fundamental disagreement on human rights and what matters. In the midst of this ongoing crisis, books have taken on a close, nearly inextricable affinity with the human body, and the language we use continually reflects such a close association: as one example, David Kastan describes modern technology as "so seemingly inevitable that we fail to see it as a mediation. It seems to contain the text as naturally as skin on a human body."[5] Books become bound up— quite literally—with the value and meaning of the human and nonhuman body. As a result, the future of the printed books and the nature of digital technology continues to be so hotly debated because it feels so deeply, even physically, personal.

Whether electronic books may be considered material objects or a type of disembodiment, they do not carry the same properties as printed books, which actively mold to our bodies—folded, creased, bent, curved, conformed to the pressure of hands and fingers, held open in two places at once, marked by writing utensils, sweat, tears, food spills, bugs, and weather—and mark the passage of time and human interaction in ways that digital books cannot. Although the digital buffer from the human body may seem like good news for the preservation of books, it is also a devastating loss for cultural historians who seek to understand a book's reception through physical evidence. As my previous chapters argue, a change in materiality changes a text's impact, message, and cultural significance in ways that may or may not be for the better.

Digitization has yet to achieve an equal bibliographic record of embedded human interaction, and although it attempts to sell its increased accessibility, many rural and reservation communities do not have the infrastructure, financial resources, or institutional resources for database subscriptions that could begin to fulfill the promises of increased accessibility.[6] In fact, the potential diminishment of the second-hand market for books, as publishers design e-books to prevent sharing or resale, may instead further erode the accessibility of books to disenfranchised communities. In Sherman Alexie's "Superman and Me" (1997), for example, he begins his reflection on the role of books in his life by emphasizing their physical presence, the accessibility of used books despite his family's poverty, and his relationship to his parents through their love of books. Describing his father as an avid reader who "bought his books by the pound" mostly at second-hand stores, he remembers his childhood home as full of books, "stacked in crazy piles in the bathroom, bedrooms, and living room." Books became a way of loving his father, Alexie writes, despite the social expectations in his life for Indian children to be silent, monosyllabic, submissive, and stupid when it comes to their education. An access to second-hand books, then, not only became a means of love but a means of Indigenous joy in the midst of survival. Alexie remembers, "I read anything that had words and paragraphs. I read with equal parts joy and desperation. I loved those books, but I also knew that love had only one purpose. I was trying to save my life." Now as an author himself, Alexie holds up books to students in reservation schools as a means of opening "their locked doors" and as a way to "save our lives."[7] The book has always functioned as an active, not passive, conduit in the relationships between human bodies, and an accessibility to books became Alexie's means of climbing out of impoverishment.

In contrast, digital books may perpetuate or further block equal access: Ted Striphas emphasizes the shift in print to digital production as a shift in commodity value, as publishers gain a new opportunity "to restrict the secondary circulation of books, from which they cannot profit." Striphas warns that the increased mediation of internet access, digital platforms, and devices, added to the other mediations of the publishing industry, gives publishers greater control of our book consumption. Robert Darnton already documents the rise of information monopoly, as Google, and Google Books, stand prepared to digitize and control access to a digitized world library.[8] Librarians and other academics warn of the exponentially rising costs of access to the digital print record, including journals, databases, and other digital materials, and even the seemingly innocuous act of searching reflects the systemic inequalities reflected in the nation.[9] In fact, Ruha Benjamin identifies a "New Jim Code," which she defines as "the employment of new technologies that reflect and reproduce existing inequities but that are promoted and perceived as more objective or progressive than the discriminatory systems of a previous era." Benjamin also links technologies and bodies as especially pertinent to discussion of digitization, countering, "The view that 'technology is a neutral tool' ignores how race also functions like a tool, structuring whose literal voice gets embodied in AI."[10] It is an illusion to think that our books, as well as their content, are *not* influenced by the systemic inequalities within which they were produced.

Digitization puts control of the cultural record in fewer, not more, hands, and it currently functions largely under the purview of for-profit entities.[11] It also remains just as vulnerable as print, if not more so, to loss, censorship, errors, and surveillance. As previously mentioned, the misunderstanding of digitization as a replacement for print copies rather than a supplemental tool actually resulted in a massive destruction of the printed cultural record. Andrew Stauffer points to material printed between 1830 and 1923, which corresponds to the Indigenous book history that I examine here, as the most vulnerable to nearly complete cultural and physical loss due to a number of combined factors: "mostly out of copyright, frequently available in full text online, usually not valuable to collectors, sometimes in deteriorating condition due to the wood pulp paper and cheaper production values of the era, and often assumed even by scholars to be standard, identical copies created by machines in the age of the stereotype and the steam press." Moreover, Stauffer adds, "there is a lot of it, and it is little-used by patrons."[12]

Literature from marginalized communities faces even more challenges, as they may have been less rigorously collected, less canonized, less preserved, and historically less valued by research institutions. For example, while a first edition of McNickle's *The Surrounded* with its dust jacket currently sells for around $2,500, the more affordable editions may not be collected. My own institution, a small regional university classified with an R1 status, does not own a copy, and neither does my public library. Digitization may provide greater access in certain ways and to certain communities, but the pre-existing and continuing vulnerability of Indigenous books is even greater: for the nineteenth- and early twentieth-century Indigenous books I examine here, only one first edition of the first known novel published by a Native man survives, and less than a handful of copies of the first known novel published by a Native woman. The Indigenous books that first entered the American literary marketplace in increasing numbers over the course of the nineteenth and early twentieth centuries, some of them recovered only recently, now face a winnowing of accessibility that may include deaccession, off-site storage, or a digitization that reduces or even eliminates material copies. Not only do these losses endanger the largely understudied Indigenous books from this era, but they also jeopardize the emergent scholarship of Indigenous book history, periodicals, and print culture. From the book medium to electronic mediums, the fight for sovereignty—over knowledge, over resources, and over bodies—remains at the heart of these debates.

In arguing for the importance of printed books I am not arguing for their exclusive rights to package a text. In some cases, electronic media may indeed greatly increase access to materials and otherwise help readers achieve a relationship to a text that they may not otherwise have had. Additionally, Indigenous activists have made enormous strides in language preservation and other types of cultural preservation through electronic media. And to argue for the primacy of printed books seems as futile to me as arguing for the primacy of electronic media—each serve their readers in different ways, and to bring about a complete absence of either medium would be a loss to society. No medium has ever succeeded in wholly eradicating another long-standing medium. Yet my analysis of the narrative framing and control exercised by paratextual elements demonstrates the power of paratextual mediation, which increases three-fold with the paratextual, publishing, and social mediations of internet access, digital platforms, and electronic devices. Indigenous literature and nonwhite literature continue to be historically under-represented in the publishing industry, and digitization does not rectify this historical injustice.[13] Rather, technology stages a new arena in which to continue fighting for Indigenous representation and control, both on our bookshelves and on our screens. In doing so, caretakers of the cultural record must remain vigilant to what Andrew Stauffer identifies as the "bibliodiversity" not only of representation, but also of the full spectrum of editions, reprints, paratextual matter, singular copies, and marginalia that compose Indigenous book history and all other book history traditions to avoid a "flattening of the human record in all of its variability."[14]

Contemporary Indigenous literature already emphasizes that the physicality of books matters. In his semi-autobiographical novel, *The Absolutely True Diary of a Part-Time Indian*, Alexie's protagonist feels outraged when he discovers that his mother had written her maiden name over thirty years ago in his geometry book's inside front cover and he realizes "with the force of a nuclear bomb" his school and his tribe's deep poverty and oppression. In reaction, Alexie hurls the book across the room in a public, physical reaction to the systemic violence the outdated text now represents. The materiality of the text provides the documentation, easily seen and accessed, of the inequity Alexie is set up to experience in his life. In Louise Erdrich's *Books & Islands in Ojibwe Country* (2003), she muses that "Books. Why?" has been a question that has "defined my life, the question that has saved my life, and the question that most recently has resulted in the questionable enterprise of starting a bookstore," and she offers the book as a journey through what the medium of the book has meant to her life and to the Ojibwe Nation.[15]

As these authors and many more testify, material books document assertions of authority and sovereignty, as well as creative and literary talent. Engagement with the written word provided an additional venue for Indigenous political and intellectual contributions on a global scale. Archival recovery projects continue to change the scope of Indigenous literary history and alter the landscape of what we know, expanding the canon of both oral and written traditions. In fact, an increasing number of contemporary Indigenous literature takes up and reimagines the archive "against the grain" and in support of Indigenous epistemologies: for example, Deborah Miranda's *Bad Indians* (2013, Leslie Marmon Silko's *Storyteller* (1981), and N. Scott Momaday's *The Names* (1976) all combine memoir and tribalography with mixed-genre archival elements such as family photographs and oral history.[16] D'Arcy McNickle's *The Surrounded* (1936), David Treuer's *The Translation of Dr. Apelles* (2006), and Louise Erdrich and Michael Dorris's *The Crown of Columbus* (1991) reimagine archival documents such as a priest's diary, interleaved manuscripts, and Columbus's diary to critique and repurpose Western institutions. Alongside recently recovered, foundational works of fiction by authors such as John Joseph Matthews, an engagement with the archive influences contemporary Indigenous literature and criticism. Yet while the last three decades of Indigenous literary recovery have reproduced significant texts, few recovery projects have reproduced essential paratextual matter, especially in regard to the scope of reprints and editions. Its absence leaves a large gap in the field's understanding of Indigenous literary production, marketing, and reception.

Transformative archival recovery projects have certainly come from or have been assisted by the digital humanities, but digital archives have yet to prove their durability. Data studies, in fact, thus far indicate the extremely fragile and evanescent nature of digital records. Bugeja and Dimitrova, for example, documented in their study of three leading science and medical journals that within two years, 13 percent of the online references cited were inaccessible. Bugeja further notes that his impetus for multiple studies on the erosion of online scholarship came when he realized that by the time he submitted his book manuscript for publication, half of his online references had vanished into dead links. In light of their studies, both scholars express concern over the internet's "obliteration of place and material," elements that matter deeply to Indigenous literature and book history.[17] Most of the editions and reprints examined in the following chapters, for example, were not available online, or those that could be found online came from either the first edition or the latest, obscuring and implicitly devaluing the full bibliographic record and scope of Indigenous literary history. Rather than being more or less interchangeable, or the most recent edition as unequivocally the best, each reprint and edition we examine contains immense value that tells a story of its place in Indigenous and American literary history. For Indigenous literature especially, which has historically been subjected to institutional and archival discrimination or erasure, scholars should continue to weigh the benefits and losses of digitization and print technologies and remain vigilant to archival and digital gaps.

The consolidations of books, and therefore of vast bodies of knowledge, into a few institutions or corporations always disadvantages the dissemination of and access to that knowledge. It poses a looming and arguably unprecedented threat to the education of the world's population, disguised behind a ubiquitous and seemingly democratic electronic screen. In *Censors at Work*, Darnton provocatively questions the special interest backers of digitization and writes to "provoke reflection on the problem posed by the convergence of two kinds of power—that of the state, ever-expanding in scope, and that of communication, constantly increasing with changes in technology." Darnton exposes what he describes as "systems of censorship" historically conducted by the state into literary realms, and asks readers to consider, "If states wielded such power in the age of print, what will restrain them from abusing it in the age of the Internet?"[18]

As a case in point, the Modern Language Association imposed a structural violence on Indigenous book history when the 8th edition of its citation style announced that it no longer requires documentation of a source's place of publication. Despite a foreword which claims that the newest style "*embodies* so many of the values that define the association" (emphasis mine), in most storytelling traditions, especially Indigenous ones, stories are inextricably tied to place, and to remove them enacts and embeds a type of violence within the story and the book itself.[19] By way of explanation, the 8th edition now considers the identification and citation of a book's city of publication a traditional practice that "usually serves little purpose today."[20] In contrast, however, books are made by communities, not solely by authors, and *where* those communities are located and what they produce matters. The places of book production should not be omitted or abstracted, because to do so occludes both labor and community, and to erase such a foundational acknowledgment from book history obscures structures of power in the publishing industry. As Katherine Hayles argues, "Information, like humanity, cannot exist apart from the embodiment that brings it into being as a material entity in the world; and embodiment is always instantiated, local, and specific."[21] Even diasporic archives require a physical presence in community that is negated with digitization, and an increasing disembodiment from place and community should remain a concern even as digital recovery and access provides benefits for Indigenous communities and scholars.

In addition, the physical locations of archives matter. Travel to an archive entails a response-ability, in Toni Morrison's sense of the word, to the communities who house and preserve the items, not merely in the economic support of the community, but also socially and politically in experiencing the community and gaining a knowledge of it. Travel to or research within a specific archive, despite the financial burden and sometimes the inconvenience, also encourages a responsibility to consider archival provenance—who owns what, and why. Such questions become more immediate and pressing when a researcher finds she must arrange funding and travel to an archive in New England to view a text written and produced in the West, for instance, and causes one to consider the imperial structures of book collecting that may escape one's notice within a digital catalogue. Finally, a researcher must be responsible to the field of bibliography and the integrity of their own work to examine multiple copies of a text before drawing conclusions, a practice that digitization often does not make possible at the present. Material archives require readers to interact bodily not only with the materials but also with the communities that maintain and surround the archive.

As has always been the case, we—academics librarians, institutions, organizations, bibliophiles, booksellers, publishers, and readers—will be accountable to future generations for the decisions we make now about printed books. Our first responsibility as scholars is not knowledge production but toward human and nonhuman beings in community. Does my work encourage or deepen a greater responsibility to place? Does it encourage or extend responsibilities to the communities in which I research, work, and live? As our generation and the ones to come debate the nature of the digital, I propose that such a debate will be unsuccessful without a critical reflection of the value and full scope of printed editions in Indigenous book history. While we might never definitively know what future generations will cherish, our commitment to social justice calls upon us to think carefully about the equity of what we preserve, what we discard, what we value, and why. It is our responsibility to continue to weigh these questions going forward.

NOTES

Introduction: Material Matters

1 Throughout my book I choose the less bibliographically precise term "reprint" when referring to either an edition or an impression. My interest here remains less in the specialized terminology of descriptive bibliography and more in building bridges for an interdisciplinary audience between book history and Native literary studies. I also interchange "Indigenous" and "Native" for two reasons: first, while the texts I choose here come from Native Americans, within the boundaries of what is now the United States, I hope to build momentum toward a global Indigenous book history scholarship using common methodologies and in acknowledgment of the book as inherently global. In addition, while contemporary scholars have typically used the term "Indigenous" to refer to tribal peoples across the world and "Native" to refer to tribal peoples in the United States, in the past few years Native studies and Native literary studies have begun to use "Indigenous" and "Native" more interchangeably. For example, see Calcaterra, *Literary Indians*; Estes, *Our History*; Tatonetti, *Written by the Body*.

2 Coupal, Hanson, and Sarah Henzi, "Sovereign Histories," viii. While I would not presume to compare Indigenous books to sacred objects, Amy Lonetree's description here articulates the agency and embodied layers of meaning that I contemplate in books: "Objects in museums are living entities. They embody layers of meaning, and they are deeply connected to the past, present, and future of Indigenous communities. Every engagement with objects in museum cases or in collection rooms should begin with this core recognition. We are not just looking at interesting pieces. In the presence of objects from the past, we are privileged to stand as witnesses to living entities that remain intimately and inextricably tied to their descendant communities." Lonetree, *Decolonizing Museums*, xv.

3 Multigraph Collective, *Interacting with Print*, 222.

4 McCoy, "Race," 157; McKenzie, *Bibliography*, 1. See Dinius, "Look!!"; Fielder and Senchyne, "Against a Sharp White"; Goldsby, "Book Faces"; Jackson, "Talking Book"; Nishikawa, "Black Pagecraft"; Radus, "Margaret Boyd" and "Printing Native History"; Round, "Bibliography" and *Removable Type*; Wigginton, *Indigenuity*.

5 Linderman, *Pretty-shield*, n.p.

6 Matthews, "Framing," 26; Butler, *Bodies That Matter*, x.

7   Both McNickle and Ridge had additional books published posthumously. I also limited my analysis to prose and to editions printed in English, although the growing number of Native books translated and published in languages such as Hungarian, French, and Italian warrants further study.

8   Warner, *Letters of the Republic*, 8, 17. On the complexity of authenticity and introductions, see Raibmon, *Authentic Indians*; Sekora, "Black Message/White Envelope."

9   Lopenzina, *Looking-Glass*, 3.

10 See for example Darnton, *Case for Books*; Seeber, "Legacy Systems"; Stauffer, *Book Traces* and "My *Old Sweethearts*."

11 MLA, "Significance of Primary Records," 27 (my italics); Fuchs, "Diaries," 38. In referencing the archive, I employ it broadly here to refer to both archival collections, rare books, and special collections.

12 Dale and Ryan, *Body in the Library*, 2.

13 Apess, *A Son of the* Forest (1831), 3. See Lopenzina's *Looking-Glass* for his insightful discussion of Apess's trauma.

14 See O'Connell, Introduction to *A Son of the Forest*.

15 Gustafson, *Eloquence Is Power*, 1; Lopenzina, *Looking-Glass*, 37. See also Weyler, *Empowering Words*.

16 McLean, *Typographers on Type*, 41. Meynell numbers twenty-five letters in the English alphabet rather than twenty-six because seventeenth-century printers omitted the letter "w," easily created by two "v's." See also Deloria, *Custer*, 10; Febvre and Martin, *Coming of the Book*, 11; Loxley, *Type*, 208.

17 Warner, *Letters of the Republic*, 13, 47.

18 Rezek, "Racialization of Print," 418.

19 Warner, *Letters of the Republic*, 14; Berlant, *Anatomy of National Fantasy*, 11.

20 Young, *Black Writers*, 7; Roy, "Slave Narrative Unbound," 264.

21 Putzi, *Identifying Marks*, 2, italics in original; Harris, "Construction of Race," 1725.

22 Grosz, *Volatile Bodies*, xi; Elshtain and Cloyd, *Politics*, xv. See also Block, *Colonial Complexions*; Butler, *Bodies That Matter*; Chiles, "Becoming Colored" and *Transformable Race*; Dain, *Hideous Monster*; Esposito, *Persons and Things*; Fear-Segal and Tillett; *Indigenous Bodies*; Johnson, *Persons and Things*; Sorisio, *Fleshing Out America*; Sweet, *Bodies Politic*; Tucker, *Moment of Racial Sight*; I limit myself in this study to a discussion of books and *human* bodies, but my analysis could well extend into other types of bodies, including the animal, plant, water, and mineral bodies out of which books are made.

23 Esposito, *Persons and Things*, 13.

24 Rasmussen, *Queequeg's Coffin*, 113.

25 Lopenzina, *Red Ink*, 45.

26 In one particularly horrific example, a General Daniel Morgan used the skin of a Native man he had killed in combat to bind a book called *The History of Christianity*. See McElroy, "Book Bound."

27 Brylowe, "Flood," 37.

28 Piper, *Dreaming in Books*, 46.

29 Qtd. in Zanjani, *Sarah Winnemucca*, 103–4.

30 Cohen, *Networked Wilderness*, 2; Carpenter and Sorisio, *Newspaper Warrior*, 2.

31 For one review of the lack of critical attention to earlier centuries of Native literary production, see Fitzgerald and Wyss, "Land and Literacy."
32 For an exemplary model of how to teach and frame historical "firsts," see Collins,
"More Than a Name."
33 McCoy, "Race," 156–57.

Chapter One: Dispossessed

1 Linguistically, the correct spelling should be "Murrieta." In his note on the various
(mis)spellings of "Murrieta," Hausman notes that the American misspellings of the
name with a single "r" have signaled to some Spanish-speaking scholars not only a
simple mistake but larger linguistic and cultural misunderstandings. Therefore, I use
"*Murieta*" to refer to the novel and Murrieta in all other cases, except when quoting
from a source that utilizes the "Murieta" spelling. I also retain the diacritical mark in
"Joaquín" unless quoting from a source that omits it. See Hausman, "Becoming," iii.
2 Certainly, other Native tribes outside of California and the Cherokee Nation
experienced unjust seizure during this era as well, but I focus here on the communities linked to Ridge's novel and biography.
3 See McGill, *American Literature*. Reprints of newspaper articles and other
formats received different treatment than books in the history of copyright law.
On the history and limitations of copyright, see Hofmeyr, "Colonial Copyright";
McGill, *American Literature* and "Copyright"; Rose, *Authors and Owners*;
Slauter, *Who Owns the News?*; Spoo, *Without Copyrights*.
4 See Round, *Removeable Type*, Chapter Six, for earlier Native copyright holders.
In addition, the *California Police Gazette* had not only reprinted his book but
stripped it of Ridge's authorial byline as well, which did not reflect a common practice within the culture of reprinting books. Kevin Taylor distinguishes between
plagiarism and piracy in the publishing world as follows: "broadly speaking we can
define plagiarism as the appropriation of another person's words or ideas without
proper permission or acknowledgement, while piracy refers to the large-scale reproduction of whole books, whether in print or electronic form, to substitute for
legitimate copies." Ridge himself uses the term "spurious" in his preface to the 1871
edition. For an overview of piracy, plagiarism, and intellectual property, see Johns,
Piracy; Spoo, *Without Copyrights*; Taylor, "Plagiarism and Piracy," 259. My thanks
to my anonymous reviewer for their productive critique of my terminology.
5 Scafidi, *Who Owns Culture?*. Scafidi proposes that we evaluate a potential cultural appropriation by using three "S's": source, significance, and similarity. For
example, with my paraphrasing, is the item ethically and respectfully sourced,
with consent, collaboration, and acknowledgment? What is the item's significance or sacredness to the cultural group from which it comes? How similar is the
item to its original source, involving a direct copy or one's own creativity? See also
Metcalf, "Native Appropriations."
6 Alemán, "Assimilation," 73; Rifkin, "'For the wrongs,'" 29; Rowe, "Highway
Robbery" and "Nineteenth-Century"; Stevens, "Three-Fingered Jack," 81; Streeby,
American Sensations, 275; Irwin, *Bandits*, 66, 90. See also Havard, "John Rollin
Ridge's 'Joaquín Murieta.' [*sic*]"; Sandell, "John Rollin Ridge's *Joaquín Murieta*."

7 Watts, *Packaging*, 5.
8 Some sources claim Ridge murdered a tribal member who had been involved in the assassination of his father. Others claim he had been incited and assaulted by someone sent by Ridge's enemies. Clyde Ellis provides what is likely the best information possible, that Ridge shot and killed a man named David Kell, a political enemy and local judge, after an angry exchange of words. Ridge never stood trial, and likely for this reason avoided returning to Cherokee jurisdiction for the remainder of his life. Ellis, "Our Ill Fated," 380. See also Debo, "John Rollin Ridge," 63; Kennedy, *Strange Nation* 366; Powell, *Ruthless Democracy*, 57.
9 The extent to which his book influenced, or was influenced by, regional oral storytelling and *corridos* remains undetermined, although some scholars argue for the former. See Irwin, *Bandits*, 67; Streeby, *American Sensations*, 262. For a selection of Ridge's other writings, see *A Trumpet of our Own*, edited by Farmer and Strickland.
10 See Andes, *Zorro's Shadow*; Grabarchuk, "Bridging"; Hausman's "Becoming"; Thornton, *Searching for Joaquin*. To my knowledge, no scholar as yet has completed a bibliography of the vast corpus of the Murrieta legend.
11 Ridge, *Murieta*, 8–12, 136. All textual references refer to the 2018 edition unless otherwise stated. References to texts with Ridge's byline I cite as *Murieta*, the *Gazette* plagiarism I cite as *Life of Joaquin Murieta*, and the Grabhorn texts I cite as *Joaquin Murieta*. In keeping with my argument, I list all textual versions of *Murieta* under Ridge's name in my bibliography.
12 Franklin Walker confirms and delineates these revisions in his "Ridge's *Life of Joaquin Murieta*: The First and Revised Editions Compared" (1937). For another early twentieth-century bibliographic analysis, see Wagner, "John R. Ridge," 51.
13 Farquhar, "Notes," iv; Wood, "Supplementary Notes," xii.
14 Streeby, *American Sensations*, 254, 275; Jackson, "Tradition," 176; Varley, *Legend*, 3; Irwin, "Joaquín," 62; Johnson, *Roaring Camp*, 46; Hausman, "Becoming" and "Indians in the Margins," 1.
15 Goeke, "Yellow Bird," 462; Walker, "Ridge's *Life*," 257; Parins, *John Rollin Ridge*, 103. For Lindley's Euroamerican identity, see Colby, "Curtis Holbrook Lindley," 87.
16 Varley, *Legend*, 138; Parins, *John Rollin Ridge*, 103. Varley does not provide citations for his claims about Lindley.
17 López, *White by Law*, xv; Harris, "Construction of Race," 1745. On copyright and citizenship, see Slauter, *Who Owns the News?*, 9.
18 Parins, *Ridge*, 21, 222. See Parins 18–21 for details of the circumstances that led to the Treaty of New Echota. For a discussion of the complexities of Cherokee identities and politics, see Nelson, *Progressive Traditions*.
19 Hsu, "Introduction," xviii–xix; Kennedy, *Strange Nation*, 365; Powell, *Ruthless Democracy*, 64–65; Walker, *Indian Nation*, 126; Meyer, *Native Removal Writing*, 59. See also Johnson, *Roaring Camp* for a history of the era's racism, violence, and legal discrimination.
20 Rose, *Authors and Owners*, 133; Harris, "Construction of Race," 1721, 1714; Hofmeyr, "Colonial Copyright," 252, 247; Berger, "Insurgencies," 181. See also Bhandar, *Colonial Lives of Property*.
21 Parins, *Ridge*, 105–6. It remains unclear as to whether Ridge received no compensation for his novel, or rather did not receive as much as he expected or hoped.

Ellis claims the former: "The book was popular (its theme and plot were widely copied), but Ridge never realized any profit from its publication. He and the others who had invested in the venture lost their money, the victims, Ridge complained, of 'these mushrooming California [publishing] concerns.'" Ellis, "Our Ill Fated," 385. Brackets inserted by Ellis.

22 Jackson, "Introduction," xxxii. See Bancroft, *Literary Industries*, 134–41 and Walker, *San Francisco's Literary Frontier*. My thanks to Travis Ross and the SHARP listserv for the Bancroft and business directory references.

23 Streeby, *American Sensations*, 263; Walker, "Ridge's Life," 257.

24 Farquhar, "Notes," v.

25 Ridge, *Murieta*, 5. Italics in the original; *Life of Joaquin Murieta*, 1.

26 Goeke, "Yellow Bird," 471; *Murieta*, 90–91 (italics in the original); *Life of Joaquin Murieta*, 116; Irwin, *Bandits*, 58.

27 Stevens credits Nahl with establishing the "image of the 'forty-niner' and the New Californian" during the Gold Rush, and he mentions that Nahl had been first commissioned for an imaginary portrait of Joaquín Murrieta for an article in the April 1853 edition of the *Sacramento Pictorial Union*. Stevens, *Charles*, 48.

28 This 1871 edition also drops the byline "Yellow Bird" and replaces it with "John R. Ridge."

29 Varley, *Legend*, 144. The preface to the 1927 Evening Free Lance edition vaguely mentions Ridge's second edition as "soon sold out." Ridge, *History of Joaquin Murieta*, 2.

30 Goeke, "Yellow Bird," 472.

31 Ridge, *Murieta* (1871).

32 Ridge, *Murieta* (1874), 4.

33 See Owen, *Selling Rights*, 2. Varley speculates that Ridge's widow may have sold the copyright after the financial strain of his death, although no documentation has been found. Varley, *Legend*, 144.

34 Harris, "Construction of Race," 1724, 1722. See Farquhar, "Notes."

35 Hausman, "Indians in the Margins," 2.

36 For Native literary studies scholarship of *Murieta*, see Cox, *Muting White Noise*; Hausman, "Becoming" and "Indians in the Margins"; Owens, *Other Destinies*; Rifkin, "'For the wrongs'"; Walker, *Indian Nation*; Weaver, *That the People*. For the question of *Murieta*'s place in Native literary history, see Debo, "John Rollin Ridge," 68, 71; Parker, *Invention*, 172. Ellis goes so far as to question Ridge's identification as an Indian, claiming that he did nothing on behalf of his people. See Ellis, "Our Ill Fated." My thanks to Diana Noreen Rivera for drawing my attention to the Arte Público edition.

37 *Joaquin Murieta*, Grabhorn Press 1932, "Publisher's Preface."

38 Farquhar, "Notes," iii; Ridge, *Murieta*, 152.

39 Farquhar, "Notes," iii–iv.

40 Walker, "Ridge's *Life*," 257; Wood, "Supplementary Notes," xi–xii.

41 Clough, "Supplementary Notes," xvi–xvii.

42 In her 2018 foreword to *Murieta*, popular fiction writer Diana Gabaldon shares that for her, "one of the most interesting aspects of the book is its charmingly casual racism." She goes on to say, "Frankly, I've seen this kind of matter-of-fact racism all my life; most people my age probably have. There's usually no particular

animus to it, it's just people calling it like they see it—and how (and why) they see it is really interesting." Rowe also points toward the similarities in the Nahl illustration between the wide-eyed horse and the wide-eyed Mexican as suggestive of their parallel animalities. Gabaldon, "Foreword," x; Rowe, "Highway Robbery," 169.

43 Ridge, *Murieta*, 135; Drysdale, "Ridge's *Joaquín Murieta*," 78; Fagan, "Ishi's Kin to Give Him Proper Burial"; McGill, *American Literature*, 7. My thanks to the MLA 2023 audience member who pointed me toward the connection between the dismemberment of Ishi and of Murrieta.

44 Gillespie, "Turk's-Head Knots," 213; Drysdale, "Ridge's *Joaquín Murieta*," 78, 80; Harjo, *Spiral to the Stars*, 10.

Chapte Two: Whiteness, Blank Space, and Gendered Embodiment in Winnemucca's *Life among the Piutes* and Callahan's *Wynema*

1 McGann, *Textual Condition*, 13. For a history of the modern development of interword spacing and its influence on reading, see Littau, *Theories of Reading*; Saenger, *Space between Words*. For the importance of blank space to typography and graphic design, see for example Hagen and Golombisky, *White Space*; Lupton, *Thinking with Type*; McLean, *Typographers on Type*. For scholarship analyzing the blank spaces of prose, see Bernardin, "Acorn Soup"; Chute, *Graphic Women*; Gubar, "'The Blank Page'"; Harris, "Feminizing the Textual Body"; Nenno, "Projections on Blank Space"; Nishikawa, "Black Pagecraft"; Rivero, "Aphra Behn's *Oroonoko*"; Smith, *Subjectivity, Identity, and the Body*; Stout, *Strategies of Reticence*; Tsomondo, *Not So Blank*; Walker, "The Manners of the Page"; Wilhite, "Blank Spaces." For bibliographical scholarship on blank books themselves, see the first chapter of Gitelman, *Paper Knowledge*.

2 Thrush, *Indigenous London*, 35–36; Wyss, *Writing Indians*, 1–3.

3 While my focus here remains on the book, I do not mean to imply an absence of Indigenous women's literary voices in other formats. Winnemucca and Callahan's books appeared within an already rich arena of Indigenous women writers who collaborated on as-told-to narratives and ethnographies, published in newspapers and magazines, circulated letters and public documents, and produced a diverse array of literary aesthetics. Hilary Wyss does suggest, however, that Native women writers did have a more complex relationship to print culture than Native men, at least in early America, and Levy calls out the historical lack of scholarship on women's book history. See Levy, "Do Women Have a Book History?"; Wyss, "Mary Occom and Sarah Simon," 389.

4 Goeman, *Mark My Words*, 33. For more on Native women, literature, land, and colonialism through an environmental justice lens, see Fear-Segal and Tillett, *Indigenous Bodies*; Fitzgerald, *Native Women and Land*.

5 Ridge, "From the National Intelligencer," Qtd. in DiCuirci, *Colonial Revivals*, 137. For more on the colonial use of blank or empty space, see Barr and Countryman, "Introduction: Maps and Spaces"; Bhandar, *Colonial Lives*, 3; Cohen, *Networked Wilderness*, 22; Goeman, *Mark My Words*, 33–35; Harley, "Rereading the Maps"; Lopenzina, *Red Ink*, 7; Rivero, "Aphra Behn's *Oroonoko*," 445. For more on the new type of "space" colonization created for Native peoples, see Bruyneel, *Third Space*

of Sovereignty. On the concept of "virgin" land, see earlier foundational work in American literary criticism, Smith's *Virgin Land* (1950) and Kolodny's *Lay of the Land* (1975). On space and social justice, see Soja, *Postmodern Geographies* and *Seeking Spatial Justice*.

6 See Smith, *Conquest*. Although her research has not been challenged, Andrea Smith stands accused of ethnic fraud.

7 Barter, "Encrypted Citations," 58.

8 Brooks, *Common Pot*, xxii, original italics; Goeman, *Mark My Words*, 2, 5; Nishikawa, "Black Pagecraft," 448, 451. Nishikawa builds from Jacqueline Goldsby's earlier work on Black feminist typographical experimentation. See also McKittrick, *Demonic Grounds*, xvi; Salvaggio, "Theory and Space"; Wrede, "Introduction," 10–12.

9 Although Winnemucca's book uses the spelling "Piute," the contemporary spelling is "Paiute." I employ the contemporary spelling except when quoting from the text. Additionally, *Life among the Piutes* refers to the Northern Paiute rather than the distinct Southern Paiute, and it depicts the Northern Paiute as a single political entity with a shared governing structure, which strategically simplified the historical reality. While I recognize the historical complexity of the Paiute's political and organizational structures, for my purposes here I follow the book's simplified representation. See the third chapter of Rifkin's *Speaking for the People*.

10 Critics also identify *Life among the Piutes* as a tribalography, a coup tale, a captivity narrative, a biography, environmental writing, a rhetorical performance, and as "more of an extended pamphlet about the claims of the Northern Paiutes than the 'truth' of Winnemucca's life." See Sneider, "Gender, Literacy, and Sovereignty," 264; Brumble, *American Indian Autobiography*, 66; Kleist, "Sarah Winnemucca's *Life*"; Murray, *Forked Tongues*; Kilcup, *Fallen Forests*; Powell, "Sarah Winnemucca Hopkins," 74.

11 Winnemucca, *Life*, 11, 34–35, 71, 48. All textual citations come from the 1994 facsimile edition unless otherwise stated, and following the practice of other scholars I refer to the author as "Winnemucca" rather than "Hopkins."

12 Her reputation, however, remains controversial among the Paiute. See Carpenter, "Sarah Winnemucca Goes to Washington," 98 and *Seeing Red*, 93, 116–25. For more of Winnemucca's biography, see Canfield, *Sarah Winnemucca* and Zanjani, *Sarah Winnemucca*.

13 Ruoff, "Three Nineteenth-Century," 261; Georgi-Findlay, "Frontiers," 229.

14 For the diverse ways in which Winnemucca resists gender stereotypes, see Carpenter, "Choking Off That Angel Mother"; Sneider, "Gender, Literacy, and Sovereignty." For scholarship on Winnemucca's performance and negotiations, see Carpenter, "Winnemucca Goes"; Eves, "Finding Place"; Hoxie, "Denouncing"; Humud, "'Authentic Indian'"; Lape, "'I Would Rather'"; McClure, "Sarah Winnemucca"; Powell, "Sarah Winnemucca Hopkins"; Rifkin, *Speaking for the People*; Sorisio, "Playing" and "Sarah Winnemucca"; Tisinger, "Textual Performance"; Walker, *Indian Nation*.

15 Smith, *Subjectivity, Identity, and the Body*, 2, 23. See also Greyser, *On Sympathetic Grounds*.

16 Smith, *Subjectivity, Identity, and the Body*, 2, 23; Sánchez-Eppler, "Bodily Bonds," 94; Gaul, "Catharine Brown's Body," 201; Walker, *Indian Nation*, 152. Mark Rifkin also writes of *Life Among the Piutes*'s narrative as speaking of the Paiutes "as a

political body whose being and becoming gives rise to the Winnemucca family and their capacity to speak for this body." Rifkin, *Speaking for the People*, 135. See also Greyser, *On Sympathetic Grounds*; Kurzen, "Autobiographical Tradition."

17 Malea Powell poignantly remarks, "Winnemucca's text is much larger than *Life Among the Piutes*; it encompasses her lectures/performances and her personal correspondence, as well as all the stories that have been told about her, scholarly or otherwise." Powell, "Sarah Winnemucca Hopkins," 88. For scholarship on Winnemucca's engagement with genre and print culture, see Carpenter, *Seeing Red* and "Tiresias"; Carpenter and Sorisio, *Newspaper Warrior*; Kohler, "Sending Word"; Monahan, "'Rag Friends'"; Sorisio, "'I Nailed Those Lies.'"

18 Canfield, *Sarah Winnemucca*, 201, 206; Ruoff, "Three Nineteenth-Century," 262. For more on the influence of the Peabody sisters, see Elbert, Hall, and Rodier, *Reinventing the Peabody Sisters*; Marshall, *Peabody Sisters*; Ronda, "Print and Pedagogy"; Tharp, *Peabody Sisters*.

19 Powell, "Sarah Winnemucca Hopkins," 82–84; Walker, *Indian Nation*, 157. For more information regarding Rinehart, see Canfield, *Sarah Winnemucca*.

20 Qtd. in Carpenter, "*Sarah Winnemucca Goes to Washington*," 94–95.

21 Canfield does claim at least one reprinting in order to raise funds, presumably a second impression of the first edition. See Canfield, *Sarah Winnemucca*, 209, 227, 247.

22 See Quigley, "Silenced," 366.

23 Eves, "Finding Place to Speak," 2; Tisinger, "Textual Performance," 173.

24 Though Mann insists in her "Editor's Preface" of only minor interventions into Winnemucca's text that consist solely of editing the original manuscript in order to "correct orthography and punctuation," some questions arise over the extent of Mann's edits due to comments she made in a letter to a friend over Winnemucca's struggle with a legible manuscript. While we may never know the extent of Mann's editing without the discovery of a manuscript, most scholars point to the productive and lifelong collaboration of the three women, although at times their relationships undoubtedly encountered tensions and challenges. Mann and Peabody continued to support Winnemucca throughout their lives, financially and otherwise, and upon her death Mann left her small estate to Winnemucca. Unlike the dubiously shared copyright in Ridge's *Murieta*, Winnemucca registers her book's copyright exclusively in her name. Furthermore, in her study of women's literary partnerships, Bette London critiques the gender bias leveled at female collaborators that unjustly undermines their professionalism and promotes their erasure. See Carpenter and Sorisio, *Newspaper Warrior*, 10–11; Hanrahan, "'[W]orthy the imitation of the whites,'" 119; London, *Writing Double*; Rodier, "Authorizing Sarah Winnemucca?," 19; Walker, *Indian Nation*, 149; Zanjani, *Sarah Winnemucca*, 240.

25 Qtd. in Zanjani, *Sarah Winnemucca*, 103–4. For more on gender, racialized bodies, and the politics of respectability, see White, *Dark Continent of Our Bodies*.

26 Monahan, "'Rag Friends,'" 308.

27 Winnemucca, *Life among the Piutes*, 249, 259, 260; Senier, *Voices*, 79. See also Georgi-Findlay, *Frontiers of Native American Women's Writing*.

28 Zanjani, *Sarah Winnemucca*, 3, 229; Powell, "Sarah Winnemucca Hopkins," 74; Rifkin, *Speaking for the People*; Winnemucca, *Life among the Piutes*, 246.

29 Winnemucca, *Life among the Piutes*, 76.

30 Winnemucca, 78.

31 Winnemucca, 78. See also Dolan, "Cattle and Sovereignty."

32 Mennell, "(Im)penetrable Silence," 498; Sibelman, *Silence*, 16. See also Mak, *How the Page Matters*, 17.

33 Winnemucca, *Life Amaong the Piutes*, 247. Peabody reports in a letter to Edwin Monroe Bacon, editor of *The Boston Daily Advertiser*, that Winnemucca's petition had garnered over 3,000 signatures, and a letter from Mann to Miss Eleanor Lewis claims over five thousand signatures. Qtd. in Rodier, "Authoring," 118; Canfield, *Sarah Winnemucca*, 209. See also "Land of Misfortune" and "Sarah Winnemucca Hopkins Petition" for an image of the primary document.

34 Davidson, *Revolution and the Word*, 64, 147.

35 Davidson, 64, 147. For readings of signatures and the margins, see Chartier, *Frenchness in the History of the Book*; Davidson, *Revolution and the Word*; Egan, *Authorizing Experience*; Greetham; *Margins of the Text*; Harris, "Feminizing the Textual Body"; hooks, *Yearning*; Jackson, *Marginalia*; Newman, *White Women's Rights*; Orgel, *The Reader in the Book*; Postema, *Narrative Structure*; Reader, "Notebooks"; Salvaggio, "Theory and Space"; Spivak, "The New Historicism"; Tribble, *Margins and Marginality*; Tsomondo, *Not So Blank*.

36 Rezek, "Transatlantic Traffic," 299. Sarah Winnemucca also autographed copies of her book, as well as her photograph. See Canfield, *Sarah Winnemucca*, 211.

37 Monahan, "'Rag Friends,'" 309.

38 For the immediate legislative aftermath of the petition, see Canfield, *Sarah Winnemucca*, 214–20.

39 Harris, *Executing Race*, 69; Ginzberg, *Untidy Origins*, 9. White women activists, however, often had far greater access to public political platforms than women of color. See also Newman, *White Women's Rights*, 121; Zaeske, *Signatures of Citizenship*.

40 Brooks, "'This Indian World,'" 217.

41 Brooks, "'This Indian World,'" 217; Brooks, *Common Pot*, 52, 224–26.

42 See Rifkin, *Speaking for the People*, 146.

43 Intriguingly, neither Winnemucca nor her father ever tell us what the text of the "rag friend" says, which invokes it as another symbolic type of blank space.

44 Winnemucca, *Life*, 88, 89, 95.

45 I borrow here from Reader's discussion of the blank notebook as a "space of possibility." Reader, "Notebooks," 359.

46 Ruoff, "Introduction to *Wynema*," xvii, xxvi; "E. A. Weeks." See also "H.J. Smith & Co," 121. For information about Callahan's biography, see Ruoff, "Introduction"; Van Dyke, "Introduction."

47 The Mvskoke Nation are also known as the Muscogee or the Creek. I follow most contemporary scholarship with the use of "Mvskoke." For an overview of Mvskoke history, including a brief distinction between the terms Creek, Muscogee, and Mvskoke, see Harjo, *Spiral to the Stars*, 5–14, 253.

48 Callahan, *Wynema*, 16–17 and 27–29. Unless otherwise stated, all textual citations come from the second edition of the novel produced by the University of Nebraska in 1997. Due to pandemic and funding-related issues, I was not able to view the rare first edition of *Wynema* in person. I did view, however, digital images of the first edition's paratextual elements, kindly sent to me by Jolie Braun

at Ohio State University, as well as the Weeks reprint that was likely made from stereotyped plates. The University of Nebraska Press edition is a new typeset and not a facsimile, and as such the layout of paragraph breaks and chapters breaks differ. While I have not conducted a collation of the two editions and the Weeks reprint, only the paratextual elements appear to be changed, and therefore my claims about the significance of the breaks come from their place in the textual narrative rather than the layout of the page.

49 Womack, *Red on Red*, 107–9. Teuton also considers Callahan's *Wynema* as an "unparalleled as a story of Indigenous cultural shame and wholesale conversion to white Christian America," although he does find an experimentation with genre as valuable for Indigenous writers. See Teuton, "Indigenous Novel."

50 To date, the literary criticism of *Wynema* remains oddly divided along gender lines: the male scholars of the novel, who currently number four, largely critique and some-times disparage it, while female scholars, who currently number thirteen, offer more balanced critiques or argue for its attempted political advocacy. For male scholar-ship, see Womack, *Red on Red*; Teuton, "Indigenous Novel"; Sligh, *Native American Women Novelists*; and Cox, *Muting White Noise*. For female scholars, see Alves, "Reading"; Bernardin, "On the Meeting Grounds"; Carpenter, *Seeing Red*; Fore-man, "S. Alice Callahan"; Gore, "Gothic Silence"; Mollis, "Teaching 'Dear Mihia'"; Piatote, *Domestic Subjects*; Ruoff, "Justice for Indians and Women"; Ryan, "Indian Problem"; Senier, "Allotment Protest and Tribal Discourse"; Tatonetti, "Behind the Shadows"; Van Dyke, "Introduction"; Windell, "Sentimental Realisms."

51 Piatote, *Domestic Subjects*, 62; Walker, *Indian Nation*, 140; Ryan, "Indian Problem," 30.

52 Callahan, *Wynema*, ix; Watts, *Packaging*, 3–5. See Sekora, "Black Message/White Envelope."

53 Strangely, the University of Nebraska Press edition places the dedication in all capital letters as a block quote, while the original capitalizes only "TO THE INDIAN TRIBES OF NORTH AMERICA" and the rest of the words appear with standard capitalization in a paragraph format.

54 Tatonetti, "Behind the Shadows," 43.

55 Piatote, *Domestic Subjects*, 50.

56 Piatote, 88.

57 Sánchez-Eppler, "Bodily Bonds," 100 and *Touching Liberty*, 26; Bernardin, "On the Meeting Grounds," 210; Sánchez-Eppler, "Bodily Bonds," 103. See also Bur-gett, *Sentimental Bodies*; Carpenter, *Seeing Red*; Dobson, "Reclaiming Sentimental Literature"; Greyser, *On Sympathetic Grounds*; Mollis, "Teaching 'Dear Mihia'"; Piatote, *Domestic Subjects*; Rich, *Transcending the New Woman*; Ryan, "Indian Prob-lem"; Samuels, "Introduction"; Sánchez-Eppler, *Touching Liberty*; Tompkins, *Sensational Designs*; Windell, "Sentimental Realisms."

58 Callahan, *Wynema*, 1. Traditionally the Mvskoke did not live in teepees, which Womack points out as one of the many cultural inaccuracies of the novel. See *Red on Red*, 107–15.

59 Ibid. Ryan critiques the description here of a forest, linking it with the novel's subtitle as appealing to a literary stereotype rather than an accurate depiction of Mvskoke homelands. See Ryan, "Indian Problem," 27.

60 Callahan, *Wynema*, 1.

61 Callahan, 1, 5; Bernardin, "Acorn Soup," 16.

62 Posetma, *Narrative Structure in Comics*, 50; Mak, *How the Page Matters*, 17.

63 Callahan, *Wynema*, 95–96.

64 Tatonetti, "Behind the Shadows," 20.

65 Tatonetti, "Behind the Shadows," 20; Bernardin, "On the Meeting Grounds," 221. Rifkin offers a similar reading for William Apess's scant referents to the Mashantucket Pequot reservation in *A Son of the Forest* (1829, 1831) when he interprets such omissions as an "invocation of histories of Native dispossession" and the "silent surround" of the textual narrative. Rifkin, *Speaking for the People*, 92.

66 Gore, "Gothic Silence"; Lopenzina, *Through an Indian's Looking Glass*, 110. See also Luciano, *Arranging Grief*.

67 Heneghan, *Whitewashing America*, xiv; McClintock, *Imperial Leather*, 211. See also Bushman, *Refinement of America*; Harris, "Construction of Race."

68 Weeks, *Paper-Manufacturing*, 69; Senchyne, *Intimacy of Paper*, 125–26; Tschichold, *Form of the Book*, 169. See also Multigraph Collective, *Interacting with Print*, 260–64; Senchyne, "Bottles of Ink." For histories of paper, see Baker, *From the Hand to the Machine*; Haggith, *Paper Trails*; Kurlansky, *Paper*; Müller, *White Magic*.

69 Senchyne, *Intimacy of Paper*, 125–28; Benton, "Typography and Gender"; Mills, *Racial Contract*, 41. See also McKee, *Producing American Races*, 11–13; Young, *Black Writers, White Publishers*, 26–30. On the falsity and elusiveness of whiteness, both for paper and as a skin color, see Calhoun, "Word Made Flax," 331; Dyer, *White*, especially 45–78.

70 Moreton-Robinson, *The White Possessive*, xix; Carpenter, *Seeing Red*, 102.

71 The 1997 edition of *Wynema* also provides a lengthy historical and biographical introduction, notes to the text, works cited and recommended reading, and a new typeset.

72 Canfield mentions that some first editions had red, as well as green, cloth bindings. However, to my knowledge, the only surviving copies are those bound in green. See Canfield, *Sarah Winnemucca*, 209.

73 Senchyne, "Bottles of Ink," 149.

74 Tanselle, *Bibliographic Analysis*, 14; Barker, *Tremulous Private Body*, 63.

Chapter Three: Pretty Shield's Thumbprint

1 Following current tribal practice and contemporary scholarship, this chapter uses "Pretty Shield" to refer to the person and *"Pretty-shield"* to refer to the text. I use the tribal designation "Crow" to match the text and current common usage, although the term Apsáalooke is also currently used. For a history of the Crow/Apsáalooke name and nation, see Medicine Crow, *From the Heart of Crow Country*.

2 Linderman, *Pretty-shield*, 2. Textual references come from the 2021 edition, unless otherwise stated, and I primarily refer to the text as *Pretty-shield* rather than *Red Mother*, following the revised title.

3 Sellers, *Native American Autobiography Redefined*, 79, 78–82; Bataille and Sands, *American Indian Women*, 45–46. See also Kurzen, "Autobiographical Tradition."

4 Raheja and Fitzgerlad, "Literary Sovereignties," 1; Carlson, *Sovereign Selves*, 14. Italics in the original. On the complications of "authenticity," see also Raibmon, *Authentic Indians*.

5 Wong, *Sending My Heart Back*, 90.

6   The 1972 *Pretty-shield* is a facsimile edition.

7   Linderman, *Pretty-shield*, 5, 35.

8   See Turner's "Significance of the Section" for the beginnings of the "frontier thesis" and his argument for the West as "closed." See also Slotkin's *Regeneration through Violence* and Campbell's *Rhizomatic West*.

9   Johnston, "Minds and Bodies," 4.

10 Owens, *Other Destinies*, 26. Owens also attempts to delineate between a "frontier" and a "territory," the latter of which he defines as "clearly mapped, fully imagined as a place of containment, invented to control and subdue the dangerous potentialities of imagined Indians." He images the concept of the frontier as the "zone of the trickster" and as such contains more Indigenous agency than a "territory." Though I take up Owens's argument that the frontier contains Indigenous agency, I am not convinced by his distinction between the two terms, aside from the political distinction of "territory" that preceded U.S. statehood. Both labels describe colonized and contested Indigenous space, and for the purposes of my chapter's argument I do not draw a distinction between frontier and territory.

11 Krupat, *For Those Who Come After*, 33; Karell, *Writing Together/Writing Apart*, 66. Krupat invents the term "bicultural composite composition" to describe as-told-to narratives in order to signal the conflict and collaboration between writer and informant. On Native autobiography, see also Brumble, *American Indian Autobiography*; Murray, *Forked Tongues*. For the term "contact zone" that underpins much of the theory utilized here, see Pratt, *Imperial Eyes*.

12 Genette, *Paratexts*, 1–2; Macksey, "Foreword," xii; McCoy, "Race," 156.

13 Pryor, "John Day Company," 106; Berlatsky, "Lost in the Gutter," 177. See also Kolodny's *Lay of the Land* and *Land Before Her*; Detsi-Diamanti's "Politicizing Aesthetics."

14 For the representational importance of Indigenous motherhood during this era, see Piatote, *Domestic Subjects*, especially Chapter Two.

15 Goldsby, "Book Faces"; Rezek, "Racialization of Print," 418.

16 Snell and Matthews, "Preface," xi. HarperCollins reprints the Snell and Matthews preface as a foreword to their 2021 edition.

17 With the exception of the 2003 edition, in which the Snell and Matthews "Preface" precedes the thumbprint.

18 Thank you to my anonymous reviewer for this point.

19 Moylan and Stiles, "Introduction," 6.

20 Lyons, *X-Marks*, 1–3, 170; Linderman, *Pretty-shield*, 7.

21 Miranda, *Bad Indians*, 28; Erdrich, *Tracks*, 99–100; Zitkala-Šá, "Widespread Enigma."

22 Blaver, "California Imagery in Context," 198–99. Blaver mentions that for a Paiute man named Young Charlie, his thumbprint along with his "X" were used on his deed of sale to identify him. Other sources claim that the practice of Native thumbprints on government documents continues today. See Berkowitz, *Case of the Indian Trader*. Despite the presence of thumbprints on other government documents, to date I have not yet found any treaties, between Montana tribal nations or any others, that record a thumbprint rather than an x-mark as a signature.

23 See Cole, *Suspect Identities*, 3; "Fingerprints"; Kofman, "Anthropometric Detective"; Tattoli, "Surprising History"; Uenuma, "First Criminal Trial." Cole also mentions fingerprints as a means of "controlling dangerous bodies." Thank you

to my anonymous reviewer who pointed me towards this additional historical information.

24 On Jemison's autobiography, see Namias's exemplary introduction to the text as well as Walsh, "'With Them was My Home'" and Wyss, "Captivity and Conversion." Thank you to my anonymous reviewer for mentioning the comparison between Jemison and Pretty Shield.

25 Lyons, *X-Marks*, 12–13.

26 Linderman, *Pretty-shield*, xxiii, 9–10; Glover, *Paper Sovereigns*, 6; Colasurdo, "'Tell Me a Woman's Story,'" 391.

27 Mullen Sands, "Collaboration or Colonialism," 42–43; Kollin, "Re-envisioning," 359–60; Portillo, *Sovereign Stories*, 100–101; Twomey, "More Than One Way," 47. See also Glenn, *Unspoken*; Rader, "'. . . just crushing silence.'"

28 Linderman, *Pretty-shield*, 2.

29 Farnell, *Do You See What I Mean?*, 2, 4. Farnell also writes, "My consultants prefer the designation 'sign talk' over 'sign language' because the latter is felt to denote a system altogether separate from speech, which is not the case here" (4). Plains Indian Sign Language (PISL) is also known as Plains Sign Language or Plains Indian Sign Talk. See Baynton's *Forbidden Signs* and Farnell's *Do You See*, especially Chapter 1: "The Nineteenth-Century Legacy," for a historical overview of sign language and its denigration in American culture because in part of its association with "savage" signs and "primitive" communication. While a sustained discussion of Plains Indian Sign Language is unfortunately absent in Baynton's book, both Farnell's work and Davis's *Hand Talk* add significantly to the historical record while laboring to bring PISL the recognition it deserves.

30 Perley, "Indigenous Sign Languages"; Hilleary, "Native American Hand Talkers."

31 Linderman, *Pretty-shield*, 105, 69–70, 16, 66, 39. Here Pretty Shield also demonstrates her skillful use of humor as a storytelling technique. For more on rhetorical strategies of Native humor, especially coming from a Native woman's body, see Carpenter, "Choking Off."

32 Young, *Presence in the Flesh*, 141; Yandell, "Moccasin Telegraph," 535–36.

33 Linderman, *Pretty-shield*, 213, 227–31.

34 Linderman, *Pretty-shield*, 1–2, 4, 7, 9; Wong, *Sending My Heart Back*, 95.

35 Bauerle, *Way of the Warrior*, xxi.

36 Wong, *Sending My Heart Back*, 98.

37 Tsomondo, *Not So Blank*, 11; Andrews, "Editing 'Minority' Texts," 47; Old Coyote and Bauerle, "Introduction," xiv.

Chapter Four: Citational Relations and the Paratextual Vision of D'Arcy McNickle's *The Surrounded*

1 Sisneros cites the year of installation as often mistaken for 1939 rather than 1940. I also follow the lead of Sisneros in describing the artwork as a series of paintings, rather than a mural, because of the three reasons given by Sisneros: (1) the artwork was not painted directly onto the wall surface but rather created with oil paint on canvas offsite, (2) the artist did not interact with the space and the public while creating a mural; instead the paintings were affixed to the walls while the library

was closed during a spring break in 1940, and (3) the Mexican and Chicano mural movement "expresses a strong social and political message, primarily from the perspective of the oppressed," which is clearly missing and the source of protest for the "Three Peoples" paintings. Sisneros, "Student Activism," n1.

2 Rodriguez, "Tourism," 199–200.

3 For the history of the "Three Peoples" paintings and student protests, see Holmen, "UNM Begins Class"; Rodriguez, "Tourism"; Sisneros, "Student Activism" and "Zimmerman Library Mural"; "Three Peoples Murals." For more on the politics between Albuquerque, New Mexico, and Native peoples, see Vicenti Carpio, *Indigenous Albuquerque*.

4 Qtd. in Sisneros, "Student Activism," 30.

5 Dilworth, "Tourists and Indians," 145; Debord, *Society of the Spectacle*, 4; Rodriguez, "Tourism," 201. For more on the social and racial relationships promoted by cultural tourism and art in the Southwest, see Dilworth, "Tourists and Indians"; Hutchinson, *The Indian Craze*; Mullin, *Culture in the Marketplace*; Wilson, *The Myth of Santa Fe*; Woidat, "Indian-Detour"; Wrobel and Long, *Seeing and Being Seen*.

6 See for example Hutchinson, *The Indian Craze*; Jacobs, *Engendered Encounters*. Some white artists and authors did gain a reflective stance on their subject position in the Southwest and later ridiculed the lack of cultural insight in others. For example, Oliver La Farge mockingly writes of the Southwest cultural tourist in the 1940s: "He believes in Hiawatha. He thinks that if the Indians were only left alone they would be perfectly happy, and in his most naïve form he wants to see Indians kept as a sort of museum exhibit, uncontaminated by contact with whites, living their old life, wearing their beautiful costumes (he has never seen really dirty buckskin), preserved and protected under some dispensation which will not bar himself from going among them. Why should he be barred? He understands them." La Farge, *Raw Material*, 155.

7 Hans, "Rethinking History," 44. For manuscript and revision details of *The Surrounded*, see Hans, *D'Arcy McNickle's The Hungry Generations* and "Re-Visions." For more on the publisher, see Ames, "Dodd, Mead and Company."

8 Parker, "D'Arcy McNickle: An Annotated Bibliography," 24.

9 Parker, "D'Arcy McNickle: An Annotated Bibliography," 28; Owens, *Other Destinies*, 72; McNickle, *The Surrounded*, 296–97. All quotes from the novel come from the UNM Press 1978 reprint, using the 1993 eighth printing, unless otherwise stated.

10 See Balthaser, "'Travels of an American Indian'"; Brown, "American Indian Modernities"; Kent, *African, Native, and Jewish American Literature*, "Mourning Dove's Cogewea," and "'You can't run away nowadays'"; Keresztesi, *Strangers at Home*; Lima, "Tribal Nations." Recent developments in the scholarship of modernism, including an acknowledgment of the movement's plurality and multicultural participants, have opened up the field to many scholars interested in the relationship between modernism and Indigenous and ethnic writers but also remind us of the long-standing ethnocentrism of the field. For examples of such work, see Booth and Rigby, "Introduction"; Bornstein, *Material Modernism*; Doyle and Winkiel, *Geomodernisms*; Mao and Walkowitz, "New Modernist Studies"; Rowe, "Other Modernisms." Other scholarship of the novel includes readings based on gender or genre: for the former, see Hoefel, "Gendered Cartography"; Lim, "End in Tears";

Parker, *Invention of Native American Literature* and "Who Shot the Sheriff." For the latter, see Kent, *African, Native, and Jewish American Literature*; Keresztesi, *Strangers at Home*; Lima, "Uneven Development"; Owens, *Other Destinies*; Ruppert, "Textual Perspectives"; Vigil, *Indigenous Intellectuals*.

11 For a comprehensive biography of McNickle, see Parker, *Singing an Indian Song*.

12 Kent, *African, Native, and Jewish American Literature*, 18. See also Cobb, Fields, and Cheatle, "'born in the opposition'"; Dietrich, *Writing Across the Color Line*.

13 Gercken, "Visions of Tribulation," 633; Balthaser, "Killing the Documentarian," 357–58; Hyde, *Bodies of Law*, 231; Bhabha, *Location of Culture*, 60; Crary, *Techniques of the Observer*, 18; Dyer, *White*, 44; Pratt, *Imperial Eyes*; Wiegman, *American Anatomies*, 6.

14 Brownlee, *Commerce of Vision*, 2. Brownlee traces visual culture in antebellum America; for visual culture's development during the early twentieth century, see Jacobs, *Eye's Mind*; Smith, *Photography on the Color Line* and "Visual Culture and Race."

15 Hurston, "What White Publishers Won't Print," 152. On the expectations and conceptualization of "Indians" in modernity, see Brown, "American Indian Modernities"; Deloria, *Indians in Unexpected Places*; Dymond, "Modernism(s) Inside Out"; Hutchinson, *Indian Craze*; Kent, *African, Native, and Jewish American Literature*; Keresztesi, *Strangers at Home*; O'Brien, *Firsting and Lasting*; Pfister, *Individuality Incorporated*.

16 So and Wezerek, "Just How White Is the Book Industry?". See also Jiménez and Beckert, "Where Is the Diversity in Publishing?"

17 Barkan and Bush, *Prehistories of the Future*, 3, 18. Lears uses the term "antimodernism" to describe the turn toward preindustrial culture as an antidote to modernity. See Lears, *No Place of Grace*.

18 Torgovnick, *Primitive Passions*, 4–5; Rony, *Third Eye*, 8.

19 Qtd. in Owens, *Other Destinies*, 60–61.

20 Qtd. in Sorenson, *Ethnic Modernism*, 197; Hans, "Rethinking History," 44.

21 Ames, "Dodd, Mead and Company," 129–30.

22 Qtd. in Owens, *Other Destinies*, 78.

23 Qtd. in Parker, "D'Arcy McNickle: Native American Author," 12.

24 Eils, "Narrative Privacy," 30, 34.

25 McNickle, *Surrounded*, 1.

26 McNickle, 1–3.

27 McNickle, 5–6.

28 McNickle, 35. For a history of the formation of the Flathead Reservation and the Confederated Salish and Kootenai Tribes (which consist of Salish, Kootenai, and Pend d'Oreille peoples), see Bigart and Woodcock, *In the Name*; Salish Kootenai College's *Challenge to Survive*.

29 McNickle, *Surrounded*, 35, 59.

30 Piatote, *Domestic Subjects*, 133–35.

31 McNickle, *Surrounded*, 118.

32 Eils, "Narrative Privacy," 31. For comments on surveillance at work within *The Surrounded*, see Holton, "The Politics of Point of View"; Nason, "Carceral Power"; Zulli, "Perception."

33 Keresztesi, *Strangers at Home*, 139; McNickle, "Interpreting Native America," 599. Italics mine.

34 McNickle, *Surrounded*, 203, 214.

35 McNickle, 215–16. My italics.

36 McNickle, 217, 225, 219.

37 McNickle, 102.

38 See Deloria, *Playing Indian*.

39 Peers, "Playing Ourselves," 46. See also Evans-Pritchard, "How 'They' See 'Us'."

40 Parker, *Invention*, 74, caption for Fig. 4.

41 Besides the UNM Press reprints, there also exists another edition produced in 1998 as a Fire Keepers book by the Quality Paperback Book Club. The edition is now out of print, but its cover unfortunately represents an elderly woman with her face aesthetically chopped in half, facing two different directions, with what appears to be an *horno* behind her. She does not make eye contact with the viewer and overall seems disturbingly objectified. For more on photography and Native representations, see Sandweiss, *Print the Legend*, especially Chapter 6.

42 Justice, *Why Indigenous Literatures Matter*, 241; Eils, "Narrative Privacy," 34.

43 Vigil, *Indigenous Intellectuals*, 310. See also Michaelsen, *Limits of Multiculturalism*.

44 Owens, *Other Destinies*, 78; Parker, "D'Arcy McNickle: An Annotated Bibliography," 6.

45 Kent, *African, Native, and Jewish American Literature*, 98.

46 Mayali, "Political Economy of Annotation," 185–86; Brown, "*The Surrounded*," 75; Kent, *African, Native, and Jewish American Literature*, 105.

47 Cox, *Muting White Noise*, 49, 50. My italics.

48 McNickle, *Surrounded*, 20–21.

49 McNickle, 69, 70, 73.

50 Sollors, *Beyond Ethnicity*, 249–50; Benstock, "Margin of Discourse," 204; Zerby, *Devil's Details*, 3. For more on the historical and paratextual function of footnotes, see Barney, *Annotation*; Bugeja and Dimitrova, *Vanishing Act*; Grafton, *Footnote*; Mallam, "A Focus on Footnotes"; Mayali, "Political Economy of Annotation"; and Zerby, *Devil's Details*. For more on the paratextual interventions of footnotes in literature, see Barter, "Encrypted Citations"; Benstock, "Margin of Discourse"; Cheng, "On the Margins"; Schachterle, "James Fenimore Cooper"; and Treat, "Introduction," 1.

51 Ahmed, "Making Feminist Points"; King et al., "Men Set Their Own Cites High," 15. See also Delgado, "Imperial Scholar";12 Woman Scholars, "Disturbing Pattern"; Ray, "Racial Politics of Citation"; Smith, *Cite Black Women*; Vettese, "Sexism in the Academy"; Williams and Collier, *CiteASista*.

52 King, "Men Set Their Own Cites High," 17; Benstock, "Margin of Discourse," 204.

53 Justice, *Why Indigenous Literatures Matter*, 241.

54 Bruner, "Introduction," 3.

55 Gates, "Belafonte's Balancing Act," 160.

56 Despite their vital public service record, U.S. libraries also participated in systemic segregation and economic inequalities, which further blocked intellectual and educational access for Black and other historically disenfranchised communities. See Knott, *Not Free, Not for All*; Selby, *Freedom Libraries*.

57 See 12 Woman Scholars, "Disturbing Pattern"; Smith, "Cite Black Women"; Williams and Collier, *CiteASista*; and Zurn, Bassett, and Rust, "The Citation Diversity Statement."

58 Parker, *Singing an Indian Song*, 68.

59 As two examples, see also Jojola, "On Revision and Revisionism" and the recent controversy in New Mexico over the Zia symbol: Schmitt, "Discussions to be Held"; and "Zia Pueblo Upset."

60 Kent, *African, Native, and Jewish American Literature*, 101.

61 Grafton, *Footnote*, 234; Mayali, "Political Economy of Annotation," 186.

62 "Three Peoples Murals"; Rao, "University of New Mexico May Remove." See also Holmen, "UNM Begins Class"; Rodriguez, "Tourism," esp. 199–201; Sisneros, "Student Activism."

63 Keresztesi, for example, writes of the "characters' lack of understanding [about] why things happen to them" and the novel's "trajectory of inescapable determinism." Owens writes of the characters as being "hopelessly trapped," and Rains describes the ending as raising the hopes of the reader before "finally dashing them with a conventional tragic conclusion." Keresztesi, *Strangers at Home*, 143; Owens, *Other Destinies*, 66; Rains, "'He Never Wanted to Forget It.'" See also Owens, "'Map of the Mind'" and "Red Road to Nowhere."

64 McNickle, *Surrounded*, 294–97.

65 Herman, "'Whole in Small Compass,'" 364.

66 Keresztesi, *Strangers at Home*, 143.

67 Allen, *Voice of the Turtle*, 15–16.

68 Ruppert, "Politics and Culture," 96.

69 Peers, "'Playing Ourselves,'" 57; Deloria, *Indians in Unexpected Places*, 14; Piper, *Book Was There*, 26.

Conclusion: Paratextual Futures

1 For reading's impact on the brain, see Goldman, "This Is Your Brain." For digital reading and the brain, see Baron, "Why Do We Remember"; Carr, *Shallows*; Lossin, "Against the Universal Library"; Mangen, Olivier, and Velay, "Comparing Comprehension"; Mueller and Oppenheimer, "Pen Is Mightier"; Munzer et al., "Differences in Parent-Toddler Interactions" and "Tablets, Toddlers and Tantrums"; Wolf, *Proust and the Squid*.

2 Sconce, *Haunted Media*, 9, 19.

3 Zuboff expresses these concerns under twenty-first century surveillance, writing, "Just as industrial civilization flourished at the expense of nature and now threatens to cost us the Earth, an information civilization shaped by surveillance capitalism and its new instrumentarian power will thrive at the expense of human nature and will threaten to cost us our humanity." Zuboff, *Age of Surveillance Capitalism*, 11–12.

4 Simpson, *As We Have Always Done*, 220–24.

5 Kastan, *Shakespeare and the Book*, 115. For a discussion of potential Indigenous dis/embodied kinships with machines, see Lewis et al., "Making Kin with the Machines." See also Hansen, *Embodying Technesis*.

6 See Duarte, *Network Sovereignty*; Guzmán, "The Great Disconnect"; Kickingwoman, "Indian Country Receives Broadband"; Mangan, "Cost of Connection."

7 Alexie, "Superman and Me," 4–6. In citing Alexie, I do not ignore the accusations of sexual harassment made against him. At the current moment, I continue to cite

his work while attaching this conversation to it in the hopes of future productive conversations about the intersections of race, gender violence, patriarchy, and privilege.

8 Striphas, *Late Age of Print*, qtd. in Levy and Mole, "Introduction," xix–xx. See Darnton, *Case for Books*, esp. Chapter 1, "Google and the Future of Books."

9 See DiCuirci, *Colonial Revivals*, 185; Seeber, "Legacy Systems"; Stauffer, *Book Traces*, 173; Manoff, "Human and Machine Entanglement" and "Unintended Consequences," 275; Noble, *Algorithms of Oppression*.

10 Benjamin, Ruha. *Race after Technology*, 5–6, 29. Ivy Schweitzer addresses the potential pitfalls as well as benefits in Native literary digital humanities projects specifically, within the greater context of a racially inequitable digital humanities sphere. See Schweitzer, "Introduction" and "Native Sovereignty and the Archive."

11 McGann, *New Republic*, 20. See also Darnton, *Case for Books*; Ovenden, *Burning the Books*.

12 Stauffer, "My *Old Sweethearts*." See DiCuirci, *Colonial Revivals*, 185; McKenzie, *Bibliography*, 270; MLA, "Statement on the Significance"; Orgel, *Reader in the Book*; Ovenden, *Burning the Books*; Stauffer, *Book Traces*; Zuboff, *Age of Surveillance Capitalism*.

13 See So and Wezerek, "Just How White?"

14 Stauffer, *Book Traces*, 137; Stauffer, "My *Old Sweethearts*."

15 Alexie, *Absolutely True Diary*, 30–31; Erdrich, *Books and Islands*, 4.

16 See Stoler, *Along the Archival Grain*; Caswell, *Urgent Archives*; Howe, *Choctalking on Other Realities* for her discussion of "tribalography." My thanks to Furlan, Beth Piatote, the ASAIL listserv, and the 2018 MLA on "The Indigenous Archive" for inspiration and suggestions along this theme.

17 Bugeja and Dimitrova, *Vanishing Act*, 5, 6, 12.

18 Darnton, *Censors at Work*, 20.

19 Feal, "Foreword," vii.

20 Modern Language Association, *MLA Handbook*, 51.

21 Hayles, *How We Became Posthuman*, 49.

BIBLIOGRAPHY

12 Woman Scholars. "A Disturbing Pattern." *Inside Higher Ed.* August 27, 2021. https://www.insidehighered.com/advice/2021/08/27/entrenched-inequity-not-appropriately-citing-scholarship-women-and-people-color.

Ahmed, Sara. "Making Feminist Points." *Feministkilljoys* (blog). https://feministkilljoys.com/2013/09/11/making-feminist-points/.

Akins, Damon B., and William J. Bauer, Jr. *We Are the Land: A History of Native California.* Oakland: University of California Press, 2021.

Alemán, Jesse. "Assimilation and the Decapitated Body Politic in *The Life and Adventures of Joaquín Murieta.*" *Arizona Quarterly* 60, no. 1 (2004): 71–98.

Alexie, Sherman. *The Absolutely True Diary of a Part-Time Indian.* New York: Little, Brown, and Company, 2007.

———. "Superman and Me." In *Approaching Literature: Reading, Thinking, and Writing.* 3rd ed., edited by Peter Schakel and Jack Ridl, 4–6. Boston: Bedford/St. Martin's, 2012.

Allen, Paula Gunn, ed. *Voice of the Turtle: American Indian Literature, 1900–1970.* New York: Ballantine Books, 1994.

Alves, Jaime Osterman. *Fictions of Female Education in the Nineteenth Century.* New York: Routledge, 2009.

Ames, Gregory. "Dodd, Mead and Company." In *Dictionary of Literary Biography.* Vol. 49, *American Literary Publishing Houses, 1638–1899,* Part I: A–M, edited by Peter Dzwonkoski. Detroit: Gale Research Company, 1986.

Andes, Stephen J. C. *Zorro's Shadow: How a Mexican Legend Became America's First Superhero.* Chicago: Chicago Review Press, 2020.

Andrews, William. "Editing 'Minority' Texts." In *The Margins of the Text,* edited by D. C. Greetham, 45–55. Ann Arbor: University of Michigan Press, 1997.

Apes[s], William. *A Son of the Forest: The Experience of William Apes, A Native of the Forest.* New York: Published by the Author, 1829.

———. *A Son of the Forest: The Experience of William Apes, A Native of the Forest*. 2nd ed., revised and corrected. New York: Published by the Author, Printed by G.F. Bunce, 1831.

Baker, Cathleen A. *From the Hand to the Machine: Nineteenth-Century American Paper and Mediums: Technologies, Materials, and Conservation*. Ann Arbor, MI: The Legacy Press, 2010.

Balthaser, Benjamin. "Killing the Documentarian: Richard Wright and Documentary Modernity." *Criticism* 55, no. 3 (2013): 357–90.

———. "'Travels of an American Indian into the Hinterlands of Soviet Russia': Rethinking Indigenous Modernity and the Popular Front in the Work of Archie Phinney and D'Arcy McNickle." *American Quarterly* 66, no. 2 (2014): 385–416.

Bancroft, Hubert Howe. *Literary Industries*. Vol. 34 of *The Works of Hubert Howe Bancroft*. San Francisco: The History Company, 1890. https://archive.org/stream/bwlitindustries39bancroft#page/n11/mode/2up/search/Cooke.

Barkan, Elazar, and Ronald Bush. Introduction to *Prehistories of the Future: The Primitivist Project and the Culture of Modernism*, 1–19. Edited by Elazar Barkan and Ronald Bush. Stanford: Stanford University Press, 1995.

Barker, Francis. *The Tremulous Private Body: Essays on Subjection*. New York: Methuen, 1984.

Barney, Stephen A., ed. *Annotation and Its Texts*. New York: Oxford University Press, 1991.

Baron, Naomi S. "Why Do We Remember More by Reading in Print Vs. on a Screen?." *Neurophysch* May 9, 2021. Accessed December 7, 2022.

Barr, Juliana, and Edward Countryman. "Introduction: Maps and Spaces, Paths to Connect, and Lines to Divide." In *Contested Spaces of Early America*, edited by Julian Barr and Edward Countryman, 1–28. Philadelphia: University of Pennsylvania Press, 2014.

Barter, Faith. "Encrypted Citations: *The Bondwoman's Narrative* and the Case of Jane Johnson." *MELUS* 46, no. 1 (2021): 51–74.

Bataille, Gretchen M., and Kathleen Mullen Sands. *American Indian Women: Telling Their Lives*. Lincoln: University of Nebraska Press, 1984.

Bauerle, Phenocia, ed. *The Way of the Warrior: Stories of the Crow People*. Complied and translated by Henry Old Coyote and Barney Old Coyote Jr. Lincoln: University of Nebraska Press, 2003.

Baynton, Douglas C. *Forbidden Signs: American Culture and the Campaign against Sign Language*. Chicago: University of Chicago Press, 1996.

Bellin, Joshua David. *The Demon of the Continent: Indians and the Shaping of American Literature*. Philadelphia: University of Pennsylvania Press, 2001.

Benjamin, Ruha. *Race after Technology*. Medford, MA: Polity, 2019.

Benstock, Shari. "At the Margin of Discourse: Footnotes in the Fictional Text." *PMLA* 98, no. 2 (1983): 204–25.

Benton, Megan L. "Typography and Gender: Remasculating the Modern Book." In *Illuminating Letters: Typography and Literary Interpretation*, edited by Paul C. Gutjahr and Megan L. Benton, 71–93. Amherst: University of Massachusetts Press, 2001.

Berger, Jason. "Insurgencies from *There There*." *MELUS* 47, no. 1 (2022): 175–99.

Bergland, Renée L. *The National Uncanny: Indian Ghosts and American Subjects*. Hanover, NH: University Press of New England, 2000.

Berkowitz, Paul D. *The Case of the Indian Trader: Billy Malone and the National Park Service Investigation at Hubbell Trading Post*. Albuquerque: University of New Mexico Press, 2011.

Berlant, Lauren. *The Anatomy of National Fantasy: Hawthorne, Utopia, and Everyday Life*. Chicago: University of Chicago Press, 1991.

Berlatsky, Eric. "Lost in the Gutter: Within and Between Frames in Narrative and Narrative Theory." *Narrative* 17, no. 2 (2009): 162–87.

Bernardin, Susan. "Acorn Soup Is Good Food: L. Frank, *News from Native California*, and the Intersections of Literary and Visual Arts." *Studies in American Indian Literatures* 27, no. 3 (2015): 1–33.

———. "On the Meeting Grounds of Sentiment: S. Alice Callahan's 'Wynema, A Child of the Forest'." *American Transcendental Quarterly* 15, no. 3 (2001): 209–24.

Bhabha, Homi K. *The Location of Culture*. New York: Routledge, 1994.

Bhandar, Brenna. *Colonial Lives of Property: Law, Land, and Racial Regimes of Ownership*. Durham: Duke University Press, 2018.

Bigart, Robert, and Clarence Woodcock. *In the Name of the Salish & Kootenai Nation: The 1855 Hell Gate Treaty and the Origin of the Flathead Indian Reservation*. Pablo, MT: Salish Kootenai College Press, 1996.

Blaver, Angela D. "California Imagery in Context: The Mono Basin Kutzadika'a Paiutes." In *Indigenous Symbols and Practices in the Catholic Church: Visual Culture, Missionization and Appropriation*, edited by Kathleen J. Martin, 185–202. Burlington: Ashgate, 2010.

Block, Sharon. *Colonial Complexions: Race and Bodies in Eighteenth-Century America*. Philadelphia: University of Pennsylvania Press, 2018.

Booth, Howard J., and Nigel Rigby. "Introduction." In *Modernism and Empire*, edited by Howard J. Booth and Nigel Rigby, 1–12. New York: Manchester University Press, 2000.

Bornstein, George. *Material Modernism: The Politics of the Page*. New York: Cambridge University Press, 2001.

Bringhurst, Robert. "Introduction." In *The Form of the Book: Essays on the Morality of Good Design*, by Jan Tschichold, Translated by Hajo Hadeler. Point Roberts, WA: Hartley & Marks, 1991.

Brooks, Joanna. "'This Indian World': An Introduction to the Writings of Samson Occom." In *The Collected Writings of Samson Occom, Mohegan: Leadership and Literature in Eighteenth-Century Native America*, edited by Joanna Brooks, 3–39. New York: Oxford University Press, 2006.

Brooks, Lisa. *The Common Pot: The Recovery of Native Space in the Northeast*. Minneapolis: University of Minnesota Press, 2008.

———. *Our Beloved Kin: A New History of King Philip's War*. New Haven: Yale University Press, 2018.

Brown, Kirby. "American Indian Modernities and New Modernist Studies' 'Indian Problem.'" *Texas Studies in Literature and Language* 59, no. 3 (2017): 287–318.

Brown, William. "*The Surrounded*: Listening between the Lines of Inherited Stories." In *The Legacy of D'Arcy McNickle: Writer, Historian, Activist*, edited by John Lloyd Purdy, 69–84. Norman: University of Oklahoma Press, 1996.

Brownlee, Peter John. *The Commerce of Vision: Optical Culture and Perception in Antebellum America*. Philadelphia: University of Pennsylvania Press, 2019.

Brumble, David. *American Indian Autobiography*. Berkeley: California University Press, 1988.

Bruner, Edward M. "Introduction: The Ethnographic Self and the Personal Self." In *Anthropology and Literature*, edited by Paul Benson, 1–26. Urbana: University of Illinois Press, 1993.

Bruyneel, Kevin. *The Third Space of Sovereignty: The Postcolonial Politics of U.S.-Indigenous Relations*. Minneapolis: University of Minnesota Press, 2007.

Brylowe, Thora. "The Flood, the Mill, and the Body of the Book." In *Codex*, edited by Micah Bloom, 30–37. Grand Forks, ND: The Digital Press at the University of North Dakota, 2017.

Buck, Pearl S. *The Good Earth*. New York: John Day Company, 1931.

Bugeja, Michael, and Daniela V. Dimitrova. *Vanishing Act: The Erosion of Online Footnotes and Implications for Scholarship in the Digital Age*. Duluth, MN: Litwin Books, 2010.

Burgett, Bruce. *Sentimental Bodies: Sex, Gender, and Citizenship in the Early Republic*. Princeton: Princeton University Press, 1998.

Bushman, Richard L. *The Refinement of America: Persons, Houses, Cities*. New York: Knopf, 1992.

Butler, Judith. *Bodies That Matter: On the Discursive Limits of "Sex."* New York: Routledge, 1993.

Calcaterra, Angela. *Literary Indians: Aesthetics & Encounter in American Literature to 1920*. Chapel Hill: University of North Carolina Press, 2018.

Calhoun, Joshua. "The Word Made Flax: Cheap Bibles, Textual Corruption, and the Poetics of Paper." *PMLA* 126, no. 2 (2011): 327–44.

Callahan, S. Alice. *Wynema: A Child of the Forest.* Chicago: H. J. Smith, 1891.

———. *Wynema: A Child of the Forest.* Chicago: E.A. Weeks, 1893.

———. *Wynema: A Child of the Forest.* Lincoln: University of Nebraska Press, 1997.

Campbell, Neil. *The Rhizomatic West: Representing the American West in a Transnational, Global, Media Age.* Lincoln: University of Nebraska Press, 2008.

Canfield, Gae Whitney. *Sarah Winnemucca of the Northern Paiutes.* Norman: University of Oklahoma Press, 1983.

Carlson, David J. *Sovereign Selves: American Indian Autobiography and the Law.* Urbana: University of Illinois Press, 2006.

Carpenter, Cari M. "Choking Off That Angel Mother: Sarah Winnemucca Hopkins's Strategic Humor." *Studies in American Indian Literatures* 26, no. 3 (2014): 1–24.

———. "Sarah Winnemucca Goes to Washington: Rhetoric and Resistance in the Capital City." *American Indian Quarterly* 40, no. 2 (2016): 87–108.

———. *Seeing Red: Anger, Sentimentality, and American Indians.* Columbia: Ohio State University Press, 2008.

———. "Tiresias Speaks: Sarah Winnemucca's Hybrid Selves and Genres." *Legacy* 19, no. 1 (2002): 71–80.

Carpenter, Cari M., and Carolyn Sorisio. *The Newspaper Warrior: Sarah Winnemucca Hopkins's Campaign for American Indian Rights, 1864–1891.* Lincoln: University of Nebraska Press, 2015.

Carr, Nicholas. *The Shallows: What the Internet Is Doing to Our Brains.* New York: Norton, 2010.

Caswell, Michelle. *Urgent Archives: Enacting Liberatory Memory Work.* New York: Routledge, 2021.

Chartier, Roger. *Frenchness in the History of the Book: From the History of Publishing to the History of Reading.* Worcester, MA: American Antiquarian Society, 1988.

Cheng, Eileen. "On the Margins: The Mediating Function of Footnotes in Thomas Hutchinson's 'History of Massachusetts-Bay.'" *Early American Studies* 11, no. 1 (2013): 98–116.

Chiles, Katy L. "Becoming Colored in Occom and Wheatley's Early America." *PMLA* 123, no. 5 (2008): 1398–417.

———. *Transformable Race: Surprising Metamorphoses in the Literature of Early America.* New York: Oxford University Press, 2014.

Chute, Hillary L. *Graphic Women: Life Narrative and Contemporary Comics.* New York: Columbia University Press, 2010.

Clough, Charles W. "Supplementary Notes of Joaquin Murieta: Part II." In *Joaquin Murieta, The Brigand Chief of California,* xiii–xvii. Fresno, CA: Valley Publishers, 1969.

Cobb, Daniel M., Kyle D. Fields, and Joseph Cheatle. "'born in the opposition': D'Arcy McNickle, Ethnobiographically." In *Beyond Two Worlds: Critical Conversations on Language and Power in Native North America*, edited by James Joseph Buss and C. Joseph Genetin-Pilawa, 253–67. Albany: State University of New York Press, 2014.

Cohen, Matt. *The Networked Wilderness: Communicating in Early New England*. Minneapolis: University of Minnesota Press, 2009.

Colasurdo, Christine. "'Tell Me a Woman's Story': The Question of Gender in the Construction of *Waheenee*, *Pretty-shield*, and *Papago Woman*." *American Indian Quarterly* 21, no. 3 (1997): 385–407. Web. *JSTOR*. 25 May 2016.

Colby, William E. "Curtis Holbrook Lindley." *California Law Review* 9, no. 2 (1921): 87–99.

Cole, Simon A. *Suspect Identities: A History of Fingerprinting and Criminal Identification*. Cambridge: Harvard University Press, 2001.

Collins, Cory. "More Than a Name: Teaching Historic Firsts." *Learning for Justice*. Nov. 27, 2018. Accessed July 13, 2021.

Coupal, Michelle, Aubrey Jean Hanson, and Sarah Henzi. "Sovereign Histories, Gathering Bones, Embodying Land: Visiting with Contributors." *Studies in American Indian Literatures* 32, no. 3–4 (2020): vii–xv.

Cox, James H. *Muting White Noise: Native American and European American Novel Traditions*. Norman: University of Oklahoma Press, 2006.

Crary, Jonathan. *Techniques of the Observer: On Vision and Modernity in the Nineteenth Century*. Cambridge: MIT Press, 1990.

Dain, Bruce. *A Hideous Monster of the Mind: American Race Theory in the Early Republic*. Cambridge: Harvard University Press, 2002.

Dale, Leigh, and Simon Ryan, eds. *The Body in the Library*. Amsterdam, Netherlands: Rodopi B.V., 1998.

Darnton, Robert. *The Case for Books: Past, Present, and Future*. New York: Public Affairs, 2009.

———. *Censors at Work: How States Shaped Literature*. New York: W. W. Norton, 2014.

Davidson, Cathy N. *Revolution and the Word: The Rise of the Novel in America*. Expanded edition. New York: Oxford University Press, 2004.

Davis, Jeffrey E. *Hand Talk: Sign Language among American Indian Nations*. New York: Cambridge University Press, 2010.

Debo, Angie. "John Rollin Ridge." *Southwest Review* 17, no. 1 (1932): 59–71.

Debord, Guy. *Society of the Spectacle*. Detroit: Black & Red, 1983.

Delgado, Richard. "The Imperial Scholar: Reflections on a Review of Civil Rights Literature." *University of Pennsylvania Law Review* 132, no. 3 (1984): 561–78.

Deloria, Philip J. *Indians in Unexpected Places*. Lawrence: University Press of Kansas, 2004.

————. *Playing Indian*. New Haven: Yale University Press, 1998.

Deloria, Vine, Jr. *Custer Died for Your Sins: An Indian Manifesto*. 1969. Norman: University of Oklahoma Press, 1988.

Detsi-Diamanti, Zoe. "Politicizing Aesthetics: The Politics of Violence and Sexuality in Colonial and Revolutionary Representations of America as an Indian Woman." *The AnaChronisT* (2006): 61–78.

DiCuirci, Lindsay. *Colonial Revivals: The Nineteenth-Century Lives of Early American Books*. Philadelphia: University of Pennsylvania Press, 2019.

Dietrich, Lucas A. *Writing across the Color Line: U.S. Print Culture and the Rise of Ethnic Literature, 1877–1920*. Amherst: University of Massachusetts Press, 2020.

Dilworth, Leah. "Tourists and Indians in Fred Harvey's Southwest." In *Seeing and Being Seen: Tourism in the American West*, edited by David M. Wrobel and Patrick T. Long, 142–64. Lawrence: University Press of Kansas, 2001.

Dinius, Marcy J. "'Look!! Look!!! at This!!!!': The Radical Typography of David Walker's 'Appeal.'" *PMLA* 126, no. 1 (2011): 55–72.

Dobson, Joanne. "Reclaiming Sentimental Literature." *American Literature* 69, no. 2 (1997): 263–88.

Dolan, Kathryn Cornell. "Cattle and Sovereignty in the Work of Sarah Winnemucca." *American Indian Quarterly* 44, no. 1 (2020): 86–114.

Doyle, Laura, and Laura Winkiel. *Geomodernisms: Race, Modernism, and Modernity*. Bloomington: Indiana University Press, 2005.

Drysdale, David J. "Ridge's *Joaquín Murieta*: Banditry, Counterinsurgency, and Colonial Power after Guadalupe-Hidalgo." *Canadian Review of American Studies* 45, no. 1 (2016): 62–85.

Duarte, Marisa Elena. *Network Sovereignty: Building the Internet across Indian Country*. Seattle: University of Washington Press, 2017.

Dyer, Richard. *White*. New York: Routledge, 1997.

Dymond, Justine. "Modernism(s) Inside Out: History, Space, and Modern American Indian Subjectivity in *Cogewea, the Half-Blood*." In *Geomodernisms: Race, Modernism, Modernity*, edited by Laura Doyle and Laura Winkiel, 297–312. Bloomington: Indiana University Press, 2005.

"E. A. Weeks (1893–1898): A Chicago Publisher." May 24, 2021. https://www.henryaltemus.com/Weeks/index.html.

Egan, Jim. *Authorizing Experience: Refigurations of the Body Politic in Seventeenth-Century New England Writing*. Princeton: Princeton University Press, 1999.

Eils, Colleen Gleeson. "Narrative Privacy: Evading Ethnographic Surveillance in Fiction by Sherman Alexie, Rigoberto González, and Nam Le." *MELUS* 42, no. 2 (2017): 30–52.

Elbert, Monika M., Julie E. Hall, and Katharine Rodier, eds. *Reinventing the Peabody Sisters*. Iowa City: University of Iowa Press, 2006.

Ellis, Clyde. "Our Ill Fated Relative: John Rollin Ridge and the Cherokee People." *Chronicles of Oklahoma* 68, no. 4 (1991): 376–95.

Elshtain, Jean Bethke, and J. Timothy Cloyd, eds. *Politics and the Human Body: Assault on Dignity.* Nashville: Vanderbilt University Press, 1995.

Emery, Jacqueline, ed. *Recovering Native American Writings in the Boarding School Press.* Lincoln: University of Nebraska Press, 2017.

Erdrich, Louise. *Books and Islands in Ojibwe Country.* Washington, DC: National Geographic Directions, 2003.

———— and Michael Dorris. *The Crown of Columbus.* New York: Harper Collins, 1991.

————. *Tracks.* 1988. New York: Harper Perennial, 2004.

Esposito, Roberto. *Persons and Things: From the Body's Point of View.* Translated by Zakiya Hanafi. Malden, MA: Polity Press, 2015.

Estes, Nick. *Our History Is the Future: Standing Rock versus the Dakota Access Pipeline, and the Long Tradition of Indigenous Resistance.* New York: Verso, 2019.

Evans-Pritchard, Deirdre. "How 'They' See 'Us': Native American Images of Tourists." *Annals of Tourism Research* 16, no. 1 (1989): 89–105.

Eves, Rosalyn Collings. "Finding Place to Speak: Sarah Winnemucca's Rhetorical Practices in Disciplinary Spaces." *Legacy* 31, no. 1 (2014): 1–22.

Fagan, Kevin. "Ishi's Kin to Give Him Proper Burial." *SFGate.* August 10, 2000. Accessed January 16, 2023. https://www.sfgate.com/bayarea/article/Ishi-s-Kin-To-Give-Him-Proper-Burial-Indians-to-2744424.php#ixzz1wBvJxpTg.

Farnell, Brenda. *Do You See What I Mean?: Plains Indian Sign Talk and the Embodiment of Action.* Lincoln: University of Nebraska Press, 1995.

Farquhar, Francis P. "Notes on Joaquin Murieta." In *Joaquin Murieta, The Brigand Chief of California,* i–viii. Fresno, CA: Valley Publishers, 1969.

Feal, Rosemary G. Foreword to *MLA Handbook.* 8th ed. New York: The Modern Language Association of America, 2016.

Fear-Segal, Jacqueline, and Rebecca Tillett, eds. *Indigenous Bodies: Reviewing, Relocating, Reclaiming.* Albany: State University of New York Press, 2013.

Febvre, Lucien, and Henri-Jean Martin. *The Coming of the Book: The Impact of Printing 1450–1800.* Translated by David Gerard. New York: Verso, 1990.

Fielder, Brigitte, and Jonathan Senchyne. "Introduction: Infrastructures of African American Print." In *Against a Sharp White Background: Infrastructures of African American Print,* edited by Brigitte Fielder and Jonathan Senchyne, 3–26. Madison, WI: University of Wisconsin Press, 2019.

"Fingerprints: The Convoluted Patterns of Racism." In *The Dickinsonia History Project.* Dickinson College Digital Museum. Carlisle, PA:

Dickinson College. Accessed June 17, 2022. https://dh.dickinson.edu
/digitalmuseum/exhibit-artifact/babes-in-the-woods/fingerprints.

Fitzgerald, Stephanie. *Native Women and Land: Narratives of Dispossession and Resurgence*. Albuquerque: University of New Mexico Press, 2015.

Fitzgerald, Stephanie, and Hilary E. Wyss. "Land and Literacy: The Textualities of Native Studies." *Early American Literature* 45, no. 2 (2010): 241–50.

Foreman, Carolyn Thomas. "S. Alice Callahan: Author of *Wynema, A Child of the Forest*." *Chronicles of Oklahoma* 33, no. 3 (1955): 306–15.

Fuchs, Miriam. "The Diaries of Queen Lili'uokalani." *Profession* 95 (1995): 38–40.

Gabaldon, Diana. Foreword to *The Life and Adventures of Joaquín Murieta, the Celebrated California Bandit*, by John Rollin Ridge, vii–xiii. New York: Penguin Books, 2018.

Galton, Sir Francis. *Finger Prints*. New York: Macmillan, 1892.

Gates, Henry Louis, Jr. "Belafonte's Balancing Act." In *Thirteen Ways of Looking at Black Man*, 154–79. New York: Random House, 1997.

Gaul, Theresa Strouth. "Catharine Brown's Body: Missionary Spiritualization and Cherokee Embodiment." In *Women's Narratives of the Early Americans and the Formation of Empire*, edited by Mary McAleer Balkun and Susan C. Imbarrato, 201–14. New York: Palgrave Macmillan, 2016.

Genette, Gérard. *Paratexts: Thresholds of Interpretation*. Translated by Jane E. Lewin. Foreword by Richard Macksey. Cambridge: Cambridge University Press, 1997.

Georgi-Findlay, Brigitte. "The Frontiers of Native American Women's Writing: Sarah Winnemucca's *Life among the Piutes*." In *New Voices in Native American Literary Criticism*, edited by Arnold Krupat, 222–52. Washington, DC: Smithsonian Institution Press, 1993.

Gercken, Becca. "Visions of Tribulation: White Gaze and Black Spectacle in Richard Wright's *Native Son* and *The Outsider*." *African American Review* 44, no. 4 (2011): 633–48.

Gillespie, Alexandra. "Turk's-Head Knots." *The Unfinished Book*, edited by Alexandra Gillespie and Deidre Lynch, 203–18. New York: Oxford University Press, 2021.

Ginzberg, Lori D. *Untidy Origins: A Story of Woman's Rights in Antebellum New York*. Chapel Hill: University of North Carolina Press, 2005.

Gitelman, Lisa. *Paper Knowledge: Toward a Media History of Documents*. Durham: Duke University Press, 2014.

Glenn, Cheryl. *Unspoken: A Rhetoric of Silence*. Carbondale: Southern Illinois University Press, 2004.

Glover, Jeffrey. *Paper Sovereigns: Anglo-Native Treaties and the Law of Nations, 1604–1664*. Philadelphia: University of Pennsylvania Press, 2014.

Goeke, Joe. "Yellow Bird and the Bandit: Minority Authorship, Class, and Audience in John Rollin Ridge's *The Life and Adventures of Joaquín Murieta*." *Western American Literature* 37, no. 4 (2003): 452–78.

Goeman, Mishuana. *Mark My Words: Native Women Mapping Our Nations.* Minneapolis: University of Minnesota Press, 2013.

Goldman, Corrie. "This Is Your Brain on Jane Austen, and Stanford Researchers Are Taking Notes," *Stanford News.* September 7, 2012. https://news.stanford.edu/news/2012/september/austen-reading-fmri-090712.html.

Goldsby, Jacqueline. "Book Faces." In *The Unfinished Book,* edited by Alexandra Gillespie and Deidre Lynch, 151–65. New York: Oxford University Press, 2021.

Golombisky, Kim, and Rebecca Hagen. *White Space Is Not Your Enemy: A Beginner's Guide to Communicating Visually through Graphic, Web, & Multimedia Design.* Burlington, MA: Focal Press, 2010.

Gore, Amy. "Gothic Silence: S. Alice Callahan's *Wynema,* the Battle of the Little Bighorn, and the Indigenous Unspeakable." *Studies in American Indian Literatures* 30, no. 1 (2018): 24–49.

Grabarchuk, Alexandra. "Bridging Deep Chasms: The Soviet Third Direction in Alexsei Rybnikov's Rock Opera *The Star and Death of Joaquin Murieta.*" *Musicologica Olomucensia* 22 (2015): 39–60.

Grafton, Anthony. *The Footnote: A Curious History.* Cambridge: Harvard University Press, 1997.

Greenblatt, Stephen. *Marvelous Possessions: The Wonder of the New World.* Chicago: University of Chicago Press, 1991.

Greetham, D. C., ed. *The Margins of the Text.* Ann Arbor: University of Michigan Press, 1997.

Greyser, Naomi. *On Sympathetic Grounds: Race, Gender, and Affective Geographies in Nineteenth-Century North America.* New York: Oxford University Press, 2018.

Grosz, Elizabeth. *Volatile Bodies: Toward a Corporeal Feminism.* Bloomington: Indiana University Press, 1994.

Gubar, Susan. "'The Blank Page' and the Issues of Female Creativity." *Writing and Sexual* Difference. Spec. Issue of *Critical Inquiry* 8, no. 2 (1981): 243–63.

Gustafson, Sandra M. *Eloquence Is Power: Oratory & Performance in Early America.* Chapel Hill: University of North Carolina Press, 2000.

Guzmán, Alicia Inez. "The Great Disconnect." *NM Political Report.* June 21, 2021. https://nmpoliticalreport.com/2021/06/21/the-great-disconnect/. Accessed February 1, 2023.

Hagen, Rebecca, and Kim Golombisky. *White Space Is Not Your Enemy: A Beginner's Guide to Communicating Visually Through Graphic, Web, and Multimedia Design.* 2nd ed. New York: Focal Press, 2013.

Haggith, Mandy. *Paper Trails: From Trees to Trash—The True Cost of Paper.* London: Virgin Books, 2008.

Hanrahan, Heidi M. "'[W]orthy the imitation of the whites': Sarah Winnemucca and Mary Peabody Mann's Collaboration." *MELUS* 38, no. 1 (2013): 119–36.

Hans, Birgit, ed. *D'Arcy McNickle's The Hungry Generations: The Evolution of a Novel*. Albuquerque: University of New Mexico Press, 2007.

———. "Rethinking History: A Context for *The Surrounded*." In *The Legacy of D'Arcy McNickle: Writer, Historian, Activist*, edited by John Lloyd Purdy, 33–52. Norman: University of Oklahoma Press, 1996.

———. "Re-Visions: An Early Version of *The Surrounded*." *Studies in American Indian Literatures* 4, no. 2/3 (1992): 181–95.

Hansen, Mark. *Embodying Technesis: Technology beyond Writing*. Ann Arbor: University of Michigan Press, 2000.

Harjo, Laura. *Spiral to the Stars: Mvskoke Tools of Futurity*. Tucson: University of Arizona Press, 2019.

Harley, J. Brian. "Rereading the Maps of the Columbian Encounter." *Annals of the Association of American Geographers* 82, no. 3 (1992): 522–36.

Harris, Cheryl I. "The Construction of Race and the Emergence of Whiteness as Property." *Harvard Law Review* 106, no. 8 (1993): 1715–44.

Harris, Katherine D. "Feminizing the Textual Body: Female Readers Consuming the Literary Annual." *The Papers of the Bibliographical Society of America* 99, no. 4 (2005): 573–622.

Harris, Sharon M. *Executing Race: Early American Women's Narratives of Race, Society, and the Law*. Columbus: Ohio State University Press, 2005.

Havard, John C. "John Rollin Ridge's 'Joaquín Murieta': Sensation, Hispanicism, and Cosmopolitanism." *Western American Literature* 49, no. 4 (2015): 321–49.

Hausman, Blake Michael. "Becoming Joaquin Murrieta: John Rollin Ridge and the Making of an Icon." PhD diss., University of California–Berkeley, 2011.

———. "Indians in the Margins: Teaching the Native American Characters in John Rollin Ridge's *Joaquín Murieta*." *Studies in American Indian Literatures* 28, no. 2 (2016): 1–24.

Hayles, N. Katherine. *How We Became Posthuman: Virtual Bodies in Cybernetics, Literature, and Informatics*. Chicago: The University of Chicago Press, 1999.

Heneghan, Bridget T. *Whitewashing America: Material Culture and Race in the Antebellum Imagination*. Jackson: University Press of Mississippi, 2003.

Herman, Matthew. "'The Whole in Small Compass': D'Arcy McNickle's Social Vision in *The Surrounded*." *Modern Fiction Studies* 65, no. 2 (2019): 354–75.

Hilleary, Cecily. "Native American Hand Talkers Fight to Keep Sign Language Alive." *Voices of America (VOA) News*. April 3, 2017. https://www

.voanews.com/a/native-american-hand-talker-fight-to-keep-signed
-language-alive/3794333.html.

"H.J. Smith & Co," In *A Business Tour of Chicago, Depicting Fifty Years' Pro-gress*, 121. Chicago: E. E. Barton, 1887.

Hoefel, Roseanne. "Gendered Cartography: Mapping the Mind of Female Characters in D'Arcy McNickle's *The Surrounded*." *Studies in American Indian Literatures* 10, no. 1 (1998): 45–64.

Hofmeyr, Isabel. "Colonial Copyright, Customs, and Indigenous Textualities: Literary Authority and Textual Citizenship." In *Indigenous Textual Cultures: Reading and Writing in the Age of Global Empire*, edited by Tony Ballantyne, Lachy Paterson and Angela Wanhalla, 245–62. Durham: Duke University Press, 2020.

Holmen, Megan. "UNM Begins Class on 'Three Peoples' Mural." *The Daily Lobo*. January 31, 2018. http://www.dailylobo.com/article/2018/01/three-peoples-class.

Holton, Robert. "The Politics of Point of View: Representing History in Mourning Dove's *Cogewea* and D'Arcy McNickle's *The Surrounded*." *Studies in American Indian Literatures* 9, no. 2 (1997): 69–80.

hooks, bell. *Yearning: Race, Gender, and Cultural Politics*. Boston: South End Press, 1990.

Howe, LeAnne. *Choctalking on Other Realities*. San Francisco, Aunt Lute Books, 2013.

Hoxie, Frederick E. "Denouncing American's Destiny: Sarah Winnemucca's Assault on US Expansion." *Cultural and Social History* 9, no. 4 (2012): 549–67.

Hsu, Hsuan L. Introduction to *The Life and Adventures of Joaquín Murieta, the Celebrated California Bandit*, by John Rollin Ridge, xv–xxx. New York: Penguin Books, 2018.

Humud, Sarah Bonnie. "The 'Authentic Indian': Sarah Winnemucca's Resistance to Colonial Constructions of Indianness." *American Indian Culture and Research Journal* 42, no. 2 (2018): 57–76.

Hurston, Zora Neale. "How It Feels to Be Colored Me." In *I Love Myself When I Am Laughing . . . And Then Again When I Am Looking Mean and Impressive*, edited by Alice Walker, 152–55. New York: The Feminist Press, 1979.

———. "What White Publishers Won't Print." In *Zora Neale Hurston: Folklore, Memoirs, and Other Writings*, edited by Cheryl A. Wall, 950–55. New York: Library of America, 1995.

Hutchinson, Elizabeth. *The Indian Craze: Primitivism, Modernism, and Transculturation in American Art, 1890–1915*. Durham: Duke University Press, 2009.

Hyde, Alan. *Bodies of Law*. Princeton: Princeton University Press, 1997.

Irwin, Robert McKee. *Bandits, Captives, Heroines, and Saints: Cultural Icons of Mexico's Northwest Borderlands*. Minneapolis: University of Minnesota Press, 2007.

Jackson, H. J. *Marginalia: Readers Writing in Books*. New Haven: Yale University Press, 2001.

Jackson, Joseph Henry. Introduction to *The Life and Adventures of Joaquín Murieta, The Celebrated California Bandit*, by Yellow Bird/John Rollin Ridge, xi–l. 1955. Norman: University of Oklahoma Press, 1977.

———. "Tradition and the Skeptic: The Creation of Joaquin Murieta." *The Pacific Spectator* II, no. 2 (1948): 176–81.

Jackson, Leon. "The Talking Book and the Talking Book Historian: African American Cultures of Print: The State of the Discipline." *Book History* 13, no. 1 (2010): 251–308.

Jacobs, Karen. *The Eye's Mind: Literary Modernism and Visual Culture*. Ithaca: Cornell University Press, 2001.

Jacobs, Margaret. *Engendered Encounters: Feminism and Pueblo Cultures, 1879–1934*. Lincoln: University of Nebraska Press, 1999.

Jiménez, Laura M., and Betsy Beckert. "Where Is the Diversity in Publishing: The 2019 Diversity Baseline Survey Results." *Lee and Low Books*. January 28, 2020. https://blog.leeandlow.com/2020/01/28/2019diversitybaselinesurvey/.

Johns, Adrian. *Piracy: The Intellectual Property Wars from Gutenberg to Gates*. Chicago: University of Chicago Press, 2009.

Johnson, Barbara. *Persons and Things*. Cambridge: Harvard University Press, 2008.

Johnson, Susan Lee. *Roaring Camp: The Social World of the California Gold Rush*. New York: Norton, 2000.

Johnson v. McIntosh, 21 U.S. (8 Wheat.) 543 (1823).

Johnston, Jessica R. "Minds and Bodies." In *The American Body in Context: An Anthology*, edited by Jessica R. Johnston, 1–10. Wilmington, DE: Scholarly Resources, 2001.

Jojola, Theodore S. "On Revision and Revisionism: American Indian Representations in New Mexico." In *Natives and Academics: Researching and Writing about American Indians*, edited by Devon A. Mihesuah, 172–80. Lincoln: University of Nebraska Press, 1998.

Justice, Daniel Heath. *Why Indigenous Literatures Matter*. Waterloo: Wilfrid Laurier University Press, 2018.

———. *Our Fire Survives the Storm: A Cherokee Literary History*. Minneapolis: University of Minnesota Press, 2005.

Karell, Linda K. *Writing Together/Writing Apart: Collaboration in Western American Literature*. Lincoln: University of Nebraska Press, 2002.

Kastan, David Scott. *Shakespeare and the Book*. New York: Cambridge University Press, 2001.

Kennedy, J. Gerald. *Strange Nation: Literary Nationalism and Cultural Conflict in the Age of Poe*. New York: Oxford University Press, 2016.

Kent, Alicia A. *African, Native, and Jewish American Literature and the Reshaping of Modernism*. New York: Palgrave Macmillan, 2007.

———. "Mourning Dove's *Cogewea*: Writing Her Way into Modernity." *MELUS* 24, no. 3 (1999): 39–66.

———. "'You can't run away nowadays': Redefining Modernity in D'Arcy McNickle's *The Surrounded*." *Studies in American Indian Literatures* 20, no. 2 (2008): 22–46.

Keresztesi, Rita. *Strangers at Home: American Ethnic Modernism between the World Wars*. Lincoln: University of Nebraska Press, 2005.

Kickingwoman, Kolby. "Indian Country Receives Broadband 'Down Payment.'" *Indian Country Today*. June 3, 2021. https://indiancountrytoday.com/news/indian-country-receives-broadband-down-payment?fbclid=IwAR289bsYTgpJr3FAS2EdoZZdMGkUILDRGAK6YBxcMOlvgs8TkJZBQWBRufM.

Kilcup, Karen. *Fallen Forests: Emotion, Embodiment, and Ethics in American Women's Environmental Writing, 1781–1924*. Athens: University of Georgia Press, 2013.

King, Molly M., Carl T. Bergstrom, Shelley J. Correll, Jennifer Jacquet, and Jevin D. West. "Men Set Their Own Cites High: Gender and Self-citation Across Fields and Over Time." *Socius* 3 (2017): 1–22.

Kleist, Jacquelynn. "Sarah Winnemucca's *Life among the Piutes: Their Wrongs and Claims* as Captivity Narrative." *CEA Critic* 75, no. 2 (2013): 79–92.

Knott, Cheryl. *Not Free, Not for All: Public Libraries in the Age of Jim Crow*. Amherst: University of Massachusetts Press, 2015.

Kofman, Ava. "The Anthropometic Dectective and His Racial Clues." *The Public Domain Review*. February 24, 2016. https://publicdomainreview.org/essay/the-anthropometric-detective-and-his-racial-clues.

Kohler, Michelle. "Sending Word: Sarah Winnemucca and the Violence of Writing." *Arizona Quarterly* 69, no. 3 (2013): 49–76.

Kollin, Susan. "Re-envisioning the Big Sky: Regional Identity, Spatial Logics, and the Literature of Montana." In *A Companion to the Regional Literatures of America*, edited by Charles L. Crow, 344–62. Malden, MA: Blackwell Publishing, 2003.

Kolodny, Annette. *The Land Before Her: Fantasy and Experience of the American Frontiers, 1630–1860*. Chapel Hill: University of North Carolina Press, 1984.

———. *The Lay of the Land: Metaphor as Experience and History in American Life and Letters*. Chapel Hill: University of North Carolina Press, 1975.

Krupat, Arnold. *For Those Who Come After: A Study of Native American Autobiography*. Berkeley: University of California Press, 1985.

Kurlansky, Mark. *Paper: Paging Through History*. New York: Norton, 2016.

Kurzen, Crystal M. "Toward a Native American Women's Autobiographical Tradition: Genre as Political Practice." In *The Oxford Handbook of Indigenous American Literature*, edited by James H. Cox and Daniel Heath Justice, 202–14. New York: Oxford University Press, 2014.

La Farge, Oliver. *Laughing Boy*. Boston: Houghton Mifflin, 1929.

———. *Raw Material*. Boston: Houghton Mifflin, 1945.

"Land of Misfortune: Sarah Winnemucca Petitions Congress." *History, Art & Archives: United States House of Representatives*. March 26, 2018. Access December 16, 2022.

Lape, Noreen Groover. "'I Would Rather Be with My People, but Not to Live with Them as They Live': Cultural Liminality and Double Consciousness in Sarah Winnemucca Hopkins's *Life among the Piutes: Their Wrongs and Claims*." *American Indian Quarterly* 22, no. 3 (1998): 259–79.

Lears, T. J. Jackson. *No Place of Grace: Antimodernism and the Transformation of American Culture, 1880–1920*. Chicago: University of Chicago Press, 1981.

Levy, Michelle. "Do Women Have a Book History?" *Studies in Romanticism* 53, no. 3 (2014): 296–317.

Levy, Michelle, and Tom Mole. Introduction to *The Broadview Reader in Book History*. Edited by Michelle Levy and Tom Mole, ix–xx. Toronto: Broadview Press, 2015.

Lewis, Jason Edward, Noelani Arista, Archer Pechawis, and Suzanne Kite. "Making Kin with the Machines." *Journal of Design and Science*. July 16, 2018. https://doi.org/10.21428/bfafd97b.

Lim, January. "End in Tears: Understanding Grief and Loss in D'Arcy McNickle's *The Surrounded*." *English Studies in Canada* 35, no. 2–3 (2009): 145–64.

Lima, Enrique. "Tribal Nations, Transnational Indigenous Movements, and D'Arcy McNickle." *Settler Colonial Studies* 3, no. 3–4 (2013): 414–25.

———. "The Uneven Development of the 'Bildungsroman': D'Arcy McNickle and Native American Modernity." *Comparative Literature* 63, no. 3 (2011): 291–306.

Linderman, Frank B. *American: The Life Story of a Great Indian*. New York: John Day Company, 1930.

———. [*Plenty-coups: Chief of the Crows*]. Lincoln: University of Nebraska Press, 1969.

———. [*Plenty-coups: Chief of the Crows*]. Introduction by Barney Old Coyote, Jr. and Phenocia Bauerle. Afterword by Timothy McCleary. Lincoln: University of Nebraska Press, 2002.

———. *Red Mother: The Life Story of Pretty-Shield, a Medicine Woman of the Crows*. New York: John Day Company, 1932.

———. [*Pretty-shield: Medicine Woman of the Crows*]. Lincoln: University of Nebraska Press, 1972.

———. [*Pretty-shield: Medicine Woman of the Crows*]. Preface by Alma Snell and Becky Matthews. Lincoln: University of Nebraska Press, 2003.

———. [*Pretty-shield: Medicine Woman of the Crows*]. Foreword by Alma Snell and Becky Matthews. New York: Harper Perennial, 2021.

Littau, Karin. *Theories of Reading: Books, Bodies, and Bibliomania*. Malden, MA: Polity Press, 2006.

London, Bette. *Writing Double: Women's Literary Partnerships*. Ithaca: Cornell University Press, 1999.

Lonetree, Amy. *Decolonizing Museums: Representing Native America in National and Tribal Museums*. Chapel Hill: University of North Carolina Press, 2012.

Lopenzina, Drew. *Through an Indian's Looking-Glass: A Cultural Biography of William Apess, Pequot*. Amherst: University of Massachusetts Press, 2017.

———. *Red Ink: Native Americans Picking Up the Pen in the Colonial Period*. Albany: State University of New York, 2012.

López, Ian Haney. *White by Law: The Legal Construction of Race*. Revised and updated. 2006. New York: New York University Press, 1996.

Lossin, Rebecca. "Against the Universal Library." *New Left Review*, no. 107 (2017): 99–114.

Loxley, Simon. *Type: The Secret History of Letters*. New York: I.B. Tauris, 2004.

Luciano, Dana. *Arranging Grief: Sacred Time and the Body in Nineteenth-Century America*. New York: New York University Press, 2007.

Lupton, Ellen. *Thinking with Type: A Critical Guide for Designers, Writers, Editors, and Students*. 2nd ed. New York: Princeton Architectural Press, 2010.

Lyons, Scott Richard. *X-Marks: Native Signatures of Assent*. Minneapolis: University of Minnesota Press, 2010.

Macksey, Richard. Foreword to *Paratexts: Thresholds of Interpretation*, by Gérard Genette, xi–xxii. Cambridge: Cambridge University Press, 1997.

Mak, Bonnie. *How the Page Matters*. Toronto: University of Toronto Press, 2011.

Mallam, William D. "A Focus on Footnotes." *The Journal of Higher Education* 31, no. 2 (1960): 99–102.

Mangan, Katherine. "The Cost of Connection." *The Chronicle of Higher Education*. April 22, 2022. Accessed December 7, 2022.

Mangen, Anne, Gérard Olivier, and Jean-Luc Velay. "Comparing Comprehension of a Long Text Read in Print Book and on Kindle: Where in the Text and When in the Story?" *Frontiers in Psychology* 10 (2019): 38.

Manoff, Marlene. "Human and Machine Entanglement in the Digital Archive: Academic Libraries and Socio-Technical Change." *portal: Libraries and the Academy* 15, no. 3 (2015): 513–30.

————. "Unintended Consequences: New Materialist Perspectives on Library Technologies and the Digital Record." *portal: Libraries and the Academy* 13, no. 3 (2013): 273–82.

Mao, Douglas, and Rebecca L. Walkowitz. "The New Modernist Studies." *PMLA* 123, no. 3 (2008): 737–48.

Marshall, Megan. *The Peabody Sisters: Three Women Who Ignited American Romanticism*. Boston: Houghton Mifflin, 2005.

Matthews, John T. "Framing in *Wuthering Heights*." *Texas Studies in Literature and Language* 27, no. 1 (1985): 25–61.

Mayali, Laurent. "For a Political Economy of Annotation." In *Annotation and Its Texts*, edited by Stephen A. Barney, 185–91. New York: Oxford University Press, 1991.

McClintock, Anne. *Imperial Leather: Race, Gender and Sexuality in the Colonial Contest*. New York: Routledge, 1995.

McClure, Andrew S. "Sarah Winnemucca: [Post]Indian Princess and Voice of the Paiutes." *MELUS* 24, no. 2 (1999): 29–51.

McCoy, Beth A. "Race and the (Para)Textual Condition." Special Issue, *PMLA* 121, no. 1 (2006): 156–69.

McCulley, Johnston. *The Curse of Capistrano*. All-Story Weekly, 100, no. 2 (Aug. 9, 1919)—101, no. 2 (Sept. 6, 1919).

————. *The Mark of Zorro*. New York: Grosset & Dunlap, 1924.

McElroy, Erin, ed. "Book Bound from Native American Skin Controversy." *Iliff Digital Collections*. Iliff School of Theology, Denver, CO. http://archives.iliff.edu/drupal/islandora/object/controversies%3A50?page=1. Accessed December 2, 2022.

McGann, Jerome. *A New Republic of Letters: Memory and Scholarship in the Age of Digital Reproduction*. Cambridge: Harvard University Press, 2014.

————. *The Textual Condition*. Princeton: Princeton University Press, 1991.

McGill, Meredith L. *American Literature and the Culture of Reprinting, 1834–1853*. Philadelphia: University of Pennsylvania Press, 2003.

————. "Copyright." In *The Industrial Book, 1840–1880*. Vol. 3 of *A History of the Book in America*, edited by Scott E. Casper et al., 158–78. Chapel Hill: American Antiquarian Society and University of North Carolina Press, 2007.

McKee, Patricia. *Producing American Races: Henry James, William Faulkner, Toni Morrison*. Durham: Duke University Press, 1999.

McKenzie, D. F. *Bibliography and Sociology of Texts*. London: The British Library, 1986.

McKittrick, Katherine. *Demonic Grounds: Black Women and the Cartographies of Struggle*. Minneapolis: University of Minnesota Press, 2006.

McLean, Ruari, ed. *Typographers on Type: An Illustrated Anthology from William Morris to the Present Day*. New York: W.W. Norton & Company, 1995.

McNickle, D'Arcy. "Interpreting Native America." *The Nation* 219 (December 7, 1974): 599–600.

———. *The Surrounded.* New York: Dodd, Mead & Company, 1936.

———. *The Surrounded.* Albuquerque: University of New Mexico Press, 1978.

———. *The Surrounded.* Albuquerque: University of New Mexico Press, 1993.

———. *The Surrounded.* New York: Quality Paperback Book Club, 1998.

———. *Wind from an Enemy Sky.* Albuquerque: University of New Mexico Press, 1978.

Medicine Crow, Joseph. *From the Heart of the Crow Country: The Crow Indians' Own Stories.* New York: Orion Books, 1992.

Mennell, D. Jan. "(Im)penetrable Silence: The Language of the Unspeakable in Manuela Fingueret's *Hija del Silencio.*" *Revista Canadiense de Estudios Hispánicos* 27, no. 3 (2003): 485–507.

Metcalf, Jessica. "Native Appropriations: Why Representations Matter." National Bioneers Conference, Indigeneity Forum. YouTube video, 18:23. Filmed 2015. https://bioneers.org/native-appropriations-why-representations-matter/. Accessed August 24, 2022.

Meyer, Sabine N. *Native Removal Writing: Narratives of Peoplehood, Politics, and Law.* Norman: University of Oklahoma Press, 2022.

Meynell, Francis. *Typography.* London: Pelican Press, 1923.

Michaelsen, Scott. *The Limits of Multiculturalism: Interrogating the Origins of American Anthropology.* Minneapolis: University of Minnesota Press, 1999.

Mills, Charles W. *The Racial Contract.* Ithaca: Cornell University Press, 1997.

Miranda, Deborah A. *Bad Indians: A Tribal Memoir.* Berkeley, CA: Heyday, 2013.

Modern Language Association of America. *MLA Handbook.* 8th ed. New York: The Modern Language Association of America, 2016.

———. "Statement on the Significance of Primary Records." *Profession* 95 (1995): 27–28.

Mollis, Kara. "Teaching 'Dear Mihia': Sentimentalism and Cross-Cultural Education in S. Alice Callahan's *Wynema: A Child of the Forest.*" *MELUS* 33, no. 3 (2008): 111–29.

Momaday, N. Scott. *The Names: A Memoir.* New York: Harper & Row, 1976.

Monahan, Sara. "'Rag Friends': Literacy, Embodiment, and the Talking Letter in Sarah Winnemucca's *Life among the Piutes.*" *College Literature* 48, no. 2 (2021): 292–313.

Moreton-Robinson, Aileen. *The White Possessive: Property, Power, and Indigenous Sovereignty.* Minneapolis: University of Minnesota Press, 2015.

Mourning Dove [Hum-Ishu-Ma]. *Cogewea, The Half-Blood: A Depiction of the Great Montana Cattle Range.* Boston: Four Seas Company, 1927.

Moylan, Michele, and Lane Stiles. Introduction to *Reading Books: Essays on the Material Text and Literature in America.* Edited by Michele Moylan and Lane Stiles, 1–15. Amherst: University of Massachusetts Press, 1996.

Mueller, Pam A., and Daniel M. Oppenheimer. "The Pen Is Mightier Than the Keyboard: Advantages of Longhand over Laptop Note Taking." *Psychological Science* 25, no. 6 (2014): 1159–68.

Mullen Sands, Kathleen. "Collaboration or Colonialism: Text and Process in Native American Women's Autobiographies." *MELUS* 22, no. 4 (1997): 39–59.

Müller, Lothar. *White Magic: The Age of Paper.* Translated by Jessica Spengler. Malden, MA: Polity Press, 2014.

Mullin, Molly H. *Culture in the Marketplace: Gender, Art, and Value in the American Southwest.* Durham: Duke University Press, 2001.

Multigraph Collective. *Interacting with Print: Elements of Reading in the Era of Print Saturation.* Chicago: University of Chicago Press, 2018.

Munzer, Tiffany G., Alison L. Miller, Heidi M. Weeks, Niko Kaciroti, and Jenny Radesky. "Differences in Parent-Toddler Interactions with Electronic Versus Print Books." *Pediatrics* 143, no. 4 (2019).

Munzer, Tiffany G., Alison L. Miller, Yujie Wang, Niko Kaciroti, and Jenny S. Radesky. "Tablets, Toddlers and Tantrums: The Immediate Effects of Tablet Device Play." *Acta Paediatrica* 110, no. 1 (2020): 255–56.

Murray, David. *Forked Tongues: Speech, Writing and Representation in North American Indian Texts.* Bloomington: Indian University Press, 1991.

Namias, June. Introduction to *A Narrative of the Life of Mrs. Mary Jemison,* by James E. Seaver, edited by June Namias. Norman: University of Oklahoma Press, 1995.

Nason, Dory. "Carceral Power and Indigenous Feminist Resurgence in D'Arcy McNickle's *The Surrounded* and Janet Campbell Hale's 'Claire.'" *American Indian Culture and Research Journal* 40, no. 1 (2016): 141–60.

Nelson, Joshua B. *Progressive Traditions: Identity in Cherokee Literature and Culture.* Norman: University of Oklahoma Press, 2014.

Nenno, Nancy P. "Projections on Blank Space: Landscape, Nationality, and Identity in Thomas Mann's *Der Zauberberg.*" *The German Quarterly* 69, no. 3 (1996): 305–21.

Newman, Louise Michele. *White Women's Rights: The Radical Origins of Feminism in the United States.* New York: Oxford University Press, 1999.

Nishikawa, Kinohi. "Black Pagecraft." *PMLA* 136, no. 3 (2021): 447–54.

Noble, Safiya Umoja. *Algorithms of Oppression: How Search Engines Reinforce Racism.* New York: New York University Press, 2018.

O'Brien, Jean M. *Firsting and Lasting: Writing Indians out of Existence in New England.* Minneapolis: University of Minnesota Press, 2010.

O'Connell, Barry. Introduction to *"A Son of the Forest" and Other Writings,* by William Apess, edited by Barry O'Connell, ix–xxii. Amherst: University of Massachusetts Press, 1992.

Old Coyote Jr., Barney, and Phenocia Bauerle. Introduction to *Plenty-coups: Chief of the Crows*, by Frank B. Linderman, ix–xv. Lincoln: University of Nebraska Press, 2002.

Orgel, Stephen. *The Reader in the Book: A Study of Spaces and Traces*. New York: Oxford University Press, 2015.

Ovenden, Richard. *Burning the Books: A History of the Deliberate Destruction of Knowledge*. Cambridge: Belknap Press of Harvard University Press, 2020.

Owen, Lynette. *Selling Rights*. 3rd ed. New York: Routledge, 1997.

Owens, Louis. "The 'Map of the Mind': D'Arcy McNickle and the American Indian Novel." *Western American Literature* 19, no. 4 (1985): 275–83.

———. *Other Destinies: Understanding the American Indian Novel*. Norman: University of Oklahoma Press, 1992.

———. "The Red Road to Nowhere: D'Arcy McNickle's 'The Surrounded' and 'The Hungry Generations.'" *American Indian Quarterly* 13, no. 3 (1989): 239–48.

Parins, James W. *John Rollin Ridge: His Life & Works*. Lincoln: University of Nebraska Press, 1991.

Parker, Dorothy R. "D'Arcy McNickle: An Annotated Bibliography of His Published Articles and Book Reviews in a Biographical Context." In *The Legacy of D'Arcy McNickle: Writer, Historian, Activist*, edited by John Lloyd Purdy, 3–29. Norman: University of Oklahoma Press, 1996.

———. "D'Arcy McNickle: Native American Author, Montana Native Son." *Montana: The Magazine of Western History* 45, no. 2 (1995): 2–17.

———. *Singing an Indian Song: A Biography of D'Arcy McNickle*. Lincoln: University of Nebraska Press, 1992.

Parker, Robert Dale. *The Invention of Native American Literature*. Ithaca: Cornell University Press, 2003.

———. "Who Shot the Sheriff: Storytelling, Indian Identity, and the Marketplace of Masculinity in D'Arcy McNickle's *The Surrounded*." *Modern Fiction Studies* 43, no. 4 (1997): 898–932.

Peers, Laura. "'Playing Ourselves': First Nations and Native American Interpreters at Living History Sites." *The Public Historian* 21, no. 4 (1999): 39–59.

Perley, Logan. "Indigenous Sign Languages Once Used to Help Nations Communicate Still Being Used Today." *CBC Radio*, November 13, 2020, https://www.cbc.ca/radio/unreserved/breaking-barriers-unreserved-marks-indigenous-disability-awareness-month-1.5796873/indigenous-sign-languages-once-used-to-help-nations-communicate-still-being-used-today-1.5796874?fbclid=IwAR2m5dtCD34JC8voLfHjdh4BVNjkSarEOzdnnrAaa2UAbFm3b9ulTsxCuBg.

Pfister, Joel. *Individuality Incorporated: Indians and the Multicultural Modern*. Durham: Duke University Press, 2004.

Piatote, Beth H. *Domestic Subjects: Gender, Citizenship, and Law in Native American Literature*. New Haven: Yale University Press, 2013.

Piper, Andrew. *Book Was There: Reading in Electronic Times*. Chicago: The University of Chicago Press, 2012.

———. *Dreaming in Books: The Making of the Bibliographic Imagination in the Romantic Age*. Chicago: University of Chicago Press, 2009.

Portillo, Annette Angela. *Sovereign Stories and Blood Memories: Native American Women's Autobiography*. Albuquerque: University of New Mexico Press, 2017.

Postema, Barbara. *Narrative Structure in Comics: Making Sense of Fragments*. Rochester, NY: RIT Press, 2013.

Powell, Malea D. "Sarah Winnemucca Hopkins: Her Wrong and Claims." In *American Indian Rhetorics of Survivance: Word Medicine, Word Magic*, edited by Ernest Stromberg, 69–94. Pittsburgh: University of Pittsburgh Press, 2006.

Powell, Timothy B. *Ruthless Democracy: A Multicultural Interpretation of the American Renaissance*. Princeton: Princeton University Press, 2000.

Pratt, Mary Louise. *Imperial Eyes: Travel Writing and Transculturation*. 2nd ed. New York: Routledge, 1992.

Pryor, Elizabeth. "The John Day Company." In *American Literary Publishing Houses, 1900–1980: Trade and Paperback*. Vol. 46 of *Dictionary of Literary Biography*, edited by Peter Dzwonkoski. Detroit: Gale Research Company, 1986.

Putzi, Jennifer. *Identifying Marks: Race, Gender, and the Marked Body in Nineteenth-Century America*. Athens: University of Georgia Press, 2006.

Queen Lili'uokalani. *Hawaii's Story by Hawaii's Queen*. Boston: Lee and Shephard, 1898.

Quigley, Dawn. "Silenced: Voices Taken from American Indian Characters in Children's Literature." *American Indian Quarterly* 40, no. 4 (2016): 364–78.

Rader, Pamela J. "'. . . just crushing silence like the inside of a drum before the stick drops': *Zwischenraum* as a Site for Productive Silences in Louise Erdrich's *The Painted Drum*." *The Rocky Mountain Review* 69, no. 1 (2015): 49–67.

Radus, Daniel. "Margaret Boyd's Quillwork History." *Early American Literature* 53, no. 2 (2018): 513–37.

———. "Printing Native History in David Cusick's *Sketches of Ancient History of the Six Nations*." *American Literature* 86, no. 2 (2014): 217–43.

Raheja, Michelle, and Stephanie Fitzgerald. "Literary Sovereignties: New Directions in American Indian Autobiography." Special issue, *American Indian Culture and Research Journal* 30, no. 1 (2006): 1–3.

Raibmon, Paige. *Authentic Indians: Episodes of Encounter from the Late-Nineteenth-Century Northwest Coast*. Durham: Duke University Press, 2005.

Rains, Jim. "'He Never Wanted to Forget It': Contesting the Idea of History in D'Arcy McNickle's *The Surrounded*." In *All Our Stories Are Here: Critical Perspectives on Montana Literature*, edited by Brady Harrison, 141–59. Lincoln: University of Nebraska Press, 2009.

Rao, Sameer. "University of New Mexico May Remove Murals That Ignore Indigenous POV." *ColorLines*. October 9, 2018. Accessed August 12, 2022. https://www.colorlines.com/articles/university-new-mexico-may-remove-murals-ignore-indigenous-pov.

Rasmussen, Birgit Brander. *Queequeg's Coffin: Indigenous Literacies an Early American Literature*. Durham: Duke University Press, 2012.

Ray, Victor. "The Racial Politics of Citation." *Inside Higher Ed*, April 27, 2018.

Reader, Simon. "Notebooks: The Lichtenberg Way." *The Unfinished Book*, edited by Alexandra Gillespie and Deidre Lynch, 357–69. New York: Oxford University Press, 2021.

Rezek, Joseph. "The Racialization of Print." *American Literary History* 32, no. 3 (2020): 417–45.

——. "Transatlantic Traffic: Phillis Wheatley and Her Books." In *The Unfinished Book*, edited by Alexandra Gillespie and Deidre Lynch, 289–302. New York: Oxford University Press, 2021.

Rich, Charlotte J. *Transcending the New Woman: Multiethnic Narratives in the Progressive Era*. Columbia: University of Missouri Press, 2009.

Ridge, John. "From the National Intelligencer." *Cherokee Phoenix and Indians' Advocate*, March 19, 1831: 2, column 2b–3a. https://www.wcu.edu/library/DigitalCollections/CherokeePhoenix/Vol3/no41/from-the-national-intelligencer-page-2-column-2b-3a.html.

Ridge, John Rollin. *The Life and Adventures of Joaquin Murieta, the Celebrated California Bandit*. San Francisco: W.B. Cooke, 1854. http://beinecke1.library.yale.edu/pdf/Zc95_R429_L6_complete.pdf.

[——]. *The Life of Joaquin Murieta, The Brigand Chief of California; A Complete History of His Life, From the Age of Sixteen to the Time of His Capture and Death at the Hands of Capt. Harry Love, in the Year 1853*. San Francisco: California Police Gazette, 1859.

[John R. Ridge]. *The Life and Adventures of Joaquin Murieta, the Celebrated California Bandit*. "Third Edition: Revised and Enlarged by the Author." San Francisco: F. MacCrellish, 1871.

[John R. Ridge]. *The Life and Adventures of Joaquin Murieta, the Celebrated California Bandit*. "Third Edition: Revised and Enlarged by the Author." Bound with *Career of Tiburcio Vasquez, the Bandit of Soledad, Salinas and Tres Pinos, with Some Account of His Capture by Sheriff Rowland of Los Angeles*. San Francisco: F. MacCrellish, 1874.

[John R. Ridge]. *The History of Joaquin Murieta, The King of California Out-laws, Whose Band Ravaged the State in the Early Fifties*. Hollister, CA: Evening Free Lance, 1927.

[————]. *Joaquin Murieta, The Brigand Chief of California*. San Francisco: The Grabhorn Press, 1932.

[Yellow Bird (John Rollin Ridge)]. *The Life and Adventures of Joaquín Murieta, the Celebrated California Bandit*. Introduction by Joseph Henry Jackson. Norman: University of Oklahoma Press, 1955. Reprint 1977.

[————]. *Joaquin Murieta, The Brigand Chief of California*. San Francisco: The Grabhorn Press, 1932. Reprinted with Supplementary Notes of Joaquin Murieta and Illustrations. 1969.

[John Rollin Ridge]. *The Life and Adventures of Joaquín Murieta, the Celebrated California Bandit*. Foreword by Diana Gabaldon. Introduction and Notes by Hsuan L. Hsu. New York: Penguin Books, 2018.

[John Rollin Ridge]. *A Trumpet of Our Own: Yellow Bird's Essays on the North American Indian, Selections from the Writings of the Noted Cherokee Author John Rollin Ridge*. Compiled and edited by David Farmer and Rennard Strickland. San Francisco: The Book Club of California, 1981.

Rifkin, Mark. "'For the wrongs of our poor bleeding country': Sensation, Class, and Empire in Ridge's *Joaquín Murieta*." *Arizona Quarterly* 65, no. 2 (2009): 27–56.

————. *Speaking for the People: Native Writing and the Question of Political Form*. Durham: Duke University Press, 2021.

Rivero, Albert J. "Aphra Behn's *Oroonoko* and the 'Blank Spaces of Colonial Fiction.'" *Studies in English Literature, 1500–1900* 39, no. 3 (1999): 443–62.

Rodier, Katharine. "Authoring Sarah Winnemucca?: Elizabeth Peabody and Mary Peabody Mann." In *Reinventing the Peabody Sisters*, edited by Monika M. Elbert, Julie E. Hall, and Katharine Rodier, 108–25. Iowa City: University of Iowa Press, 2006.

Rodriguez, Sylvia. "Tourism, Whiteness, and the Vanishing Anglo." In *Seeing and Being Seen: Tourism in the American West*, edited by David M. Wrobel and Patrick T. Long, 194–210. Lawrence: University Press of Kansas, 2001.

Ronda, Bruce A. "Print and Pedagogy: The Career of Elizabeth Peabody." In *A Living of Words: American Women in Print Culture*, edited by Susan Albertine, 35–48. Knoxville: University of Tennessee Press, 1995.

Rony, Fatimah Tobing. *The Third Eye: Race, Cinema, and Ethnographic Spectacle*. Durham: Duke University Press, 1996.

Rose, Mark. *Authors and Owners: The Invention of Copyright*. Cambridge: Harvard University Press, 1993.

Rosenbloom, Megan. *Dark Archives: A Librarian's Investigation into the Science and History of Books Bound in Human Skin*. New York: Farrar, Straus, and Giroux, 2020.

Round, Phillip. "Bibliography and the Sociology of American Indian Texts." *Textual Cultures* 6, no. 2 (2011): 119–32.

———. *Removable Type: Histories of the Book in Indian Country, 1663–1880.* Chapel Hill: University of North Carolina Press, 2010.

Rowe, John Carlos. "Highway Robbery: 'Indian Removal,' the Mexican-American War, and American Identity in *The Life and Adventures of Joaquín Murieta.*" *Novel: A Forum on Fiction* 31, no. 2 (1998): 149–73.

———. "Nineteenth-Century United States Literary Culture and Transnationality." *PMLA* 118, no. 1 (2003): 78–89.

———. "Other Modernisms." In *A Concise Companion to American Fiction*, edited by Peter Stoneley and Cindy Weinstein, 275–94. New York: Wiley-Blackwell, 2008.

Roy, Michaël. "The Slave Narrative Unbound." In *Against a Sharp White Background: Infrastructures of African American Print*, edited by Brigitte Fielder and Jonathan Senchyne, 259–76. Madison, WI: University of Wisconsin Press, 2019.

Ruoff, A. LaVonne Brown. Introduction to *Wynema: A Child of the Forest*, by S. Alice Callahan, xiii–xlviii. Lincoln: University of Nebraska Press, 1997.

———. "Justice for Indians and Women: The Protest Fiction of Alice Callahan and Pauline Johnson." *World Literature Today* 66, no. 2 (1992): 249–55.

———. "Three Nineteenth-Century American Indian Autobiographers." In *Redefining American Literary History*, edited by A. LaVonne Brown Ruoff and Jerry W. Ward, Jr., 251–69. New York: The Modern Language Association of America, 1990.

Ruppert, James. "Politics and Culture in the Fiction of D'Arcy McNickle." *Rocky Mountain Review of Language and Literature* 42, no. 4 (1988): 185–95.

———. "Textual Perspectives and the Reader in *The Surrounded.*" In *Narrative Chance: Postmodern Discourse on Native American Indian Literatures*, edited by Gerald Vizenor, 91–100. Albuquerque: University of New Mexico Press, 1989.

Ryan, Melissa. "The Indian Problem as a Woman's Question: S. Alice Callahan's *Wynema: A Child of the Forest.*" *The American Transcendental Quarterly* 21, no. 1 (2007): 23–45.

Saenger, Paul. *Space between Words: The Origins of Silent Reading.* Stanford: Stanford University Press, 1997.

Salish Kootenai College. *Challenge to Survive: History of the Salish Tribes of the Flathead Indian Reservation.* Pablo, MT: Salish Kootenai College Tribal History Project, 2008.

Salvaggio, Ruth. "Theory and Space, Space and Woman." *Tulsa Studies in Women's Literature* 7, no. 2 (1988): 261–82.

Samuels, Shirley. Introduction to *The Culture of Sentiment: Race, Gender, and Sentimentality in Nineteenth-Century America.* Edited by Shirley Samuels, 3–8. New York: Oxford University Press, 1992.

Sánchez-Eppler, Karen. "Bodily Bonds: The Intersecting Rhetorics of Feminism and Abolition." In *The Culture of Sentiment: Race, Gender, and Sentimentality in Nineteenth-Century America*, edited by Shirley Samuels, 92–114. New York: Oxford University Press, 1992.

———. *Touching Liberty: Abolition, Feminism, and the Politics of the Body.* Berkeley: University of California Press, 1993.

Sandell, David P. "John Rollin Ridge's *Joaquín Murieta* and the Legacy of the Mexican American Frontier." *Aztlán: A Journal of Chicano Studies* 28, no. 2 (2003): 21–55.

Sandweiss, Martha A. *Print the Legend: Photography and the American West.* New Haven: Yale University Press, 2002.

"Sarah Winnemucca Hopkins Petition." *History, Art & Archives: United States House of Representatives.* Accessed December 16, 2022.

Scafidi, Susan. *Who Owns Culture?: Appropriation and Authenticity in American Law.* New Brunswick, NJ: Rutgers University Press, 2005.

Schachterle, Lance. "James Fenimore Cooper on the Languages of the Americans: A Note on the Author's Footnotes." *Nineteenth-Century Literature* 66, no. 1 (2011): 37–68.

Schmitt, Madeline. "Discussion to Be Held on New Mexico's Appropriation of the Zia Symbol." KRQE, May 18, 2018. https://www.krqe.com/news/discussion-to-be-held-on-new-mexicos-appropriation-of-zia-symbol/.

Schweitzer, Ivy. "Introduction: The Afterlives of Indigenous Archives." In *Afterlives of Indigenous Archives: Essay in Honor of the* Occom Circle, edited by Ivy Schweitzer and Gordon Henry, 1–20. Hanover, NH: Dartmouth College Press, 2019.

———. "Native Sovereignty and the Archive: Samson Occom and Digital Humanities." *Resources for American Literary Study* 38 (2015): 21–52.

Sconce, Jeffrey. *Haunted Media: Electronic Presence from Telegraphy to Television.* Durham: Duke University Press, 2000.

Seeber, Kevin. "Legacy Systems." June 15, 2018. https://kevinseeber.com/blog/legacy-systems/. Accessed March 23, 2021.

Sekora, John. "Black Message/White Envelope: Genre, Authenticity, and Authority in the Antebellum Slave Narrative." *Callaloo* 32 (1987): 482–515.

Selby, Mike. *Freedom Libraries: The Untold Story of Libraries for African Americans in the South.* Lanham, MD: Rowan & Littlefield, 2019.

Sellers, Stephanie A. *Native American Autobiography Redefined: A Handbook.* New York: Peter Lang, 2007.

Senchyne, Jonathan. "Bottles of Ink and Reams of Paper: *Clotel*, Racialization, and the Material Culture of Print." In *Early African American Print*

Culture, edited by Lara Langer Cohen and Jordan Alexander Stein, 140–58. Philadelphia: University of Pennsylvania Press, 2012.

———. *The Intimacy of Paper in Early and Nineteenth-Century American Literature*. Amherst: University of Massachusetts Press, 2020.

Senier, Siobhan. "Allotment Protest and Tribal Discourse: Reading *Wynema*'s Successes and Shortcomings." *American Indian Quarterly* 24, no. 3 (2000): 420–40.

———. *Voices of American Indian Assimilation and Resistance: Helen Hunt Jackson, Sarah Winnemucca, and Victoria Howard*. Norman: University of Oklahoma Press, 2001.

Sibelman, Simon P. *Silence in the Novels of Elie Wiesel*. New York: St. Martin's Press, 1995.

Silko, Leslie Marmon. *Ceremony*. New York: Seaver Books, 1981.

Simpson, Leanne Betasamosake. *As We Have Always Done: Indigenous Freedom through Radical Resistance*. Minneapolis: University of Minnesota Press, 2017.

Sisneros, Samuel. "Student Activism and the *Three Peoples* Paintings: Challenging Settler Mythology at the University of New Mexico." *Aztlán: A Journal of Chicano Studies* 44, no. 1 (2019): 19–52.

———. "Zimmerman Library Mural in the National Register of Historic Places: A Working Paper and Timeline." *University Libraries & Learning Sciences Faculty and Staff Publications* (2020). https://digitalrepository.unm.edu/ulls_fsp/143.

Slauter, Will. *Who Owns the News?: A History of Copyright*. Stanford: Stanford University Press, 2019.

Sligh, Gary Lee. *A Study of Native American Women Novelists: Sophia Alice Callahan, Mourning Dove, and Ella Cara Deloria*. Lewiston, NY: Edwin Mellen Press, 2003.

Slotkin, Richard. *Regeneration through Violence: The Mythology of the American Frontier, 1600–1860*. Norman: University of Oklahoma Press, 2000.

Smith, Andrea. *Conquest: Sexual Violence and American Indian Genocide*. Durham: Duke University Press, 2015.

Smith, Christen A. "Cite Black Women." Cite Black Women Collective. Accessed August 4, 2022. http://citeblackwomencollective.org.

Smith, Henry Nash. *Virgin Land: The American West as Symbol and Myth*. New York: Vintage Books, 1950.

Smith, Shawn Michelle. *Photography on the Color Line: W. E. B. Du Bois, Race, and Visual Cuture*. Durham: Duke University Press, 2004.

———. "Visual Culture and Race." *MELUS* 39, no. 2 (2014): 1–11.

Smith, Sidonie. *Subjectivity, Identity, and the Body: Women's Autobiographical Practices in Twentieth Century*. Bloomington: Indian University Press, 1993.

Sneider, Leah. "Gender Literacy, and Sovereignty in Winnemucca's *Life among the Piutes*." *American Indian Quarterly* 36, no. 3 (2012): 257–87.

Snell, Alma Hogan. *Grandmother's Grandchild: My Crow Indian Life*. Edited by Becky Matthews. Lincoln: University of Nebraska Press, 2000.

Snell, Alma Hogan, and Becky Matthews. Preface to *Pretty-shield: Medicine Woman of the Crows*, by Frank B. Linderman, v–xiii. Lincoln: University of Nebraska Press, 2003.

So, Richard Jean, and Gus Wezerek. "Just How White Is the Book Industry?" *The New York Times*, December 11, 2020.

Soja, Edward W. *Postmodern Geographies: The Reassertion of Space in Critical Social Theory*. New York: Verso, 1989.

———. *Seeking Spatial Justice*. Minneapolis: University of Minnesota Press, 2010.

Sollors, Werner. *Beyond Ethnicity: Consent and Descent in American Culture*. New York: Oxford University Press, 1986.

Sorensen, Leif. *Ethnic Modernism and the Making of US Literary Multiculturalism*. New York: Palgrave Macmillan, 2016.

Sorisio, Carolyn. *Fleshing Out America: Race, Gender, and the Politics of the Body in American Literature, 1833–1879*. Athens: The University of Georgia Press, 2002.

———. "'I Nailed Those Lies': Sarah Winnemucca Hopkins, Print Culture, and Collaboration." *J19* 5, no. 1 (2017): 79–106.

———. "Playing the Indian Princess?: Sarah Winnemucca's Newspaper Career and Performance of American Indian Identities." *Studies in American Indian Literatures* 23, no. 1 (2011): 1–37.

———. "Sarah Winnemucca, Translation, and US Colonialism and Imperialism." *MELUS* 37, no. 1 (2012): 35–60.

Spivak, Gayatri Chakravorty. "The New Historicism: Political Commitment and the Postmodern Critic." In *The New Historicism*, edited by H. Aram Veeser, 277–92. New York: Routledge, 1989.

Spoo, Robert. *Without Copyrights: Piracy, Publishing, and the Public Domain*. New York: Oxford University Press, 2013.

Stauffer, Andrew M. *Book Traces: Nineteenth-Century Readers and the Future of the Library*. Philadelphia: University of Pennsylvania Press, 2021.

———. "My *Old Sweethearts*: On Digitization and the Future of the Print Record." In *Debates in the Digital Humanities 2016*, edited by Matthew K. Gold and Lauren F. Klein. Minneapolis: University of Minnesota Press, 2016. https://dhdebates.gc.cuny.edu/read/untitled/section/16446b2e-6dc7-49b0-baeb-3c1e050234cf#ch19.

Stevens, Erica. "Three-Fingered Jack and the Severed Literary History of John Rollin Ridge's *The Life and Adventures of Joaquín Murieta*." *ESQ: A Journal of the American Renaissance* 61, no. 1 (2015): 73–112.

Stevens, Moreland L. *Charles Christian Nahl: Artist of the Gold Rush, 1818–1878*. Sacramento: E.B. Crocker Art Gallery, 1976.

Stoler, Ann Laura. *Along the Archival Grain: Epistemic Anxieties and Colonial Common Sense*. Princeton: Princeton University Press, 2009.

Stout, Janis P. *Strategies of Reticence: Silence and Meaning in the Works of Jane Austen, Willa Cather, Katherine Anne Porter, and Joan Didion*. Charlottesville: University Press of Virginia, 1990.

Stowe, Harriet Beecher. *Uncle Tom's Cabin; or, Life among the Lowly*. Boston: John P. Jewett & Company, 1852.

Streeby, Shelley. *American Sensations: Class, Empire, and the Production of Popular Culture*. Berkeley: University of California Press, 2002.

Striphas, Ted. *The Late Age of Print: Everyday Book Culture from Consumerism to Control*. New York: Columbia University Press, 2011.

Sweet, John Wood. *Bodies Politic: Negotiating Race in the American North, 1730–1830*. Baltimore: Johns Hopkins University Press, 2003.

Tanselle, G. Thomas. *Bibliographic Analysis: A Historical Introduction*. New York: Cambridge University Press, 2009.

Tatonetti, Lisa. "Behind the Shadows of Wounded Knee: The Slippage of Imagination in *Wynema: A Child of the Forest*." *Studies in American Indian Literatures* 16, no. 1 (2004): 1–31.

———. *Written by the Body: Gender Expansiveness and Indigenous Non-Cis Masculinities*. Minneapolis: University of Minnesota Press, 2021.

Tattoli, Chantel. "The Surprising History (and Future) of Fingerprints." *The Paris Review*, May 15, 2018. https://www.theparisreview.org/blog/2018/05/15/the-surprising-history-and-future-of-fingerprints/.

Taylor, Kevin. "Plagiarism and Piracy: A Publisher's Perspective." *Learned Publishing* 19, no. 4 (2006): 259–66.

Teuton, Sean Kicummah. "The Indigenous Novel." In *Oxford Handbook of Indigenous American Literature*, edited by James H. Cox and Daniel Heath Justice, 318–32. New York: Oxford University Press, 2014.

Tharp, Louise Hall. *The Peabody Sisters of Salem*. Boston: Little, Brown and Company, 1988.

Thiong'o, Ngũgĩ wa. *Re-membering Africa*. Nairobi: East African Educational Publishers, 2009.

Thornton, Bruce S. *Searching for Joaquín: Myth, Murieta and History in California*. San Francisco: Encounter Books, 2003.

"Three Peoples Murals in Zimmerman Library." University of New Mexico University Libraries Research Guides. Accessed August 4, 2022. https://libguides.unm.edu/c.php?g=1168686&p=8535451.

Thrush, Coll. *Indigenous London: Native Travelers at the Heart of Empire*. New Haven: Yale University Press, 2016.

Tisinger, Danielle. "Textual Performance and the Western Frontier: Sarah Winnemucca Hopkins's *Life Among the Piutes: Their Wrongs and Claims*." *Western American Literature* 37, no. 2 (2002): 171–95.

Tompkins, Jane. *Sensational Designs: The Cultural Work of American Fiction, 1790–1860*. New York: Oxford University Press, 1985.

Torgovnick, Marianna. *Primitive Passions: Men, Women, and the Quest for Ecstasy*. New York: Alfred A. Knopf, 1997.

Treat, James. "Introduction: Native Christian Narrative Discourse." *Native and Christian: Indigenous Voices on Religious Identity in the United States and Canada*, edited by James Treat, 1–26. New York: Routledge, 1996.

Treuer, David. *The Translation of Dr. Apelles: A Love Story*. St. Paul, MN: Greywolf Press, 2006.

Tribble, Evelyn. *Margins and Marginality: The Printed Page in Early Modern England*. Charlottesville: University Press of Virginia, 1993.

Tschichold, Jan. *The Form of the Book: Essays on the Morality of Good Design*. Translated by Hajo Hadeler. Edited by Robert Bringhurst. Point Roberts, WA: Hartley & Marks, 1991.

Tsomondo, Thorell Porter. *Not So Blank "Blank Page": The Politics of Narrative and the Woman Narrator in the Eighteenth and Nineteenth-Century Novel*. New York: Peter Lang Publishing, 2007.

Tucker, Irene. *The Moment of Racial Sight: A History*. Chicago: The University of Chicago Press, 2012.

Turner, Frederick Jackson. "The Significance of the Section in American History." *The Wisconsin Magazine of History* 8, no. 3 (1925): 255–80.

Twomey, Tish Eshelle. "More Than One Way to Tell a Story: Rethinking the Place of Genre in Native American Autobiography and the Personal Essay." *Studies in American Indian Literatures* 19, no. 2 (2007): 22–51.

Uenuma, Francine. "The First Criminal Trial That Used Fingerprints as Evidence." *Smithsonian Magazine*. December 5, 2018. https://www.smithsonianmag.com/history/first-case-where-fingerprints-were-used-evidence-180970883/.

Van Dyke, Annette. "An Introduction to *Wynema: A Child of the Forest* by Sophia Alice Callahan." *Studies in American Indian Literatures* 4, no. 2 (1992): 123–28.

Varley, James F. *The Legend of Joaquín Murrieta: California's Gold Rush Bandit*. Twin Falls, Idaho: Big Lost River Press, 1995.

Vettese, Troy. "Sexism in the Academy: Women's Narrowing Path to Tenure." *Head Case* 34 (2019). https://www.nplusonemag.com/issue-34/essays/sexism-in-the-academy/.

Vicenti Carpio, Myla. *Indigenous Albuquerque*. Lubbock: Texas Tech University Press, 2011.

Vigil, Kiara M. *Indigenous Intellectuals: Sovereignty, Citizenship, and the American Imagination, 1880–1930*. New York: Cambridge University Press, 2015.

Vizenor, Gerald. "Almost Browne." In *Shadow Distance: A Gerald Vizenor Reader*, edited by Gerald Vizenor, 107–14. Hanover: Wesleyan University Press, 1994.

Wagner, Henry R. "John R. Ridge." In *The Zamorano 80: A Selection of Distinguished California Books Made by Members of the Zamorano Club*, edited by Don Hill, Dana H. Jones, and Homer D. Crotty, entry #64. Los Angeles: The Zamorano Club, 1945.

Walker, Cheryl. *Indian Nation: Native American Literature and Nineteenth-Century Nationalisms*. Durham: Duke University Press, 1997.

Walker, Franklin. "Ridge's *Life of Joaquin Murieta*: The First and Revised Editions Compared." *California Historical Society Quarterly* 16, no. 3 (1937): 256–62.

———. *San Francisco's Literary Frontier*. New York: A.A. Knopf, 1939.

Walker, Sue. "The Manners of the Page: Prescription and Practice in the Visual Organization of Correspondence." *Huntington Library Quarterly* 66, no. 3/4 (2003): 307–29.

Walsh, Susan. "'With Them Was My Home': Native American Autobiography and *A Narrative of the Life of Mrs. Mary Jemison*." *American Literature* 64, no. 1 (1992): 49–70.

Warner, Michael. *The Letters of the Republic: Publication and the Public Sphere in Eighteenth-Century America*. Cambridge: Harvard University Press, 1990.

Warrior, Robert Allen. *The People and the Word: Reading Native Nonfiction*. Minneapolis: University of Minnesota Press, 2005.

Watts, Richard. *Packaging Post/Coloniality: The Manufacture of Literary Identity in the Francophone World*. Lanham, MD: Lexington Books, 2005.

Weaver, Jace. *That the People Might Live: Native American Literatures and Native American Community*. New York: Oxford University Press, 1997.

Weeks, Lyman Horace. *A History of Paper-Manufacturing in the United States, 1690–1916*. 1916. Reprint. New York: Burt Franklin, 1969.

Weyler, Karen A. *Empowering Words: Outsiders and Authorship in Early America*. Athens: University of Georgia Press, 2013.

White, E. Frances. *Dark Continent of Our Bodies: Black Feminism and the Politics of Respectability*. Philadelphia: Temple University Press, 2001.

Wiegman, Robyn. *American Anatomies: Theorizing Race and Gender*. Durham: Duke University Press, 1995.

Wigginton, Caroline. *Indigenuity: Native Craftwork and the Art of American Literatures*. Chapel Hill: University of North Carolina Press, 2022.

Wilhite, Keith. "Blank Spaces: Outdated Maps and Unsettled Subjects in Jhumpa Lahiri's *Interpreter of Maladies*." *MELUS* 41, no. 2 (2016): 76–96.

Williams, Brittany, and Joan Collier. *CiteASista* (blog). Accessed August 4, 2022. https://citeasista.com/blog/.

Wilson, Chris. *The Myth of Santa Fe: Creating a Modern Regional Tradition*. Albuquerque: University of New Mexico Press, 1997.

Windell, Maria A. "The Sentimental Realisms of S. Alice Callahan's *Wynema: A Child of the Forest*." *American Literary Realism* 49, no. 3 (2017): 246–62.

Winnemucca, Sarah. *Life among the Piutes*. Boston: Cupples, Upham; New York: G.P. Putnam, 1883.

———. *Life among the Piutes*. Preface by M.R. Harrington. Introduction by Russ and Anne Johnson. Bishop, CA: Chalfant Press, 1969.

———. *Life among the Piutes*. Reno: University of Nevada Press, 1994.

Woidat, Caroline M. "The Indian-Detour in Willa Cather's Southwestern Novels." *Twentieth-Century Literature* 48, no. 1 (2002): 22–29.

Wolf, Maryanne. *Proust and the Squid: The Story and Science of the Reading Brain*. New York: Harper Perennial, 2008.

Womack, Craig S. *Red on Red: Native American Literary Separatism*. Minneapolis: University of Minnesota Press, 1999.

Wong, Hertha Dawn. *Sending My Heart Back across the Years: Tradition and Innovation in Native American Autobiography*. New York: Oxford University Press, 1992.

Wood, Raymund F. "Supplementary Notes of Joaquin Murieta: Part I." In *Joaquin Murieta: The Brigand Chief of California*, ix–xii. Fresno, CA: Valley Publishers, 1969.

Wrede, Theda. Introduction to "Theorizing Space and Gender in the 21st Century." Special issue, *The Rocky Mountain Review of Language and Literature* 69, no. 1 (2015): 10–17.

Wrobel, David M., and Patrick T. Long. *Seeing and Being Seen: Tourism in the American West*. Lawrence: University Press of Kansas, 2001.

Wurdemann, Audrey. *Bright Ambush*. New York: John Day Company, 1934.

Wyss, Hilary E. "Captivity and Conversion: William Apess, Mary Jemison, and Narratives of Racial Identity." *American Indian Quarterly* 23, no. 3/4 (1999): 63–82.

———. "Mary Occom and Sarah Simon: Gender and Native Literacy in Colonial New England." *New England Quarterly* 79, no. 3 (2006): 387–412.

———. *Writing Indians: Literacy, Christianity, and Native Community in Early America*. Amherst: University of Massachusetts Press, 2000.

Yandell, Kay. "The Moccasin Telegraph: Sign-Talk Autobiography and Pretty-Shield, Medicine Woman of the Crows." *American Literature* 84, no. 3 (2012): 533–61.

Young, John K. *Black Writers, White Publishers: Marketplace Politics in Twentieth-Century African American Literature*. Jackson: University Press of Mississippi, 2006.

Young, Katharine. *Presence in the Flesh: The Body in Medicine*. Cambridge: Harvard University Press, 1997.

Zaeske, Susan. *Signatures of Citizenship: Petitioning, Antislavery, and Women's Political Identity*. Chapel Hill: University of North Carolina Press, 2003.

Zanjani, Sally. *Sarah Winnemucca*. Lincoln: University of Nebraska, 2001.

Zerby, Chuck. *The Devil's Details: A History of Footnotes*. New York: Simon & Schuster, 2002.

"Zia Pueblo Upset over Symbol Usage." KOAT, Jun. 4, 2014. https://www.youtube.com/watch?v=3N_jW6TyVPQ.

Zitkala-Šá. "The Widespread Enigma Concerning Blue-Star Woman." In *American Indian Stories, Legends, and Other Writings*, edited by Cathy N. Davidson and Ada Norris, 143–54. New York: Penguin Books, 2003.

Zuboff, Shoshana. *The Age of Surveillance Capitalism: The Fight for a Human Future at the New Frontier of Power*. New York: Public Affairs, 2019.

Zulli, Jeri. "Perception in D'Arcy McNickle's *The Surrounded*: A Postcolonial Reading." In *Telling the Stories: Essays on American Indian Literatures and Cultures*, edited by Elizabeth Hoffman Nelson and Malcolm A. Nelson, 71–81. New York: Peter Lang, 2001.

Zurn, Perry, Danielle S. Bassett, and Nicole C. Rust. "The Citation Diversity Statement: A Practice of Transparency, A Way of Life." *Scientific Life* 24, no. 9 (2020): 669–72.

INDEX